Fighting Fictions

FIGHTING FICTIONS
War, Narrative and
National Identity

Kevin Foster

Pluto Press
LONDON • STERLING, VIRGINIA

First published 1999 by Pluto Press
345 Archway Road, London N6 5AA
and 22883 Quicksilver Drive,
Sterling, VA 20166–2012, USA

British Library Cataloguing in Publication Data
A catalogue record for this book is available from the British Library

ISBN 0 7453 0956 9 hbk

Library of Congress Cataloging in Publication Data
Foster, Kevin, 1961–
    Fighting fictions: war, narrative, and national identity/Kevin
Foster.
        p.   cm.
    Includes bibliographical references.
    ISBN 0–7453–0956–9 (hardback: alk. paper)
    1. Falkland Islands War, 1982. 2. Nationalism—Great Britain.
3. Nationalism—Argentina.   I. Title.
F3031.5.F67   1999
997'.110241—dc21   98–36836
                                                          CIP

Designed and Produced for Pluto Press by
Chase Production Services, Chadlington, OX7 3LN
Typeset from disk by Stanford DTP Services, Northampton
Printed in the EC by T.J. International, Padstow

Contents

Illustrations

Acknowledgements

Over the years, in the course of the work and study that have led to this book, I have accumulated more debts than I could ever hope to repay. The first and greatest of these I owe to my parents, Jean and Kevin, whose love and faith in me have guided and sustained me: my first and best teachers, what follows is an inadequate expression of my love, respect and gratitude to them for all that they have given me. My brothers, Martin, Robert, David and Damien, and their partners and families, Hisako, Jane, Alex, Mandy, Polly, Tom and Trisha, have all helped at different times and in different ways – my love and thanks to all of them. I have benefited from the guidance and encouragement of some marvellous teachers, most notably Vincent Burke, David Langston, Angela Dale, Chris Dobbyn and Peter Millard. Robin Gerster's work on the cultural criticism of war writing has provided an admirable example and an exacting standard for my own research. Anne Beech, my editor, has been a model of patience, understanding and encouragement: thanks, yet again, and here it is, at last! Thanks also to Robert Webb at Pluto for so expertly taking the book through to production. I am indebted to Ravnol Gray, John and Caroline MacLelland, Sergio Tell and Claudio Uno for books – and to Claudio and family for their hospitality during my stay in Buenos Aires. I would also like to thank Louise, Tony and the Gray family, Clive and Meg Probyn, Alan Sandison, Julian Croft, Robert Dingley, Helena Davies, Wayne Murphy and Suzanne Oberhardt, Nick Leaver, Robert and Carolyn Zimmerman, Terry Penaluna, Marie Ewart, Tony Burke, Allan MacDonald, Chas Esche, R. B., and Thérèse O'Loughlin. I alone am accountable for all opinions (unless otherwise acknowledged), errors or omissions in what follows.

Parts of Chapter 4 appeared in an earlier form in *Cultural Studies* (Vol. 11, No. 2, 1997); earlier versions of other parts of the book have appeared in *Small Wars and Insurgencies*, *Southern Review*, *Meridian* and *War, Literature and the Arts*. I am grateful to the editors and publishers of these journals for their permission to reuse and rework this material.

The author and publisher gratefully acknowledge the kindness of the following for their permission to reproduce photographs and illustrations: the Trustees of the Imperial War Museum, London (1); Les Gibbard (3); Max Hastings (4); Steve Bell (5); Hermenegildo Sabat (6); the *Daily Express* (7).

In a work of nonfiction we almost never know the truth of what happened. The ideal of unmediated reporting is regularly achieved only in fiction, where the writer faithfully reports on what is going on in his imagination ... In imaginative literature we are constrained from considering alterative scenarios – there are none. This is the way it *is*. Only in nonfiction does the question of what happened and how people thought and felt remain open. (Malcolm, 1994: 154–5)

politics have to do with the nature of human association, the contract of men with men. The politics of a country can only be the extension of its idea of human relationships. (Naipaul, 1980: 151)

Every war is alike in the way its early stages replay elements of the preceding war. Everyone fighting a modern war tends to think of it in terms of the last one he knows anything about. (Fussell, 1975: 314)

The eruption of jingoism, the thunderous Churchillian rhetoric which was so readily available to politicians of all persuasions showed that this was less a matter of real territorial ambition or a desire to protect 'our own'; but, like Suez, more an affair of the heart, of who we thought we were, who we wanted to be. (McEwan, 1989: 28–9)

We are a great nation, but if we continue to behave like a Great Power we shall soon cease to be a great nation. (qtd in Clarke, 1996: 233)

For my son, James

Introduction
Facts and Fictions

What little news I got of [the Falklands War] had the cracked ring of archaic fiction. (Raban, 1986: 137)

More than a decade after Argentine troops laid down their arms on the Falklands and the islands were returned to British rule, Spencer Fitz-Gibbon set out to establish 'what *really* happened' in the first decisive land battle of the campaign, the Battle for Goose Green (Fitz-Gibbon, 1995: 139). The actual events at Goose Green had, in his view, been all but obscured by a thick coating of 'military myths' transforming what one of the participants in the battle described as 'a complete fuck-up!' into 'a feat of arms and gallantry probably unsurpassed in the glorious history of the British army' (Fitz-Gibbon, 1995: 29, 117; Frost, 1983: 178–9). Fitz-Gibbon determined to render a coldly factual account of the battle. He was interested in the myths about Goose Green only in so far as he could identify their sources, correct their errors and so 'pop the bubble of mythology with the needle of truth' (Fitz-Gibbon, 1995: 5). Indeed, throughout the book he employs the terms 'myth' and 'mythology' as antonyms for fact, signifying a mistaken or more often invented record of events.[1] Events in the Falklands, Fitz-Gibbon implies, preceded the myths which grew up around them – that is to say, things happened which by a carefully managed process of (mis)representation were then cast into more palatable forms, rewritten to accord with orthodox military doctrine, regimental tradition, fictional archetype or national myth:

One senior officer who served in the Falklands admitted to me that ever since the war he has helped maintain a facade, helped perpetuate a myth about his unit's experience for the sake of the regiment's reputation; and one of his colleagues, eyewitness to a controversial incident during the land campaign, admitted that he has often deliberately misled researchers with half-truths ... I have also heard confessions from NCOs [Non-Commissioned Officers] that they lied to their superiors when a certain event was being investigated, rather than risk their unit's reputation being sullied. (Fitz-Gibbon, 1995: xiii)

It is my contention, and my central aim in this book, to demonstrate that the reverse was the case, that events in the Falklands, how they were experienced, understood and described by both participants and observers, were preceded and shaped by certain powerful myths of national identity, that events in the Falklands were substantially predetermined by a range of narrative and historical precedents – that the war had been written before it ever took place. What Spencer Fitz-Gibbon saw as random invention was, I believe, a highly structured if on occasions hardly conscious process dedicated to the generation of particular facts about the war which, collectively, comprised an official or preferred account of its origins, aims and salient events. The myths about the Falklands War should not therefore, as Fitz-Gibbon implies, be seen in opposition to, but as one of the fundamental shaping forms of, its history.[2]

The Falklands War may seem a geographically and historically distant conflict today, but I believe, and it will be one of my aims in this book to demonstrate, that it represents a critical space – physical, mythic and narrative – in the shaping of contemporary Britain. The brash, self-confident nationalism of late 1990s 'Cool Britannia' is built on the bones of what happened in the South Atlantic in the spring of 1982 and how these events were mediated, experienced and understood back in the United Kingdom. The Falklands Conflict, as such, provides a vital (re)source for the British to understand who and what they are as a nation and where this sense of collective self-identity has come from, and for that reason, if no other, it demands our scrutiny. The war also furnishes a compelling case study of the part played by the past in the framing of contemporary experience, the role of conflicts and the myths they spawn in shaping the British experience and understanding of the present.[3] I am not, however, arguing that the mythic processes which produced the Falklands War were in any sense unique to it, merely that the Falklands provides a convenient focus for the study of more general narrative and historical processes.

Clearly, my understanding and use of the term 'myth' differs significantly from Fitz-Gibbon's, informed as it is by the work of Roland Barthes and Claude Levi-Strauss.[4] I use it in both its anthropological and semiological senses to describe a chain of associated concepts, usually rendered as a narrative, by which individuals and communities mediate their personal and collective anxieties and through which they are able to understand, express and communicate to themselves and others a sense of their identity as members of specific social, cultural and national groups. In the context of the Falklands War this process manifested itself in a series of myths about how and why the British became involved in the conflict, what they were ostensibly fighting for, the status of the islands and their occupants, and the individual and collective virtues which brought victory to the task force. These accounts of the war were, in Barthes' terms, classically mythic in that they gave 'an historical intention a natural justification, and [made] contingency appear eternal' (Barthes 1973: 155). That is to say, the decision of the British to pursue a military solution in the Falklands and the conduct of the campaign were presented not as a last ditch defence against political oblivion or an improvised and often panicky response to unexpected events, but as an expression of the essential national character, last evident with equivalent clarity during the Second World War at Dunkirk and in the Blitz. According to Barthes:

> myth is constituted by the loss of the historical quality of things: in it, things lose the memory that they once were made ... Myth does not deny things, on the contrary, its function is to talk about them; simply, it purifies them, it makes them innocent, it gives them a natural and eternal justification, it gives them a clarity which is not that of an explanation but that of a statement of fact ... In passing from history to nature, myth acts economically: it abolishes the complexity of human acts, it gives them the simplicity of human essences, it does away with all dialectics, with any going back beyond what is immediately visible. (Barthes 1973: 155–6)

It is my purpose in what follows to arrest the mythopoeic inertia and restore some corrective complexity, to move back from myth, through nature to the historical quality of things, to recover the memory of how and why these myths about the Falklands War were forged. In this wilful act of recall I will examine the component elements of the key myths of national identity, narratives of the family, heroism and the enemy; examine their roles in the celebration of the war and the promotion of a specific political agenda; and propose that the economic and social policies they served in and through the Falklands were ultimately hostile to the very ideals of nationhood purportedly upheld in and endorsed by the conflict.

In Chapter 1 I will outline and illustrate my methodological approach. My focus here is on two central questions – how and what can one know of an event like the Falklands War? and in what ways do the processes by which one's understanding of it is mediated materially (re)shape it? I will illustrate my response to these questions through a detailed analysis of George Orwell's *Homage to Catalonia* (1938), not in an effort to imply some moral or political equivalence between the Spanish Civil War and the Falklands Conflict but to illustrate how the conceptual and narrative processes by which Orwell made sense of and represented his experiences in Spain remained virtually unchanged more than forty years later in the Falklands. I will demonstrate that what Orwell knew or thought he knew about the war in Spain was a function of how he had sought to make sense of it and how he had then endeavoured to represent it; that his understanding of the war had been shaped by the historical precedent of the First World War; and that his account of it was articulated through a conventional rites of passage narrative which presented his experiences there as a political coming of age. I will compare this with the Falklands, where the organising historical precedent was provided by the Second World War and the official accounts of the conflict were articulated through and inscribed over the discursive norms of the medieval romance quest which constructed the fighting in the South Atlantic as a journey in search of the nation's 'essential identity' (Wright, 1985: 164). Yet when Orwell discoverd that his use of the First World War as a basis for organising his response to the fighting in Spain had led him fundamentally to misunderstand and misrepresent it, the primary focus of his narrative shifted from the organisation of a coherent response to the war to the provision of an accurate and honest record of its events. In the Falklands, the identification of narrative with political, military and cultural coherence implied that the defence of one entailed the maintenance of the others. Consequently, the official accounts of the war continued to draw moral, historical and cultural equivalences between events in the Falklands and the Second World War, despite growing evidence of their illegitimacy, incongruity or patent inaccuracy.

Chapter 2, drawing on the work of Patrick Wright, examines the idea of a 'national past': its embodiment in images of the countryside, its articulation in specific narratives from the Second World War, the processes whereby the Falkland Islands and their people were established as its living forms, and the mission to liberate the islanders as a means to the recovery and rejuvenation of its principles in the present (Wright, 1985: 146). It will examine how information about and from the islands was sourced, gathered and distributed, and will consider the practical effects of the reporters' long and close cohabitation with the military. It will consider why and how the representational forms of the Second World War were deployed in and so significantly shaped the coverage of the Falklands Conflict.

Chapters 3, 4 and 5 will look at three of the key narratives shaping the ideals of personal and national identity and so framing the experience of the Falklands War, narratives of the family, heroism and the enemy. Chapter 3 will analyse narratives describing, promoting and utilising various ideas about and ideals of the family. I will consider how, during the Second World War, through photography and narrative, the family was constructed as an ideal of unity, an emblem of the nation's essential identity (Wright, 1985: 164). I will examine how and to what ends this representation of the family was revived and redeployed during the Falklands Conflict. I will analyse how, through the agency of the family, the war in the Falklands was constructed as, in Patrick Wright's terms, an 'Historical' event linked with, and returning to the citizen and the nation as a whole, its essential, grander identity. I will then examine the actual communities involved in the conflict, the British nation, the Falkland Islanders, the military, the task force, their families and the journalists who covered the war, and consider how effectively they embodied and promoted the collective ideals which the task force was ostensibly upholding in the South Atlantic.

Chapter 4 will examine the role of specific narrative forms in the construction, celebration and subversion of an official model of heroic behaviour in the Falklands War. In the first instance I will examine the language of peace and demonstrate how the representation of diplomacy negated any possibility of a peaceful resolution to the dispute and so served to prepare the British nation for war and the celebration of its iconic figures. I will analyse the concept of 'mythical "History"' and consider how the soldier hero was identified during the Falklands War as the living link back to the nation's glorious national past (Wright, 1985: 176). I will describe how individual heroes in the Falklands were selected, constructed and promoted through the narrative norms of the romance quest. I will detail how these discursive patterns enhanced the achievements of a privileged minority whose actions and ideals were closely linked to the British government's own domestic policies and, accordingly, how the contribution of the military managers who planned the campaign and the ordinary soldiers who carried it through was systematically undervalued. I will examine the processes by which familiar narrative forms were used by combatants or reporters to provide themselves with a sense of reassurance in unfamiliar and frightening circumstances. I will consider how those critical of the official, celebratory line on the war articulated their dissent through the discursive norms of the romance quest. I will examine the construction of official Argentine accounts of the conflict, the representation of the recovery of the Malvinas as a crusade in defence of the true faith of Catholic nationalism and the role this narrative of the war allotted to the conscripts in the South Atlantic. I will detail how, despite the official celebration of the islands' return to Argentine rule as both the territorial and moral unification of the nation – a final triumph over the ethnic, social and political divisions of the past, its most salient physical and symbolic associations were with the darkest chapter in the nation's history of entrenched and violent division, the dirty war. I will then consider the uses to which these dissonant narratives of celebration and subversion, of unification and fragmentation, were put by the conscripts.

The final chapter will examine the construction of the enemy. It will consider the efforts of the government and the media to establish the Argentinians as a worthy enemy, to represent them as emblems of moral otherness and so promote and sustain a simple Manichean vision of the conflict. I will then plot both the origins of and the reasons for the collapse of this moral and discursive structure. I will examine how, in an effort to promote a polarised vision of the issues at stake in the South Atlantic, the individual and collective conduct of the opposing forces was symbolically sexualised, and I will consider the resultant tensions between an urgent desire for heterosexual self-affirmation and the military's long and intimate engagement with homosexual subculture, not least in its traditional reliance on homoerotic bonds as the basis of unit cohesion. I will detail why these narratives of otherness were difficult to sustain in relation to the Falklands, propose the identity of the real enemy and explain the processes by which this realisation helped finally deconstruct the official, celebratory account of the conflict.

As such, this book approaches and examines the Falklands War as a struggle for ideological rather than physical terrain, as a discursive conflict in which the most sacred myths of British and Argentine national identity were deployed in the battle for moral and cultural sovereignty over the war and for the personal reassurance and political survival this offered, as a battle to shape the fighting fictions which framed and formed the conflict.

1
Homage to the Falklands

for a creative writer possession of the 'truth' is less important than emotional sincerity. (Orwell, 1957: 45)

VIRTUAL CONFLICTS

Early in 1991, as the first allied troops returned in triumph from Kuwait and Saudi Arabia, Jean Baudrillard published the last of three essays on the coverage and representation of the war in the Gulf. Baudrillard's claim that *The Gulf War Did Not Take Place* (1995) was puzzling if not perverse – the bodies on the road to Basra told a different tale – and it was greeted with anger, incredulity and outright derision.[1] Christopher Norris' response was typical: he dismissed Baudrillard's views as 'absurd', 'ludicrous', 'sheer nonsense' and identified in the essays the 'definitive exposure of the intellectual and political bankruptcy of postmodern thought' (Norris, 1992: 23, 17, 15; Baudrillard, 1995: 15).[2] Yet for all his arch provocation and modish theorising Baudrillard had a serious point to make. The essays persistently come back to two central questions which owe as much to Plato as they do to post-structuralist high theory: how and what did the public know of events in the Gulf? and in what ways (and to what ends) did the various channels and processes of their mediation materially (re)shape them?

What the public had witnessed in the Gulf, Baudrillard proposed, was not, in any traditional sense, a war at all. It wasn't only that the allies' 'logic of deterrence', the fifty-year commitment of their resources to the avoidance and not the enactment of conflict, had rendered them 'incapable of realising their own power in the form of relations of force', but more importantly, that what they were seeking in the Gulf was not physical but narrative supremacy, not the annihilation of Saddam Hussein but his discursive subjection (Baudrillard, 1995: 8). In the Gulf, Baudrillard contended, the allies had been fighting a 'virtual war', a struggle for the hearts and minds of the global viewing public, conducted not on the field of battle but in and for control over an 'abstract, electronic and informational space' from which the victor might determine the definition, representation and reception of the conflict (Baudrillard, 1995: 56). The decisive weapon in this struggle

7

for narrative supremacy was not the indiscriminate ordnance of old but the smart weaponry of modern media technology: selected images of the war, potent narratives of national pre-eminence, sanitised, edited and fired at friend and foe alike. The media's primary concern in the Gulf then, Baudrillard argued, had not been to provide an accurate record of events but to promote a narrowly nationalistic reading of them. After all, the moral, political and narrative outcomes of the war had been secured long before the first hostile exchanges: 'Since this war was won in advance, we will never know what it would have been like had it existed. We will never know what an Iraqi taking part with a chance of fighting would have been like. We will never know what an American taking part with a chance of being beaten would have been like' (Baudrillard, 1995: 61). '[P]urged of all local and political peripeteas', its events 'devoured in advance by the parasite virus, the retro-virus of history', the war, or the highly edited version of it that the public received, served above all else to dramatise and reaffirm the dominant cultural narratives of its participating nations (Baudrillard, 1995: 26–7, 63). It was on this basis, Baudrillard contended, that there had been no war in the Gulf, merely the ritualistic reaffirmation of cultural supremacy by the warring parties, a discursive rather than a military exchange.

The care with which these mythic restatements of national dominance were crafted and the fervency with which they were pronounced was, however, very nearly fatal to both their ends and their means. The highly selective nature of the reported images of war and the further closure imposed on them by their tightly controlled con-textualisation meant, as Baudrillard noted, that the more one saw of them the less one felt one knew about the war: 'war, when it has been turned into information, ceases to be a realistic war and becomes a virtual war ... just as everything psychical becomes the object of interminable speculation, so everything which is turned into information becomes the object of endless speculation, the site of total uncertainty' (Baudrillard, 1995: 41). The more carefully the images were prepared and packaged, the more aggressively they were promoted and the more widely they were disseminated, the more the events they purported to document receded until the war, 'encrusted' with the information which purported to represent it, was rendered invisible and all but intangible.

Utopia of real time which renders the event simultaneous at all points on the globe. In fact, what we live in real time is not the event, but rather in larger than life (in other words, in the virtual size of the image) the spectacle of the degradation of the event and its spectral evocation (the 'spiritualism of information': event, are you there? Gulf War, are you there?) in the commentary, gloss, and verbose *mise en scène* of talking heads which only underlines the impossibility of the image and the correlative unreality of the war ... All that we can hope for is that some event or other should overwhelm the information instead of the information inventing the event and commenting artificially upon it ... In the meantime, we will continue with the involution and encrustation of the events in and by information, and the closer we approach the live and real time, the further we will go in this direction. (Baudrillard, 1995: 48–9)

If the images from the Gulf raised awkward questions about the nature, even the existence, of the war there, then the narratives from and about the Falklands Conflict prompt a similar range of prickly epistemological questions. That there was a war in the South Atlantic is not in dispute: my concern in what follows is with the corporeality and coherence – moral, political and social – of the nations purportedly engaged in the conflict, and the role of specific narrative forms in consecrating or contesting their existence. If the loss of the Falkland Islands in April 1982 marked a new low in Britain's post-imperial history of disengagement, retreat and rejection, then it is my conjecture that the narratives which reported that humiliation and the political and military responses to it also played a vital role in remediating it and restoring the nation's self-esteem. The Emergency Parliamentary Debate on 3 April 1982 prompted by the Argentine invasion provoked an uncharacteristically unified response, an outpouring of shame and indignation, tempered by a resolute determination to return the islands to British rule.[3] The narratives which subsequently described the dispatch and progress of the task force were as much a function of that parliamentary response as they were a record of the voyage south, in that they did more than document the recovery of the islands, they celebrated and embodied the means by which this was accomplished. As I will show, the formal structure, controlling perspective and chosen detail of these narratives realised the very principles of authority, order and harmony which had purportedly governed the actions of the task force, returned the islands to British rule and restored the nation to its former glory. Accordingly, these narratives were not just an account of the nation's triumph, they were a model and an enactment of it, offering both a record and the experience of victory. However, as the government's subsequent policies on economics, industrial relations and nationality (among others) showed, the fighting in the Falklands was no remedy for the political, regional and class divisions which became increasingly pronounced through the 1980s; indeed, one might argue that it only exacerbated them. As Arthur Marwick observed: 'in many respects British society at the end of the eighties is more polarized than at any time since 1939', and the Falklands War was both a symptom and a source of this growing fragmentation

(Marwick, 1990: 393).[4] The narratives which set out to consecrate the new order could neither escape from nor conceal the dysfunctions of the old. Accordingly, as I will show, the same narratives which celebrate a spirit of national renewal lay bare the reasons why no such redemption was possible.

There is nothing new about this attempt to remedy social and political divisions through narrative or the causes of its failure. Almost half a century before the battle for the Falklands, George Orwell undertook a similar cause in *Homage to Catalonia* (1938), the account of his experiences in the Spanish Civil War, and suffered an identical defeat. While Orwell set out in *Homage to Catalonia* to celebrate the achievements of revolutionary socialism in Spain, its increasingly evident shortcomings led him to focus in ever greater detail on how and why it had failed and to consider the role his own narrative could play in confirming or countering its collapse. The moral triumph of *Homage to Catalonia* lay in Orwell's refusal to apologise for the revolution, to resolve its failings in and through his narrative. He focused instead on a sober analysis of what the revolution had achieved and where it had gone wrong, praising its enlightened experiments in egalitarianism but condemning its political conduct. Orwell thus had the integrity to put his personal commitments to one side and to carry his unflinching examination of his own side's inefficiency, brutality and mendacity through to its illuminating if bitter conclusion. British accounts of the Falklands War, in the main, did not. Orwell's account provides both an ideological and practical model for my own homage to the Falklands. Accordingly, I will examine it at some length here in order to illustrate and foreshadow my own theoretical and methodological approach. This is not to imply any direct moral or political links between the Falklands and Spanish Civil Wars, but to demonstrate how, in two thoroughly dissimilar conflicts undertaken in pursuit of radically differing political ends, half a world and half a century apart, the epistemological concerns and the narrative responses to them remain broadly similar, if not identical.

SCRIPTING THE WAR

Just as British politicians and the media identified the Falklands Conflict as a turning point in the life of the nation, the moment and the place in which the nation rediscovered itself, so, writing in 1946, Orwell claimed that Spain embodied a similar significance in his own life: 'The Spanish Civil War and other events in 1936–7 turned the scale and thereafter I knew where I stood. Every line of serious work that I have written since 1936 has been written, directly or indirectly, *against* totalitarianism and *for* democratic Socialism, as I understand it' (Orwell, 1965: 186). Spain, he insisted, had been his personal and political 'Road to Damascus', and *Homage to Catalonia* was a detailed account of that journey. Yet as Orwell's biographer, Bernard Crick, has pointed out, Orwell's construction of himself as an innocent abroad, schooled in politics and street fighting by the hard lessons of Barcelona, though effecting, was false. Orwell had committed himself to 'democratic Socialism' long before he travelled to Catalonia. From 31 January to 30 March 1936, twelve months before he left for Spain, Orwell spent eight weeks in Wigan, Barnsley and Sheffield, living with working-class families, visiting their places of work and leisure, gathering the raw material for *The Road to Wigan Pier* (1937). It was *this* journey, Crick asserted, 'not just the actual experience of "Wigan" but the reckoning it forced on him of where he stood, which committed him to Left-wing socialism and took him to Spain in the first place. He was fully committed to "democratic Socialism" (as he so carefully typed the small "d" and the large "S") before ever he went' (Crick, 1992: 193). The national conversion ostensibly effected by the Falklands War was, I will demonstrate, no less dramatic and no less specious.

Orwell's subsequent misrepresentation of the effects that the war had on him was compounded by the mutually conflicting goals of his book. His attempts to establish a coherent and credible record of events which faithfully reflected his contradictory responses to the war, to balance narrative coherence, factual accuracy and emotional honesty, were doomed to failure. Despite his political convictions, Orwell's personal feelings about what happened to him in Spain were distinctly ambivalent: his commitment to the cause was balanced by his reluctance to kill for it; his affection for the stoicism and decency of his comrades was tinged with condescension for their comic inefficiency; while his respect for the militias was qualified by his frustration at their attachment to revolutionary principles which compromised their military performance.[5] Accordingly, he found that he was able to sustain a coherent narrative of events only by consistently retailing a less than honest version of them. Similarly, in the Falklands War the media's determination to promote the cause was often at odds with its responsibility to offer an accurate record of it – when the two collided the cause of promotion almost invariably won out.

In an effort to avoid the ambiguities of tone and the slippages of viewpoint which a faithful record of his responses would inevitably entail and so to preserve a coherent focus for his account, Orwell articulates his views about and his experience of Spain through a narrative persona, a more credulous, more naive version of himself, a figure we will call 'Blair'.[6] Through Blair, Orwell translates his confusing and contradictory experiences in Spain into a traditional rites of passage narrative, a conventional *Bildungsroman*, a straightforward linear progression from innocence to experience, military and political, by means of war. In a similar fashion, the government and the media projected an idealised vision of Britain, a nation unified, harmonious and renewed, returned to its rightful position of moral, political and military leadership by the conflict in the Falklands.

Each stage in Blair's education is marked by the recurrence of a common pattern of events in which his naive expectations are, often comically, disappointed. These expectations about what he will find in Spain are founded on Orwell's understanding of and attitudes towards the First World War. As such, while Blair provides a structurally and psychologically stable focus for his account, Orwell's responses to the First World War organise his experiences into a recurring and predictable pattern and so furnish the narrative with a stable structuring principle. The Second World War exercises a similar epistemological function in accounts of the Falklands War, though in this case the historical parallels are employed to promote patterns of congruence not contradiction.

Yet the First World War occupies more than a purely structuring role in Orwell's account, it also provides a framework within which the events in Spain can be understood and interpreted – a key to their explanation and reception. In fact, one might reasonably propose that Orwell's responses to the Civil War are more decisively shaped by his imagined construction of the First World War than by anything that happens to him in Spain – that Orwell's Spain is hardly less virtual than Baudrillard's Gulf. In a similar fashion, I will show that events in the Falklands War and the public reception of them were framed within and shaped by popular attitudes towards specific events from the Second World War.

While this might look like a calculated act of narrative distortion, it is in part a reasonable psychological response to unfamiliar experiences. Cognitive scientists have long argued that what we think of as acts of perception are really acts of recall.[7] One makes sense of new or unfamiliar experiences, they claim, not merely by perceiving, identifying and organising their component features into a composite meaning, so-called 'bottom-up' processing, but also by framing these events and experiences in accordance with expectations, assumptions and prior-knowledge, otherwise known as 'top-down' processing (MacLachlan and Reid, 1994: 70). Schank and Abelson refer to the narratives composed of such expectations, assumptions and prior-knowledge as 'scripts' (1977: 41). When one finds oneself in a situation for which one has no script – for example, when, like Orwell in Spain, or one of the many journalists who accompanied the task force to the Falkland Islands, one is first exposed to conflict – the common and, according to John Keegan, by far the most intelligent response is to order the experience and one's responses to it, to neutralise one's fear of the unexpected by making use of somebody else's script: 'Battles are extremely confusing; and confronted with the need to make sense of something he does not understand, even the cleverest, indeed pre-eminently the cleverest man, realizing his need for a language and metaphor he does not possess, will turn to look at what someone else has already made of a similar set of events as a guide for his own pen' (Keegan, 1976: 62). Accordingly, just as the Second World War provided both a model and a basis for the public's top-down processing of the Falklands War, so the origins and nature of Orwell's responses to Spain can be traced in the evolution of his attitudes towards the First World War. His adolescent rejection of the First World War as 'a meaningless slaughter', in which 'even the men who had been slaughtered were held to be in some way to blame', underwent a radical transformation through the 1930s and 1940s (Orwell, 1984: 141). Though largely worked out and expressed in the essays written during the Second World War, his revised views had their origins in the preceding decade, when the First World War's unsavoury associations with imperialist politics were peeled away and a generation untested in battle reconstructed it as a site of personal, physical and moral self-affirmation: 'As the war fell back into the past, my particular generation, those who had been "just too young", became conscious of the vastness of the experience they had missed. You felt yourself a little less than a man because you had missed it' (Orwell, 1984: 141). The men who had fought in the First World War had proven themselves by facing up to and coming through the greatest challenge of their age. Many among the 'just too young' generation believed that they could prove *their* mettle only by undergoing a comparable experience, a Test.[8] Likewise, the Falklands War was seen to offer a generation cosseted by peace the opportunity to emulate (albeit vicariously, purely as spectators of the actual fighting) its parents' and grandparents' experiences in the Second World War.

Orwell visualised the Test that he both dreaded and desired as a symbolic and physical rite of passage across an archetypal First World War battlefield: 'On and off I have been toting a rifle since I was ten, in preparation not only for war but for a particular kind of war, a war in which the guns rise to a frantic orgasm of sound and at the appointed moment you clamber out of the trench, breaking your nails on the sandbags, and stumble across mud and wire into the machine-gun barrage' (Orwell, 1984: 142). In this context, when General Mola led the rebellion against the elected government of Republican Spain in July 1936 so igniting the Civil War it is no surprise that so many of the 'just too young' generation volunteered to fight: here, after all, was the ideal opportunity to combine business with pleasure, political convictions with personal needs, to halt the march of fascism and in the process undertake the Test and supply the proof of one's personal valour. The First World War thus permeated every aspect of Orwell's expectations about and experience of Spain. It not only provided a framework for his understanding of and responses to the Spanish Civil War, but also furnished an experiential model for the resolution of fundamental personal insecurities. In this regard, as I will show, it is a model of the public and private uses to which specific narratives from the Second World War were put by governments, participants in and observers of the Falklands War. The persistent identification of the Second World War as Britain's finest hour, as a moral and behavioural model for the nation's conduct in the Falklands, provided politicians, the media, combatants and the public with a means both of making sense of the conflict and of reinventing themselves through it by returning the nation to a semblance of its heroic past. While Orwell roamed the Aragon front in search of an authentic First World War experience, during the Falklands War politicians and the media set out to replicate the conditions and thereby rekindle the collective moral and psychological certitudes of the Second World War by framing the conflict in discursive forms closely identified with the iconic triumphs of the 1940s, in particular Dunkirk and the Blitz. The Second World War thus functioned as a palimpsest over which events in the Falklands were inscribed, in the context of which they might be understood, and against which they might be measured.

ANOTHER WAR

Despite Orwell's claim that 'part of the reason for the fascination that the Spanish Civil War had for people of about my age was that it was so like the Great War', Spain's failure to live up to his imagined version of the First World War structures the record of his time there into a continual passage between the pitches and troughs of expectation, disillusionment and comic resignation (Orwell, 1984: 142).

> In the afternoon we did our first guard and Benjamin showed us round the position. In front of the parapet there ran a system of narrow trenches hewn out of the rock, with extremely primitive loopholes made of piles of limestone. There were twelve sentries, placed at various points in the trench and behind the inner parapet. In front of the trench was the barbed wire, and then the hill-side slid down into a seemingly bottomless ravine; opposite were naked hills, in places mere cliffs of rock, all grey and wintry, with no life anywhere, not even a bird. I peered cautiously through a loophole, trying to find the Fascist trench.
>   'Where are the enemy?'
>   Benjamin waved his hand expansively. 'Over zere.' (Benjamin spoke English – terrible English.)

'But *where?*'

According to my ideas of trench warfare the Fascists would be fifty or a hundred yards away. I could see nothing – seemingly their trenches were very well concealed. Then with a shock of dismay I saw where Benjamin was pointing; on the opposite hill-top, beyond the ravine, seven hundred metres away at the very least, the tiny outline of a parapet and a red-and-yellow flag – the Fascist position. I was indescribably disappointed. We were nowhere near them! At that range our rifles were completely useless ... They called this war! And we were hardly even in touch with the enemy! (Orwell, 1938: 20–1)

This pattern of expectation and disillusionment increasingly centres on Orwell's search for an appropriately Test-ing experience, for the opportunity to prove himself to himself on the field of battle. For more than fifty pages he looks in vain for action and a context appropriate to the Test, yet throughout that time the only battles he undergoes are with hunger and boredom, the only assaults he suffers are his nightly skirmishes with vermin and the cold, and the only test he endures is that of his patience.

When the moment of truth finally arrives, and Orwell goes over the top in an attack on a fascist redoubt, there are none of the vital details needed to authenticate the significance of the experience, no orgasm of sound, no sandbags to clamber over and no machine-gun barrage to march into. In fact both the props and the progress of events seem like a calculated inversion, a comic denial of Orwell's heroic expectations. He and his fellow attackers proceed through a gap in their own parapet and advance not into a hail of bullets but a line of irrigation ditches brimming with muddy water: the attack takes place in complete silence broken only by the slop, slop, slop of the militiamen's sodden boots.

In the immediate context, what Orwell seeks in the fascist trenches is single combat with the enemy, objective proof of his personal valour and his own heroic incarnation: 'We dashed up the short steep slope on which the parapet stood ... I took it for granted that there would be a Fascist waiting for me at the top. If he fired at that range he could not miss me, and yet somehow I never expected him to fire, only to try for me with his bayonet. I seemed to feel in advance the sensation of our bayonets crossing, and I wondered whether his arm would be stronger than mine' (Orwell, 1938: 68–9). Yet this achieved heroic self remains maddeningly elusive, if not a little impudent: all that Orwell ever sees of it is a blanket, a bare head and a pair of naked buttocks disappearing into the darkness, just beyond his reach:

> As I rounded the corner of the hut I saw a man ... fleeing up the com-
> munication trench that led to the other Fascist position. I must have
> been very close to him, for I could see him clearly. He was bareheaded
> and seemed to have nothing on except a blanket which he was
> clutching around his shoulders ... I gripped my rifle by the small of
> the butt and lunged at the man's back. He was just out of my reach.
> Another lunge, still out of reach. And for a little distance we
> proceeded like this, he rushing up the trench and I after him on the
> ground above, prodding at his shoulder blades and never quite
> getting there. (Orwell, 1938: 69)

Orwell's fruitless pursuit of the naked fascist offers an apposite and
suggestive conclusion to his search for heroic fulfilment in that it
implies not only how but why Spain has failed to satisfy him. What
he seeks there is the consecration of an experience predicated on the
moral, physical and narrative conditions of the First World War: by
combating the fascists in Spain he is discursively fighting a different
enemy in another war in another place. For all his rapt evocation of
the beauty of the mountains, his admiration and affection for his
comrades, the naked fascist makes it clear that in a discursive sense
Orwell is not yet in Spain – little wonder then that he is left lunging
at shadows. Similarly, despite the many expressions of outrage from
politicians and the media over the Argentine seizure of the Falklands,
it is clear that the islands and the democratic rights of their people
mattered little in and of themselves. They were significant in that they
provided a resonant context for the resolution of a range of domestic
anxieties, a site in which other battles from other wars unrelated to the
Falkland Islands and their people could be fought out again, a place
in which the values of the heroic past could be rediscovered and the
nation renewed by them. If Spain left Orwell feeling alienated from an
imaginary heroic past, then the official accounts of the Falklands War
are increasingly, triumphally overwhelmed by it.

BLIND WITNESS

In a discursive sense, the attraction of the First World War for Orwell
was that it provided him with a means of fashioning the conflict in
Spain into the image of his political convictions and the resolution of
his personal needs. Yet the process by which Orwell understood the
Spanish Civil War bred not only personal disillusionment but a
fundamental misapprehension about the nature of the conflict there.
In this regard, as I will show, it provides a striking model for the uses
that the dominant British accounts of the Falklands Conflict made of

the moral and political landscape and the discursive and historical forms of the Second World War.

Orwell's pursuit of a purely personal agenda in Spain implies that until the Barcelona street fighting of May 1937, he regarded the conflict there as morally and politically uncomplicated, a straightforward struggle between the forces of socialism and fascism, good and evil, and therefore an ideal context within which he could seek his own personal and political fulfilment. However, the collapse of the Popular Front and the bloody clashes between its competing factions demonstrated that Spain offered no such cosy polarities and brought home to Orwell how little he understood of the war, indeed that he scarcely knew what it was that he was fighting for there. This is an experience with some powerful correspondents in the Falklands when the enemy's mask of otherness slips to reveal a disturbingly familiar face.

Accordingly, after his return to Barcelona from the Aragon front, Orwell sets out to map the moral and political terrain of the war, to produce a reliable and objective record of the relative positions of the opposing parties and so counter some of the more blatant lies retailed by all sides. To this end he shifts the primary focus of his account from the maintenance of a coherent narrative of events to the provision of an accurate and honest record of them, thus abandoning any further reference to or use of the First World War as an aid either to structure or description.[9] Conversely, despite compelling evidence of their resulting speciousness, narratives from or about the fighting in the South Atlantic continued to stick doggedly to the Second World War as a moral and narrative precedent for both understanding and interpreting the events in the Falklands – discursive fidelity to the narrative norms of the Second World War, it was seen, provided a boost to the government's moral and military credentials and a buttress for its political credibility.

To begin with, the key weapon in Orwell's search for an accurate and truthful account of the war was lucid prose. Orwell believed in a direct equivalence between descriptive transparency, factual accuracy and moral probity: 'Good prose', he declared, 'is like a window pane': the immediate access to reality which it apparently affords is an implicit declaration of its moral and political integrity (Orwell, 1965: 13). Bad prose, on the other hand, obscures rather than discloses; its logic of concealment, its inherent duplicity, makes it the *lingua franca* of politics and propaganda.[10] Clear expression, as such, is more than a stylistic ideal, it is a litmus-test of moral and political virtue: 'The great enemy of clear language', Orwell averred, 'is insincerity' (Orwell, 1957: 154).

The Spanish Civil War, however, shattered Orwell's faith in language as a reliable indicator of moral or political principle, in a straightforward equivalence between good prose and a good cause. In Spain

Orwell encountered plenty of good prose advocating what seemed to him a morally indefensible cause, while the good cause's propaganda was all too often a case study in 'bad writing', if not bare-faced lies, most notably and painfully for Orwell in the denunciation of his faction, the POUM (Partido Obrero de Unificación Marxista, United Marxist Workers' Party), by its ostensible ally, the PSUC (Partido Socialista Unificado Catalunya, United Socialist Party of Catalonia): 'One of the dreariest effects of this war', he lamented, 'has been to teach me that the Left-wing press is every bit as spurious and dishonest as that of the right' (Orwell, 1938: 208).[11]

This irregular correspondence between good and bad prose and good and bad politics deconstructed the moral certainties that Orwell had invested in language and compelled him to see that the clarity of his account, his own impeccable prose, was no guarantee that his record of the war was an honest one. In order to establish its credibility he first had to prove his own integrity, to demonstrate that he was indeed telling the truth. Consequently, he spends little time comparing the relative veracity of competing accounts, dedicating his energies, both physical and narrative, to the search for evidence authenticating his own record of events. To this end, much of the second half of *Homage to Catalonia* is concerned with his pursuit of three specific texts: his discharge papers, a letter of recommendation carried by his Commandant George Kopp when he was detained after the suppression of the POUM, and a leaflet reputedly issued by an anarchist splinter group, the Friends of Durruti. These are intended to corroborate specific aspects of Orwell's account, to prove, respectively, that he had been a loyal servant of the Republican cause; that Kopp was a valued officer on his way to take up an important position with the Army of the East; and that the POUM had not instigated the factional fighting in Barcelona in May 1937. Yet as Orwell found to his dismay, documentary evidence, proof, was no more reliable an indicator of honesty than was good prose. His treatment of the Friends of Durruti leaflet is exemplary in this regard. Though he admits that he had been unable to trace the leaflet, and broadly hints that it may never have existed, he still proffers its purported contents as proof that the POUM had been the victims and not the instigators of the internecine fighting in Barcelona.[12] In contrast, the foreign press, which had had no more access to the leaflet than Orwell, denounced its 'inflammatory' tendencies and held it up as clear evidence of the POUM's culpability (Orwell, 1938: 220). Clearly, whether or not the leaflet ever actually existed is of little moment: proof, like good prose, is an ideological construct and not a self-evident, objectively identifiable material; a product and not merely the determinant of opinion which proves nothing beyond the partiality of the views it supports. Orwell's experience with the Durruti leaflet provides a model of the ways in which the government and the media used various kinds of proof to promote an official line on the Falklands Conflict.[13] As I will show, driven by contemporary political needs and the moral, historical and narrative parallels which they drew between the Falklands and the Second World War, the government and the media had determined their interpretation of the causes, progress and outcomes of the fighting in the South Atlantic long before the first shots were exchanged – that is to say, the war had been written before it ever took place. The proofs they subsequently adduced to promote their interpretation of the conflict – eyewitness testimony, objective records of events – were functions and not the determinants of the official line.

Defeated in his efforts to provide a reliable overview of the conflict, a convincing historical account of its events, Orwell determined instead to offer an authentic eyewitness record of what he saw and did there – to substitute uncertainty with immediacy. However, an eyewitness account was, he discovered, no more reliable a means to the truth of events than was documentary evidence, as what the eyewitness gained in immediacy he lost in universality. Orwell's record of how the war looked and sounded merely disclosed how little of it he saw or heard. For example, throughout *Homage to Catalonia* Orwell portrays himself in situations intended to enhance his view of his surroundings: in possession of a powerful telescope in the trenches; on the roof of a building overlooking the Ramblas where some of the fiercest fighting in the May clashes took place; in a sanatorium on Tibidabo, the prominent hill to the west of Barcelona with its panoramic views over the city. Yet on each occasion these vantage points emphasise how limited a view he had of the war. Orwell spent the first three days of the Barcelona street fighting on the roof of the Poliorama Cinema at the top of the Ramblas, the *de facto* front-line between the communist and anarchist factions, perched like an umpire over a net, sitting directly below 'a small observatory with twin domes' from the windows of which 'you could see for miles around' (Orwell, 1938: 110, 111). Despite his privileged viewpoint Orwell could see nothing of the fighting, save the occasional rifle poked from surrounding windows, and could know even less of the political manoeuvring taking place behind the scenes. Consequently, his descriptions of the fighting are a catalogue of absences and vacancy, filled only by the incessant rain of hidden gunfire, 'a nightmare of noise without movement', his eyewitness account little better than the testimony of a blind man. In this regard there were further fundamental similarities with the experience of the Falklands War in that the continued prominence of the Second World War as both a means of framing and interpreting events in the South Atlantic actually served to blind the public and many of those who participated in the fighting to the specific realities of the conflict. Those whose testimony deviated from the official line were, as Robert Lawrence and Philip Williams found, encouraged (if not coerced) to conform with its discursive norms or, failing that, pressured to hold their peace.[14]

Though Orwell can describe how he felt in Spain, he knows and persistently regrets the fact that he cannot make the reader feel or experience it. His impressions remain his own and his endeavours to confirm the nature and intensity of them are thus ultimately solipsistic. His most significant memories of the war, memories which bookend the text and are, in his own words, 'typical of Spain' – shaking hands with the Italian militiaman and the little officer's handshake at police headquarters – are both moments of silence, poignant symbols of an intensely lived experience which he can communicate fully to nobody (Orwell, 1938: 186). Yet in spite of this he refuses to tailor his honesty to his political convictions, to overlook his epistemological uncertainties and endorse the popular image of the conflict's clean, but quite imaginary polarities, moral and political. In this regard, *Homage to Catalonia* offers a striking model of what the official line on the Falklands Conflict might have been, and a testament to everything it was not.

It was Orwell's determination to document faithfully what he saw and felt in Spain no matter how it offended the personal and political illusions which had sent him there that led Crick to celebrate *Homage to Catalonia* as a model of honest reporting, an object lesson in how 'to tell the verifiable truth, the whole truth and nothing but the truth' (Crick, 1992: 365). Yet what Crick saw as a triumphal attainment of the truth was in fact an account of Orwell's lonely and fruitless pursuit of it, an analysis of how it might be fixed, framed and communicated, if not a meditation on the viability of truthfulness itself. What seemed, in Raymond Williams' terms, to be 'a problem of form', a matter of rendering a coherent narrative of the events in Spain, ultimately emerges as 'a problem of consciousness', a question of whether one could ever attain the epistemological certainty which any coherent record implies (Williams 1991: 46). In this respect, the parallels with the coverage of the Falklands Conflict are particularly significant. In his quest for truthfulness Orwell is driven to examine and ultimately to condemn the epistemological principles and discursive norms on which the coherence of his own narrative is founded. His investment in Spain is essentially ideological and emotional, yet when he finds that his moral ideals and political principles have been abused he willingly lays them on the altar of honesty in pursuit of the truth about the war. In the Falklands the stakes were far higher and yet far lower: the fundamental principle shaping the government's responses to and representation of the conflict was its survival and the promotion of its policies. As such, truth, honesty, private and public principles were piled high on the altar of political expediency. Narrative and political coherence became both symbolically and effectually linked in and through the conflict: their mutual promotion was regarded as a matter of political urgency and their mutual defence, through the suppression of material which threatened either, was a guiding principle of media policy on the war.[15] The government and the media thus directed their energies to the defence and not the deconstruction of the epistemological principles and narrative norms on which their triumphal record of the conflict rested; to the purging and not the propagation of doubt; to the celebration of victory and not the contemplation of its compromises. It will be my purpose in the succeeding chapters of this book to identify the dominant features of these triumphal narratives, to consider their cultural origins and the political ends to which they were put, to consider, in short, the conditions of their truthfulness and then to carry through the deconstructive analysis so willingly undertaken by Orwell and yet so trenchantly resisted by the proponents and beneficiaries of the official versions of the Falklands Conflict.

2
Recovering the National Past

We have ceased to be a nation in retreat. (qtd in Barnett, 1982: 152)

THE NATIONAL PAST

On the day that Special Forces returned the Malvinas to Argentine rule, 2 April 1982, Adrian Mole celebrated his fifteenth birthday. The one bright spot among a disappointing selection of cards and gifts, 'the usual load of Japanese rubbish', was a model aeroplane ('made in West Germany') and a tube of glue (Townsend, 1982: 186). Early the next morning as news of the historic events in the South Atlantic unfolded, Adrian recorded his own and his family's responses:

> 8 a.m. Britain is at war with Argentina!!! Radio Four has just announced it. I am overcome with excitement. Half of me thinks it is tragic and the other half of me thinks it is dead exciting.
> 10 a.m. Woke my father up to tell him Argentina has invaded the Falklands. He shot out of bed because he thought the Falklands lay off the coast of Scotland. When I pointed out that they were eight thousand miles away he got back into bed and pulled the covers over his head. (Townsend, 1982: 186)

Dismayed by his father's unpatriotic apathy and frustrated by his inability to take any direct part in or even witness the action, Adrian retreated to his room. There he found solace and perhaps a vicarious sense of involvement in the war in assembling his model aircraft, until a flirtation with glue-sniffing landed him in hospital, the plane firmly attached to his nose – Britain's first casualty of the Falklands War.

George and Adrian Mole's differing responses to the invasion of the Falklands, a combination of excitement, indignation, trepidation and profound indifference, do more than adumbrate the range of opinions registered in the national media at the time of the crisis. They lay bare the primary difficulty faced by those dedicated to the recuperation of the islands, the need to overcome public indifference, to establish that the Falklands *mattered*, as well as implying one of the ways in which this might be achieved, by giving the public the opportunity to play soldier. Overcoming public apathy was, at the outset of the conflict, no small task. Many people, not least the soldiers tasked with recovering them, had no idea of where the Falkland Islands were or why Argentina would want them: '"Why have the Argentinians invaded Scotland?" thought [Private] Lee Fisher. "It's a long way to go for them. Of course, I wasn't actually sure where Argentina was, let alone the Falklands"' (Jennings and Weale, 1996: 48). It was widely held that the islands could matter little if few people had heard of them and fewer still could find them in an atlas, a point economically driven home by Sue Townsend when Adrian Mole tries without success to locate the islands on a map of the world: 'I couldn't see the Falkland Islands anywhere. My mother found them; they were hidden under a crumb of fruitcake' (Townsend 1984: 13). The obscurity of the islands, it is implied, offers a full measure of their political and cultural irrelevance. The *Guardian* made a similar point in an editorial printed the day after news of the invasion broke in Britain, when it cautioned against the whipping up of 'spurious national sentiment', reminding its readers that 'the Falkland Islands do not represent any strategic or commercial British interest worth fighting over' (*Guardian*, 3 April 1982: 8).

However, the official British line on the conflict was entirely premised on the whipping up of national sentiment, spurious or otherwise, as the government recognised that the George Moles of Britain would emerge from the bedclothes to pledge their support to the task force and those who dispatched it only if they could be convinced that the Falkland Islands mattered to them, that the invasion was an issue of immediate domestic concern to every Briton. How best to achieve this? It was more than 8,000 miles from Portsmouth to Port Stanley and it would take the task force the better part of three weeks to sail the length of the Atlantic Ocean, over the equator from spring to autumn, summer to winter. Surely there was no more concrete a testament to the islands' complete otherness than their physical and cultural distance from all that was local and familiar? Ironically, it was this very obscurity that underpinned their significance, that revealed why it was that the Falklands mattered so much. Utterly removed as they were from what Anthony Barnett called 'the complications of substance', the islands were 'a perfect stage for the exercise of Principle' (Barnett, 1982: 69). As Jonathan Raban observed:

Their blankness was their point: you could make them mean nothing or everything. And England had run out of symbols. Over this windy weekend [2–4 April 1982], it was busy writing meaning into the Falklands, making that undulating desolate land *signify*. Between Friday morning and Sunday afternoon, the Falkland Islands accumulated a huge number of significations. They meant Tradition,

Honour, Loyalty, Community, Principle – they meant the whole web and texture of being British. (Raban, 1986: 113)

This inventory of the islands' new significance offers a sly dig at the moral and political tendentiousness of much of the public comment inspired by the invasion – in particular expansive editorial in *The Times* on 5 April, which portrayed Argentina's recovery of the islands as morally and politically equivalent to the Nazi invasion of Poland.[1] The seizure of the islands, the editorial claimed, was a timely reminder of Britain's vulnerability in 'a dangerous and unpredictable world ... menaced by the forces of tyranny'. Britain's response to the invasion would be a crucial test of its mettle and a measure of its right to maintain a prominent place in that world:

in 1939 we stood by Poland and went to war ... a moment had come in Europe when the consequence of not standing up to the aggressive policies of a dictatorship would have been worse than standing up to them. We are now in the same position with the Argentine dictatorship ... As in 1939, so today; the same principles apply to the Falklands. We have given our word, and we must, where we can, prevent the expansionist policies of a dictatorship affecting our interests. But there is a more important dimension now. The Poles were Poles; the Falklanders are our people. They are British citizens. The Falkland Islands are British territory. When British territory is invaded, it is not just an invasion of our land, but of our whole spirit. We are all Falklanders now.
... We are an island race, and the focus of attack is one of our islands, inhabited by our islanders. At this point of decision the words of John Donne could not be more appropriate for every Briton, for every islander, for every man and woman anywhere in a world menaced by the forces of tyranny:
'No man is an island, entire of itself. Any man's death diminishes me, because I am involved in mankind; and therefore never send to know for whom the bell tolls; it tolls for thee'.
It tolls for us; it tolls for them (*The Times*, 5 April 1982: 11)

Us? Them? It is the explicit aim of this editorial to erase these distinctions, to stress our moral, historical and geographical community with the islands and their people, to identify them as ciphers of our own past and potential experiences and so establish them both as symbols of and rallying points for 'national sentiment'. The Falklands should matter to us because there, but for the grace of God ...
The editorial also exemplifies one of the central discursive strategies deployed by the government and the media in their efforts to close the meanings of and so garner support for the war: the collapsing of

selected versions of the past into the present (and vice versa) through the elision of historical and cultural narratives from the Second World War into accounts of the loss and recovery of the Falkland Islands. In this process, the relationship between past and present, between the Falklands and the Second World War, is a complex one. As Patrick Wright points out: 'Far from being somehow "behind" the present, the past exists as an accomplished presence in public understanding. In this sense it is written into present social reality, not just implicitly as residue, precedent or custom and practice, but explicitly as itself – as History, National Heritage and Tradition' (Wright, 1985: 142). Wright identifies that sense of the past 'cultivated' and 'reproduced through a variety of public agencies (schools, television, political debate, historical fiction ...)' as 'the "national past"', and proposes that it functions 'as a controlling attribute of citizenship: something that at a generalized level enables citizens ... to find unity ... between themselves and to override unresolved socio-political contradictions and differences' (Wright, 1985: 143, 146). Seen in these terms, as a symbol of unity, a living presence in the nation's cultural life, carefully cultivated through a range of public agencies, the Second World War had, at the time of the Falklands Conflict, occupied a central place in the narrative of the 'national past' for almost forty years. In Paul Fussell's view: 'Our historical instinct about the [Second World] war, our "myth" if you will, is that it constituted a notably moral common cause, one moment at least in our history when ... greed, centrifugalism and jealous individualism briefly subdued themselves in the interests of virtue' (Fussell, 1982: 231). It had, in Paul Addison's view, 'served a generation ... as a myth which enshrined their essential purity, a parable of good and evil' (qtd in Fussell, 1982: 231). According to Peter Clarke 'this was a war in which everyone could "go to it" and do their bit on "the home front"', and as a result '[t]here was a general agreement that this was a "good war"' (Clarke, 1996: 207).[2] It was the aim of *The Times'* editorial, and the official line on the war that it endorsed, to establish the Falkland Islands, their people, and the mission to liberate them in just such terms, as both symbols of moral virtue and a source of cultural unity, as a focus for national consensus, and so to write them into a prominent place in the narrative of the national past.

This task was premised, in the first instance, on the representation of contemporary Britain as a nation ill-at-ease with itself, a nation that in political, social and economic terms, seemed to have lost its way since the heady days of 1945, a nation in exile from its authentic self. This was a collective self-image depressingly familiar to Britons in the late 1970s and early 1980s, Peter Calvocoressi's *The British Experience 1945–75* (1978) identified itself as 'the tale of hopes deflated by failures' (Calvocoressi, 1978: 253),[3] while Jeremy Seabrook's study of working people and the post-war Labour movement was tellingly titled *What Went Wrong?* (1978). The Conservative Party's 1979 election campaign was premised on a definite view of what had gone wrong and the promotion of specific social and economic policies for fixing it and returning the nation to its former greatness. According to Seabrook and Blackwell, Margaret Thatcher's electoral success stemmed, in part, from her use of ennobling narratives to establish her radical policy agenda as the means to moral and spiritual as well as political redemption:

> to offer an epic account of where we are now and an heroic vision of how our situation may be transformed. Like so many storytellers she speaks of a long journey, a quest, a pilgrimage even ... But this is not just any mythic journey. It is a particular myth of exile, and Old Testament exile at that. The search is for the Promised Land. Suddenly the metaphor becomes clear. For many years the people have languished in exile. Many have succumbed to the fleshpots ('We are reaping what was sown in the sixties' – 'the years the locusts have eaten') and whored after false gods ('those who have chosen the easier path'). But a few have kept alive a memory – or is it a dream – of a Britain that was great and free. Thatcher appears – a Moses figure – and gives the people the courage to undertake the journey through the wilderness ('the rugged road') though she warns there will be sacrifices, and it will not be easy. (Seabrook and Blackwell, 1982: 7)

The straight and narrow path to redemption lay, Conservative politicians claimed, in a return to the moral, economic and social forms of the past, to those Victorian virtues – self-help, self-improvement and the authoritarian structures of the family – which, it was persistently asserted, had been the cause of and not merely the context for Britain's social, economic and military advances during the nineteenth century.[4] The nation's triumph in the Falklands offered both a symbolic first step and a model of behaviour for the journey to recovery. In a speech to the party faithful at Cheltenham shortly after the liberation of Stanley, the Prime Minister observed that the task force's success in the Falklands had been built on the same social hierarchies that had underpinned the foundation, expansion and functioning of empire. The virtues of leadership, duty and sacrifice that had served the nation so well in India, the Carribean and Africa had, she observed, brought victory over Argentina, and could now be turned to the reconquest of Britain itself, the defeat of the enemies within and a return to the glorious national past:

technology that had guaranteed their survival.[9] The brave new world of post-war reconstruction seemingly led deep into the past. In the light of this, the contrast between file footage from the Falklands and the first images of Argentine occupation broadcast and printed in Britain – hard hats and machine guns amid the rose bushes, picket fences broken up for firewood, ransacked cottages ankle-deep in excrement, helicopters on the greensward, Morris Minors motoring in the right-hand lane – did more than register the details of life under an occupying force. They indicated that the Argentine invasion constituted an assault on the symbolic heart of the country, the desecration of its most cherished icons of nationhood, 'an invasion ... of our whole spirit' – hence Fred Halliday's observation that it was as if 'the Nazis had taken over the Archers' (qtd Barnett, 1982: 101). Like the regulars from *The Archers* (an everyday story of country folk inhabiting the fictitious English village of Ambridge, broadcast daily on BBC Radio 4 since 1951), the islanders' 'evident British accents and rural gait made a deep impression' on the public (Barnett, 1982: 101).[10] They were, Jonathan Raban declared, 'visibly, audibly, our kith and kin ... The Falklanders *were* us' (Raban, 1986: 101). Rudely evicted from their homes and gardens, cast out from a life of edenic simplicity by the brutal forces of the modern military state, the islanders offered a striking symbol of Britain's own sense of bewildered exile from its post-war pastoral, its rough handling in a world grown hostile and perilous. The endeavour to retake and so restore these people to their islands thus signified far more than the recovery of so much nostalgic real estate: it represented an attempt to recover for the nation as a whole a long-lost image of itself as a community socially coherent and morally content, to recover, and where necessary rewrite, the national past in order to conquer the enemies within and so command the national present.[11]

Consequently, the first photograph released to the media recording the return of British forces to the Falklands was not of the destruction wrought on the Royal Navy's ships by the Argentine Air Force in Falkland Sound, but Tom Smith's (chronologically) later shot of a para enjoying a cup of tea under the benign gaze of a family of Falklanders, smiling broadly behind their weather-beaten picket fence. In the sunlit background of the photo there is another wooden fence, and the corner of an inlet framed by rolling green hills. The cropping of the picture, which in the *Sunday Mirror* of 23 May 1982 tellingly excised the family's woolly-hatted patriarch, not only implied the vulnerability of the islanders (women and children, in the main, it would seem) and the brutality of the conquerors, it also emphasised the photograph's horizontal axis, and was thus central to its effective ideological functioning.[12] John Fiske notes that in photography the horizontal axis 'reinforces the connotations of confrontation: the

Figure 1 Recovering the National Past (photo by Tom Smith)

movement of the reader's eyes becomes an iconic representation of the exchanges between the two sides' (Fiske, 1990: 106). It was the specific purpose of this photograph, however, to resolve the confrontational into a celebration of the common. The picket fence and the cup of tea are both metonyms of domestic and family unity, as well as symbols of national identity: they defuse the oppositions implicit in the subjects' relative physical positions – oppositions between military and civilian culture, Britain and the Falklands, men and women, past and present – implying the social and cultural heritage common to all British peoples and signifying the fact that in recovering the Falklands and liberating their people Britain had 'found itself again in the South Atlantic'.[13]

MAKING THE NEWS

This photograph was, commendably, published less than forty-eight hours after it was taken. Yet the dispatch with which it was relayed and distributed was the exception rather than the rule in media coverage of the war. In 1854, William Howard Russell's description of The Charge of the Light Brigade took twenty days to reach London; in 1982, photos, film footage and written reports from the Falklands took up to twenty-three days. As Robert Harris observed: 'for the bulk of the Falklands War, the camera might as well not have been invented. The crisis lasted for seventy-four days, and for the first fifty-four there were no British pictures of any action' (Harris, 1983: 57). In the light of these delays, and the deliberate hindrance of news from the South Atlantic that they implied, it was alleged that the Falklands Conflict was 'the worst reported war since the Crimea' (Harris, 1983: 56).[14] However, the assumption that the less news is mediated the purer it is, that speedier and more direct communications between London and the South Atlantic would have produced better coverage of the conflict, rests on an idealised if not naive construction of the material, functions and practices of journalism.[15] It sees the news, unproblematically, as 'an objective body of truth about the world' which it is the responsibility of the journalist to faithfully record and accurately render (Windschuttle, 1988: 261). Yet as Morrison and Tumber note, 'news does not exist independently of someone defining it as news' (Morrison and Tumber, 1988: 4–5). It is not an objective material but the product of specific institutional processes in which the nomination, reporting and representation of any given event as news expresses a 'selective interpretation of society through a mediating ideology' (Windschuttle, 1988: 270).[16] In the press, this mediating ideology is articulated in a consistent editorial line which is policed and enforced by various gatekeeping systems – the reporter's own professional socialisation and subsequent selection of events as news backed up by sub-editors and editors – which ensure ideological conformity in everything from punctuation to political commentary. The news, from this perspective, is no consensual body of facts but 'a social and cultural institution' producing an ideological commodity whose function is primarily hegemonic (Hartley, 1982: 4). Shaped in the image and the interests of those who define and retail it, the news plays a vital role in shaping those who consume it, 'naturalizing dominant ideology and winning consent for hegemony' (Hartley, 1982: 62).[17]

It was from just such a functional view of the news that Philip Knightley judged the media coverage of the Falklands Conflict not a failure but an unprecedented success, a 'model' of reporting which any government with a war to wage would do well to emulate (Knightley, 1989: 438). In his study of the war correspondent from the Crimea to the Falklands, *The First Casualty* (1989), Knightley details the various efforts of governments to maintain the appearance of a free flow of information in time of war while actually managing it in their own political interests. In no conflict over the preceding 150 years, Knightley asserts, had any government succeeded in this more completely than did the British in the Falklands: 'the MoD achieved *exactly* what its political masters wanted it to do, and its role in the Falklands campaign will go down in the history of journalism as a classic example of how to manage the media in wartime' (Knightley, 1989: 434). Knightley is, clearly, advancing a technical and not a moral judgement here: what impressed him was not the zeal with which the British pursued the truth but the completeness of their control over its manufacture.

The government and the media owed this control, in no small part, to the peculiar physical circumstances of the conflict. Never an easy place to get to, Argentina's invasion of the Falklands effectively cut the islands off from the rest of the world. As of 2 April 1982, the only physical link between the UK and the Falklands was provided by the Royal Navy who, at first, were unwilling to accommodate a single media representative on the journey to the South Atlantic. It was only after what has been called 'the most violent media lobbying of No. 10 [Downing Street] in recent history' that room was grudgingly found for 29 journalists, photographers, film crew and technicians (Cockerill, 1982: 7).[18] When the news organisations were, eventually, invited to propose candidates for the voyage, the names they put forward, coupled with those correspondents nominated by the MoD, ensured that coverage of the war would be sympathetic, if not enthusiastic.[19] By and large the newspapers and broadcasters kept 'their best men', their feature writers and defence correspondents, at home to cover the domestic angle on the crisis (Morrison and Tumber, 1988: 11).[20] Of the twenty-nine reporters who sailed with the task force only Mike Nicholson and Max Hastings had had any previous experience of reporting a war, while only three of the others, Derek Hudson of the *Yorkshire Post*, Ian Bruce of the *Glasgow Herald* and Alastair McQueen of the *Daily Mirror,* were (nominally) defence correspondents. The reporters who went to the Falklands were, by their own admission, 'second choice', solid but unspectacular wordsmiths, whose professional inexperience in matters of war and personal unpreparedness for what they encountered there ensured that little evidence of the brutality of the fighting would ever make it back to London, or through to the public. As it turned out, the reporters expended the greater part of their energy keeping themselves warm and alive. Happy, in the main, to accept the information made available to them through official briefings, few went alone in pursuit of alternative versions of events – 'you didn't feel the normal sort of desire to go out and find the truth' (Kim Sabido qtd in Morrison and Tumber, 1988: 98) – hence their almost unanimous endorsement of the official line on the conflict.

The military's strict control over access to the battlefield not only dictated who among the media could go to the Falklands, what they could see when they got there, and what they were allowed to dispatch to their employers, it also decisively determined *how* they wrote about the war, as the physical conditions imposed on them by the journey south resulted in subtler, but no less influential forms of self-censorship.

As reporters, the press had a duty to render 'a reasonable amount of accuracy and a rounded presentation of the facts' about events in the South Atlantic (Morrison and Tumber, 1988: xi). However, they were able to access and observe these events only through the good offices of the men whose performance they were ostensibly there to observe and evaluate with professional detachment. They were reliant on the ships and satellite facilities of the military for the transmission of their copy and dependent on the troops for instruction, equipment, companionship and protection. Confined to the ships on the long voyage south the journalists were, quite literally, locked in with the military. If physical proximity broke down the barriers of ignorance and suspicion between the journalists and the military then the common dangers they faced bred affinity, even closeness : 'The enmeshing, the identification, the whole process of involvement had nothing to do with each individual's private views, feelings about the war, or the attitudes of his organization. The dynamics of the situation were so powerful that they overwhelmed all this' (Morrison and Tumber, 1988: 99). Once ashore, as the campaign progressed, the hostility of the weather, the build-up for the battles around Stanley and the total absence of parallel civilian facilities rendered the media ever more reliant on the military and intensified the bonding process begun on ship – so much so that Robert Fox came to describe himself and his fellow hacks as 'troopie groupies' (Morrison and Tumber, 1988: 104).[21] As David Norris of the *Daily Mail* recalled: 'I couldn't help but think of myself as part of the operation. I suppose people might say that that's a bad thing, you should still maintain some impartiality. It's very difficult. On shore I dressed like a soldier. I ate like them, I lived with them. I just began to feel a part of the whole thing' (Morrison and Tumber, 1988: 98).

Accordingly, Norris and most of his colleagues found it more and more difficult to retain any sense of distance or detachment from events. When their professional responsibilities collided with their personal loyalties and private needs it was increasingly the latter that took precedence: 'what was happening to the journalists was that their professional need to cover a story in a detached way was slowly being swamped by the very real, human need to belong, to be safe' (Morrison and Tumber, 1988: 99). Loath to criticise men and women whose personal qualities, professionalism and teamwork they had grown to admire, who, on occasions, had risked their lives in defence of them, the reporters steered clear of stories which might reflect poorly on the troops and eschewed any genuinely critical analysis of the causes, conduct or aims of the war. As a result, according to Patrick Bishop: 'there wasn't any need to put pressure on anyone to write gung-ho copy because everyone was doing it without any stimulus from the military ... that's how most of the reporters felt. They were all very patriotic and "positive" about the whole thing. So the military didn't have to lean on them ... The situation was that you were a propagandist' (Morrison and Tumber, 1988: 98).

Yet this is not to suggest that the copy from the Falklands was the predictable end product of a sophisticated information policy. Indeed, for the first few weeks of the crisis the Acting Head of Public Relations at the Ministry of Defence (MoD), Ian McDonald, was unaware that the ministry even had a policy on the management of information in the event of armed conflict. In the pandemonium that erupted at Admiralty House early on 2 April 1982 when news of the Argentine invasion of the Falklands began to filter through, the brief on information policy, last updated in 1977, was entirely overlooked. McDonald, a career civil servant with no experience of PR, was under intense pressure from the Secretary of State for Defence, John Nott, to present a workable information policy.[22] In response, he told the House of Commons Defence Committee enquiry into the handling of press and public information during the campaign, 'I closed the door of my office and locked it and sat trying to think it out for five minutes' (Harris, 1983: 96). Plenty of time to boil an egg but hardly sufficient to resolve the competing demands of news and security.[23] McDonald's response was to centralise and so consolidate his personal control over the flow, management and dissemination of information about the war: 'All his staff had been forbidden to maintain their normal relations with the press. Only he was privy to the details of task force operations through his attendance of the Chiefs of Staffs Committee ... He personally drafted the Ministry's public statements. Apart from rare occasions when a military expert was called in to provide additional information, only McDonald briefed the media' (Harris, 1983: 105).[24]

The immediate upshot of his five-minute brainstorm was the cancellation of the unattributable briefings through which the Ministry provided defence correspondents with a steady flow of information and in turn promoted itself and fought its political battles. McDonald claimed that he cancelled the briefings to deny potentially useful information to the Argentinians: 'There was a very strong feeling that in fact to talk about where the Fleet, the task force, was, how it was being split up as it sailed to the Falkland Islands, would be to give information to the Argentines about possible intentions. I did not see how, talking unattributably off the record, we would be able to avoid trespassing on those kinds of areas' (Harris, 1983: 97). Yet by this criterion alone the policy was a dismal failure. Far from warding off the media it triggered a mass trespass into sensitive areas as defence correspondents, faced with the sudden and complete withdrawal of their regular supply of information, turned to extended speculation in an effort to satisfy an insatiable demand for news about the Falklands.

This ensured a far freer treatment of security issues than would ever have been the case under the original arrangements. In the most striking demonstration of the policy's adverse effects on security, the location of the proposed British beachhead on East Falkland, the subject of the utmost secrecy prior to the invasion, was not only identified but announced in the pages of a national daily more than three weeks before the first paratroopers waded ashore to reclaim the islands. In an article discussing possible sites for the main troop landing published on 28 April, the *Guardian*'s defence correspondent David Fairhall observed that 'the most likely choice, from simply looking at the map, would seem to be somewhere round Port San Carlos, at the northern end of the Falkland Sound which divides the two main islands' (Fairhall, 1982a: 13). Fortunately for the British, the Argentine High Command was too taken up with the mythic significance of the Malvinas to look at its maps with strategy and not symbolism in mind.[25]

By mid-May, however, after a series of complaints about the management of information from both the media and the military, McDonald was replaced by the man for whom he had been deputising, Neville Taylor, a civil servant with a background as a PR professional.[26] In response to a direct request from the Commander in Chief Fleet, Sir John Fieldhouse, Taylor set about extending the reach and sophistication of the news management system. He instituted a second screen of censorship in London staffed by PR experts to back up the MoD PR Officers (PROs), the so-called 'Minders', who had accompanied the journalists to the South Atlantic and were vetting their copy at source. This ensured, among much else, that the public were served a largely sanitised version of the war. In accomplishing this task the MoD were ably abetted by the editors at Broadcasting House and Fleet Street who, when they received more graphic images of the conflict, failed to make use of them. Even the Commander of British Land Forces in the Falklands, Major General Jeremy Moore, paid tribute to 'the good taste of our journalists that they did not show anything as unpleasant as could have been available' (qtd in Harris, 1983: 60).[27] The MoD later claimed in a memorandum to the HCDC that its deodorisation of the war was not a cynical exercise in public misinformation but a principled endeavour 'to minimize distress to the families of the servicemen, merchant seamen or civilians who were killed or injured in the action' (HCDC: Vol. II, p. i, para. 2).[28] Throughout the Falklands campaign, the MoD and the media organisations themselves insistently invoked 'security' or sensitivity to the bereaved as a justification for their management of taste and tone in the depiction of the war. The first casualty of the Falklands War therefore was not truth but, as John Taylor has pointed out, realism (Taylor, 1991: 92-6).

The MoD's campaign to stifle a realistic representation of the crisis was further assisted by technical difficulties that prevented the transmission of live TV pictures from the task force while it was in the South Atlantic. An ITN engineer, Peter Heaps, embarked on HMS *Hermes*, attempted without success to broadcast live TV pictures from the task force flagship back to the UK via the British military satellite, SKYNET. The technical problems were insuperable. The shipboard military satellite terminals, SCOT, were designed to carry only voice or encrypted signal traffic: television pictures required a far greater band-width. Heaps discovered that by employing all available frequencies he could transmit black and white pictures without sound. Yet to carry out a test he would have to occupy all available channels, taking the SCOT terminals out of commission for more than an hour, thereby shutting down the command ship's communications facilities for the duration of the transmission. The MoD considered this an unacceptable security risk, the tests were abandoned, and Heaps left the task force at Ascension Island and returned to the UK.

VISIONS AND REVISIONS

The absence of live footage from the Falklands was an enormous source of relief to politicians and MoD officials who were spared the onerous and highly sensitive task of censoring large amounts of contentious material under the watchful eye of the media and the public. Freed from the demands of immediate censorship the MoD was able to commit its resources to the more subtle manipulation of information from the South Atlantic, through the selection and dissemination of those narratives and images of the conflict best calculated to promote the government's official line on it. The MoD's management of still images provides a revealing case study of its censorship policies and how these worked to impede a realistic representation of the war. Photographs, as John Taylor has observed, 'are widely accepted as standing in for the real thing. They are taken as objective records, different from experience but none the less anchored in the real world' (Taylor, 1991: 1). The MoD ensured, from the outset, a strictly rationed diet of realism in the representation of the Falklands War by embarking only two professional photographers with the task force: that, the MoD insisted, would be sufficient, and what the professionals could not handle would be managed by service photographers.[29] Conspicuous by his absence was Donald McCullin, Britain's finest photojournalist whose international reputation rested on more than twenty years covering the sharp-end of wars from the Congo to Lebanon. McCullin was under no illusion about why the ships had sailed without him – his brand of realism was not wanted on this voyage: his application for a berth had, he claimed, been 'turned down flat by a high-ranking military officer who, I suppose, considered my experience in war coverage a threat to the image that they would find comfortable' (McCullin, 1982: 17).

Martin Cleaver of the Press Association (PA) and Tom Smith of the *Daily Express*, the two photographers who travelled with the task force, encountered obstacles at every stage in their efforts to furnish a visual record of the war. Refused access to specific battles, most notably Darwin and Goose Green, when Cleaver was told falsely that there was no transport going that way, they were excluded from the fighting in the hills around Stanley by the decision to conduct these assaults under cover of darkness. Transmitting the few pictures that they were able to take threw up further obstacles. Four Muirhead facsimile machines, especially designed for the transmission of photographs, had been installed aboard SS *Canberra*. However, Smith spent the greater part of the journey to the Falklands aboard the Royal Fleet Auxiliary ship *Sir Lancelot*, while Cleaver, travelling on HMS *Hermes*, only received his machine, supplied and paid for by the PA, two days before the British landings. Until they had free and regular access to the Muirheads they had to rely on the manual transmission of film. Little wonder that six weeks after they had sailed for the South Atlantic Smith and Cleaver had returned only two batches of pictures to London and it was 18 May before the first still picture from the South Atlantic came through.[30]

In the absence of photographs or live action from the South Atlantic it was left to the domestic coverage to furnish a visual record of, and dramatise the events in, the Falklands, to engage the viewers' interest and sympathies, to involve them, morally and emotionally, in the conflict and drive home the official line on it. To this end, the structure, iconography, even the personnel for these domestic accounts were largely drawn from the Second World War. Valerie Adams singled out Peter Snow's analysis of the military situation around Mount Kent, broadcast on 1 June 1982 on *Newsnight*, as an emblem of this kind of coverage. Complete with sand maps, plasticine models, photographs and artists' impressions it transformed news about prospective events around Mount Kent into a thrilling dramatisation of them, and in the process implied vital moral, historical and discursive equivalences between the Falklands and the Second World War. Standing over a studio floor relief-map of the Mount Kent area, moving models and manipulating graphics, Snow observed: 'When you look at this from the British viewpoint with the ground forces now pushing forward on two fronts very roughly along the line of the two roads, you can see that with British troops on Mount Kent and perhaps the rest of that ridge too, Stanley is now almost cut off from the rest of the island. For the next day or two we're told British supplies will be helicoptered up to join this new front line: food, ammunition and guns' (qtd in Adams, 1986: 135–6). Snow's performance was, Adams claims, a 'fairly successful ... emulation of a formal military briefing (of the type familiar to us all from war films) ... known in the Army as a "Sitrep"' (Adams, 1986: 135–6). Instead of furnishing the public with 'historical information' about (albeit projected) events, reports of this kind 'came close to entertainment – offering the same vicarious participation as a film or play' (Adams, 1986: 106). The privileging of entertainment over information seems to have dictated the uses made by the media of so-called expert commentators, academics, defence correspondents and retired service officers who were invited onto news and current affairs programmes to comment on the sand-maps, voice over the graphics and provide their informed opinions about actual or potential operations in the South Atlantic. The service chiefs and their political masters were deeply concerned that sensitive security matters might be innocently disclosed in such discussions. Accordingly, the First Sea Lord, Vice Admiral Henry Leach, proposed to Sir Frank Cooper, Permanent Secretary at the Ministry of Defence, that the national interest would be best served by replacing expert opinion with expert propaganda, suggesting to Cooper that 'we should get the concurrence of a small number of retired naval officers and we should have them making it clear to the media that they were available for such purposes; that they themselves should be briefed; and therefore they would know a great deal more than they were entitled to by virtue of their retired position, and would be on their guard accordingly to stop the indiscriminate speculation' (HCDC, 1982: Vol. II, Q 1425–6). He needn't have worried. The experts were not there to make any substantive contribution to discussions about the actual or projected conduct of the campaign. They were there in the interests of drama and not debate, as Peter Snow confirmed to Valerie Adams: 'On the whole we found [the experts] useful just to give one a flavour of the sort of attitudes and language and temperament of the people involved in this exercise' (Adams, 1986: 59). The structure of the interviews not only imposed a decorative role on the commentators but conscripted them into the promotion of the official line on the conflict. As Adams noted, they were prevented by the nature of the questioning from contributing much that was original to the discussion, and were used instead 'to embellish or reinforce or authenticate the views being put forward by journalists and programme presenters. A common technique was for an interviewer to offer a statement in the form of a question, so that the interviewee, the commentator, could endorse it' (Adams, 1986: 59).

There were, admittedly, palpable justifications for some of the parallels which politicians, the military and the media drew between the Falklands and the Second World War. In certain instances equipment employed in the South Atlantic had remained virtually unchanged since 1945: indeed some of it was *from* the Second World War. The Argentine Light-Cruiser, *General Belgrano,* for example, had been commissioned by the US Navy in 1939 as the USS *Phoenix*: she had 'come through the Japanese attack on Pearl Harbour unscathed', survived the Second World War and enjoyed 'a remarkable career' until she was torpedoed by the submarine HMS *Conqueror* on 2 May 1982 (Dobson *et al.*, 1982: 151).[31] A few weeks earlier, watching the men storm ashore at Ascension Island rehearsing for the beach landings to come, Robert Fox recognised that any amphibious assault on the Falklands would unavoidably resemble the famous beach landings of the Second World War: 'The main vehicle for [beach landing] was the large landing craft called LCU (Landing Craft Utility), the old-fashioned high-ramped open boat which is part of the World War Two iconography in the photographs of Normandy, Anzio, Sicily and the Pacific landings' (Fox, 1982a: 29). Later, when the fighting began in earnest, the military not only relied on the equipment but also drew heavily on the tactics established and perfected during the two world wars. Looking back on the battle for Mount Longdon, Captain Willie McCracken reflected on how it had been fought and won on the 'section-level tactics that we'd been taught at Sandhurst', tactics 'based on the experiences of many through the First and Second World Wars' (McCracken, 1985: 242).

Yet in many accounts of the Falklands, the employment of forms and images from the Second World War, the framing of contemporary events within the discursive norms of the 1940s, was driven by ideological aims and not operational necessity, by the determination to elicit a particular response to, and so close the possible significance of, events under the guise of providing an objective record of them. Jonathan Raban was struck by the uncanny similarities between film footage from the task force and newsreel reports from the Second World War, in particular the 'bizarre pictures' in one broadcast of the troops at work and at play on the voyage south:

The show came to a climax with a wide-angle shot of another saloon, now an Other Ranks mess, packed with several hundred singing men:

It's a long way to Tipperary, it's a long way to go!
It's a long way to Tipperary, to the sweetest girl I know –

... The reporter's voice was as strange as the pictures themselves. It was an earnest pastiche of the Britain-can-take-it style of Movietone News in the 1940s. It left unnatural dramatic gaps between the words of the script, it was overloud, as if the reporter was addressing a camp-meeting instead of a clip-on mike in his shirt front; like the singing it was exaggerated *ff* and *allegro con spirito*. (Raban, 1986: 135–6)

In a similar vein, the Glasgow University Media Group drew attention to a BBC News bulletin which posited parallels between D-Day and the projected landings on the Falkland Islands by showing 'lengthy clips of film from 1944, complete with the original commentary ("Then we hit the beach, and we were there!") only to follow it with the current MoD account: "Now the reinvasion of the Falkland Islands, if it does happen, will look very different"' (GUMG, 1985: 124). While it may have looked different, it was the express intention of reports like these to gloss over the more obvious dissimilarities between the two conflicts, to identify their deeper moral, historical and narrative links and so promote an heroic reading of them.

The configuration of events in the South Atlantic in accordance with forms, structures and models drawn from the Second World War was, as Raban noted, not only a characteristic of domestic coverage of the conflict. Max Hastings' entire response to the Falklands War was, both literally and figuratively, framed by the Second World War. Early in April 1982 when the Argentinians invaded the islands, Hastings was, by a happy coincidence, at home working on his acclaimed history of the D-Day landings, *Overlord: D-Day and the Battle for Normandy* (1984), trying desperately 'to make the leap of imagination that is essential to books of this kind, to conceive what it was like to crouch in a landing craft approaching a hostile shore at dawn on 6 June 1944. By an extraordinary fluke of history, less than two months later I found myself crouched in a British landing craft 8,000 miles away' (Hastings, 1984: 16). The Falklands War offered Hastings a unique opportunity to research the tactics and equipment and so recreate the experience of the Second World War, to summon up through the living events in the South Atlantic the spirit of a bygone war and the lost world it implied. Writing in and about the Falklands, Hastings thus kept his gaze fixed firmly on the fighting in Normandy: 'In the weeks that followed, I had an opportunity to witness an amphibious campaign whose flavour any veteran of June 1944 would immediately have recognized, even to the bren guns, oerlikons and bofors hammering into the sky' (Hastings, 1984: 16). More immediately Hastings' vision of events in the Falklands was deeply influenced by the example of his father, Robin, who covered the D-Day landings and the Normandy campaign for the *Picture Post*. Reflecting on his responsibilities as a war reporter, Hastings senior had determined that 'When one's nation is at war, reporting becomes an extension of the war effort' (qtd in Sunday Times Insight Team, 1982: 213). Nearly forty years later, on the day that the task force faced its most serious setback of the campaign when Argentine jets bombed the landing ships *Sir Galahad* and *Sir Tristan*, like his father before him, Hastings rallied to the cause. In a front page article for the *Daily Express* titled 'WHY NONE OF US CAN BE NEUTRAL IN THIS WAR', Hastings laid out his professional credo in the Falklands, declaring that he and other task force correspondents had 'decided before landing that our role was simply to report as sympathetically as possible what the British forces are doing here today' (*Daily Express*, 8 June 1982: 1). The Second World War thus not only determined how Hastings made sense of the Falklands Conflict, it also profoundly shaped the sense he made of it. Little wonder then that the Army's Director of Public Relations, Brigadier David Ramsbotham, was keen to ensure that Hastings sailed with the task force, confirming that had he not successfully lobbied for a place on his own behalf he would 'certainly have contacted him anyway' (Morrison and Tumber, 1988: 6).

The illusion that through the Falklands War Britain had abandoned the class divisions and cultural pessimism of the late 1970s and early 1980s and was journeying back to the glorious summer of 1940, to the unity, heroism and pride it implied, was cosmetically reinforced by the strategic deployment of metonymic figures from the Second World War to promote news from or about the Falklands. Sir Arthur 'Bomber' Harris, for example, was approached for his expert opinions on prosecuting an aerial campaign against the Argentinians.[32] More significantly, Dame Vera Lynn emerged from retirement to record 'a new patriotic song' for the troops in the Falklands and the nation as a whole, which was featured on ITN's flagship *News at Ten* (GUMG, 1985: 122) Watching the broadcast, Jonathan Raban was struck both by the cynicism and the power of the gesture:

A lot of dust had gathered on Miss Lynn's voice since I'd last heard it, warbling sweetly about bluebirds *oho*ver the white cliffs of *Doho*ver, but its dustiness was like the scratchy burr of a 78 played on a horn gramophone; it made it more evocative, not less; it brought back memories of the gallant little ships, the blackout, whale meat steaks and London-can-take-it.

The song was called 'I Love This Land', and it hinged on the refrain:

'It will stay this way for e-e-ver,
Which is why I love this land!'

On each reprise, the couplet sounded slightly more drivelling than it had done the last time around. You only had to look at Vera Lynn at sixty-five to see that it enshrined a wonderful, vainglorious untruth. But there was a dotty kind of truth in it too. It stated – more nakedly than anyone had dared to do so far – the terms of the daydream in which England was living in 1982. (Raban, 1986: 186–7).

The precise terms of this daydream were predicated on the moral, historical and narrative precedents of the Second World War. It was Dame Vera Lynn's role to formalise the secular consecration of the Falklands Conflict, its transfiguration into the bloodless vintage of history: to imply, by her own musical resurrection, the renewal of those individual virtues and national ideals which had once made Britain great and strong, and would now do so again in its hour of need.

Sitting in his bedroom glueing together his model aircraft (a Spitfire, perhaps?), Adrian Mole offers both an emblem of and an ironic commentary on this painstaking process of national reassembly.

3
Families at War

The Falkland Islanders are a bunch of absolute arseholes. (Jeremy Hands qtd in Morrison and Tumber, 1983: 116)

ESSENTIAL IDENTITIES

The fiftieth anniversary of the end of the Second World War was marked, in Britain, by a busy programme of formal commemoration, culminating in the VJ Day Parade on 20 August 1995 when 18,000 veterans of the campaigns in South East Asia marched along the Mall towards Buckingham Palace 'in two hours of almost delirious cheering, applause and shouting from a crowd' estimated at more than 200,000 (*Guardian Weekly*, 27 August 1995: 9). The parade, the *Guardian* claimed, was the 'climax – and farewell – to six years of looking back at the Second World War'. In looking back the nation was encouraged to reflect on a time when its moral and military authority was secure, its place in the world a source of pride, its coherent communities and stable social structures a source of strength and comfort: 'Collectivism', John Ezard observed, 'was the spirit of the period ... This was the generation which remained, at least publicly, solid at home and stood alone in the battlefield against Hitler long enough for his mistakes and his allies' mistakes to begin his downfall' (Ezard, 1995: 7). Yet there was an elegiac quality about the whole exercise. In looking back to the past with pride the nation could not help but look around at the present with a sense of shame – its waning authority in world affairs, its retreat from collectivism and the fraying of the social fabric each a source of deep disillusionment. According to Patrick Wright, this kind of disenchantment is no incidental by-product of the commemorative process but the very aim of its forms and effects – they are calculated to breed a sense of discomfort in and about the present:

> The Establishment mode of remembrance is both militarist and nationalist. Remembrance is a state occasion structured through regimental history and parade ... The interest of this mode does not lie primarily in any selectivity which it may bring to bear on previous events – its concern, as might be imagined, with glory rather than

gore. Remembrance of this kind does not merely obliterate the 'realities' of war. Its essence lies instead in the *transfiguration* which its ceremonies bring to bear on past war, introducing order, solemnity and meaning where there was chaos, disorder and loss. Acts of commemoration re-present the glory of war, its transmutation of destruction into heroism and, above all, that previous sense of nationhood. In its contempt for society at peace, establishment remembrance tends to accuse the post-war present of mediocre survival, of ending up spineless and bent over a stick. (Wright, 1985: 136)

Consequently, one might reasonably argue that Britain's half-century love affair with the Second World War and the finest hours it enshrines has been driven and shaped less by a passionate interest in the details of long gone conquests than by an increasing anxiety about how the nation measures up in the present, a growing sense of discomfort with the nation's contemporary identity fuelled by its post-war decline.

According to Wright, the 'upsurge of public nationalism', embodied in the 1995 commemorations, 'reflects the crisis of a social system which, while its development is leading directly to the destruction of traditions and customs ... at the same time demands an ever deepening source of cultural meaning to legitimate itself' (Wright, 1985: 141). Increasingly in Britain, the wellspring of this deeper 'cultural meaning', personal and collective, has been looked for and located in the near past, in a selective history of the Second World War and the ideas of family, community and nation which it embodies – hence the 'almost delirious' response to the VJ Day marchers, after all, here was cultural meaning in the flesh, the glorious national past fleetingly incarnate.

The past which this deeper sense of cultural meaning occupies and enshrines is not, however, the simple historical past of antecedent events but a precedent and preferred identity that the Second World War, or a selected version of it, is taken to realise. It is our task in the present to rediscover and renew this authentic identity, to reinvigorate the communities which embody it and so reshape the present in the image of the past: 'For "us" the contemporary "historical" event appears increasingly to be the one which marks the *recovery* and reaffirmation of the old ways ... "History" in this contemporary sense is evidently not about the *making* of a future ... "History" is what restores the essential and grander identity of the "Imaginary Briton" to the modern subject' (Wright, 1985: 164).[1]

At a national level, the Falklands War was presented as a direct means to the recovery of the nation's essential and grander identity. Yet despite the remoteness of the fighting and the limited numbers of those directly involved in it, this was a struggle in which every member of the community could play an active role through the actual structures, historical associations and symbolic significance of the family. By restoring the traditional gender roles of Second World War Britain and their attendant power structures, by returning to the domestic norms which ostensibly prevailed and brought victory in the Second World War one could restore oneself, one's family and so help return the nation to their rightful, essential and grander identity. The fight to recover the Falklands and one's ability to take part in it through the organisation of one's domestic life affirmed the fact that 'even in the present, immobilised and bureaucratic as these times may be ... it is still possible to *be* historical ... that the power of significant action still lies with the British subject' (Wright, 1985: 174–5).[2]

The first 'significant action' sanctioned by the Falklands War was, ironically, a familiar ritual of *inaction* – listening to the radio, specifically, the broadcast of the Emergency Parliamentary Debate of 3 April 1982, when the House of Commons responded to Argentina's seizure of the Falkland Islands. The tone of the debate and the rhetorical posture of its protagonists reinforced the moral and historical links between the Falklands Conflict and the Second World War, reaffirming the symbolic significance of the family as the prime locus of and model for domestic involvement in the conflict. According to Anthony Barnett, the debate was dominated by the spirit of 'Churchillism'. He describes this, variously, as a 'structure of feeling shared by the leaders of the nation's political life', and a 'fever that inflames Parliamentary rhetoric, deliberation and decision' (Barnett, 1982: 47). Both of these definitions had their origins in a specific historical juncture, 'the national unity and coalition politics' of May 1940, when Churchill assumed the leadership of a broad-based coalition government (Barnett, 1982: 47). Over the succeeding summer and autumn, through the debacle at Dunkirk, the Battle of Britain and the Blitz, Churchill's famous broadcasts on the BBC (immediately after the *Nine O'Clock News*) cemented the image of a nation united in splendid isolation, while he himself came to symbolise its bulldog pugnacity and the promise of ultimate triumph. According to Peter Clarke: 'In the heightened atmosphere of this crisis his elevated rhetoric, the only sort he knew, was happily matched to the level of events ... In the 1930s his style had often sounded dated; in 1940 his words sounded historic' (Clarke, 1996: 195). It was this sort of historic note that many of those who rose to speak on 3 April 1982 strove after – to catch the moment and consecrate the image of a nation once again united in defiance of tyranny. But the spirit of Churchillism brought with it the shadow of his luckless predecessor, Neville Chamberlain, and the bellicosity of the Falklands debate was both fuelled and tempered by painful memories of the national humiliations over which Chamberlain had presided. Douglas Jay proposed that the origins of the current crisis were much the same as those which had led the nation into war against Germany more than forty years earlier: 'The whole story will inevitably lead some people to think that the Foreign Office is a bit too much saturated with the spirit of appeasement' (Morgan, 1982: 16). But the dominant tone was Churchillian. The Commons echoed with quotations, evocations and straightforward impersonations of the Great Man as each speaker tried to out-Churchill his neighbour. Patrick Cormack offered to shield the Prime Minister from her critics, as Churchill had done for Chamberlain, to provide her with 'the fortification that a previous Conservative Prime Minister at a time of grave international crisis did not have', that she might rise phoenix-like from this political catastrophe, shed her affiliations with Chamberlain and don the Churchillian mantle herself (Morgan, 1982: 13). Julian Emery caught the tone nicely when he described the Prime Minister's support of her foreign and defence secretaries in the very terms Lloyd George had used to commend Churchill's defence of Chamberlain before concluding with his own defiant, Churchillian flourish:

> My Right Honourable Friend the Prime Minister has done her best to serve as an air-raid shelter for her colleagues directly responsible, and that she has done with her customary loyalty. However, we should recognise that we have suffered the inevitable consequences of the combination of unpreparedness and feeble counsels.
>
> We have lost a battle, but have not lost a war. It is an old saying that Britain always wins the last battle. It will not be an easy task. (Morgan, 1982: 12)[3]

The Churchillian tenor of the broadcast and the moral and historical equivalences it implied between the Falklands and the Second World War transfigured the listeners' role. It lifted them out of their isolation and conscripted them into a virtual, national community, a vast invisible regiment whose common loyalty to the daily broadcasts from and about the Falklands bound them together in support and emulation of the task force. This ritualistic attendance on the regular bulletins from the South Atlantic not only conjured up sepia-tinted images of the 1940s nuclear family faithfully gathered around the wireless in anticipation of one of the Great Man's broadcasts, it also implied that, like their parents and grandparents before them in the Second World War, they too were living through important times, and by their identification with and interest in the broadcasts were doing their own bit in the making of history.[4] So, parallels between the Falklands and the Second World War transformed the consumption of news from the conflict into a form of participation in it, translating the spectator into an active player in the quest for 'the essential and grander identity of the Imaginary Briton'.

FAMILY TIES

These parallels between the Falklands and the Second World War were focused on a shared vision of the family as a symbol of the nation.[5] They implied that as in the heroic summer of 1940, so once again in the spring and summer of 1982 the nation would draw together with the cohesion and intimacy of a family to defeat the common enemy. This image of the family as both a metonym for and an embodiment of the nation is central to what Angus Calder calls 'The Myth of the Blitz' – a myth which is anchored in the conviction that despite the traditional divisions of region, class, race and gender, the nation, like the family, is a naturally cohesive unit.[6] It is a recurring feature in British accounts of Dunkirk and the Blitz. Anxiously awaiting news of her son Alan, serving with the British Expeditionary Force in France during the spring of 1940, Clara Milburn describes and celebrates her experience of this sense of community at a local level in her diary entry for 6 June 1940:

> The telephone rings at intervals all day with rumours and snippets of news from one or another, but nothing definite about our boys. As we sat down to dinner tonight, very tired and thirsty after digging and hoeing, Mrs Cutler rang up. She is just an acquaintance in Balsall Common whom I knew through billeting. But she said: 'Mrs Milburn, I am going to Olton Monastery tomorrow and I am having candles lit and prayers said for the safe return of your son'. Surprised and touched, I could scarcely answer properly before the voice said 'Goodnight'. The kindness and sympathy everywhere is wonderful. After dinner a rest and then as we were about to continue our gardening, Harry and Ethel Spencer came, and she and I talked of Nevill and Alan, both thinking of them as our 'little boys' – mothers always do – and wiping away a tear or two. How drawn together we all are these dark days. Tonight, as they left, we all kissed each other like brothers and sisters. (Donnelly, 1979: 41–2)

On a broader, more public canvas, Mollie Panter-Downes, London correspondent for the *New Yorker*, traced in her regular 'Letter from London' the (re)emergence of a similar spirit of unity among the people of the capital suffering the dangers and disruptions of the Blitz:

> For Londoners, there are no longer such things as good nights; there are only bad nights, worse nights, and better nights. Hardly anyone has slept at all in the past week. The sirens go off at approximately the same time every evening, and in the poorer districts, queues of people carrying blankets, thermos flasks, and babies begin to form quite early outside the air-raid shelters. The *Blitzkrieg*

continues to be directed against such military objectives as the tired shopgirl, the red-eyed clerk, and the thousands of dazed and weary families patiently trundling their few belongings in perambulators away from the wreckage of their homes ...

The East End suffered most in the night raids this week. Social workers who may have piously wished that slum areas could be razed had their wish horribly fulfilled when rows of mean dwellings were turned into shambles overnight. The Nazi attack bore down heaviest on badly nourished, poorly clothed people – the worst equipped of any to stand the appalling physical strain, if it were not for the stoutness of their cockney hearts ...

The bombers, however, made no discrimination between the lowest and the highest homes in the city. The Queen was photographed against much the same sort of tangle of splintered wreckage that faced hundreds of humbler, anonymous housewives in this week's bitter dawns. The crowd that gathered outside Buckingham Palace the morning after the picture was published had come, it appeared on close inspection, less to gape at boarded windows than to listen to the cheering notes of the band, which tootled away imperturbably at the cherished ceremony of the Changing of the Guard. This was before the deliberate second try for the Palace, which has made people furious, but has also cheered them with the thought that the King and Queen are now facing risks that are common to all ...

The behaviour of all classes is so magnificent that no observer here could ever imagine these people following the French into captivity. As for breaking civilian morale, the high explosives that rained death and destruction on the capital this week were futile. (Panter-Downes, 1972: 98–101).

Yet as Angus Calder has observed, this popular model of insouciant defiance and the new communalism on which it rested, summed up in the defiant assurance that 'London-can-take-it', had been identified as the preferred response to the bombing well before the Blitz on London began in earnest on 7 September 1940.[7] It had its origins in the Home Intelligence reports of the MoI which were 'used as a guide for action by the Departments of the Ministry [of Information] concerned with publicity at home' (Calder, 1991: 122).[8] These tended, not surprisingly at a time of national peril, to accentuate the positive, so, genuine acts of neighbourliness, real demonstrations of *sang-froid*, heartening manifestations of classlessness during the raids of May to August 1940 soon calcified into an official portrait of the nation at war and a model for behaviour under fire, a sort of script which was put to work and faithfully heeded during the blitzing of September 1940 onwards.[9] Irrespective of the actual relations between the classes and the regions, the ideals of national unity were a key feature of the government's response to the trials of 1940 and every opportunity was taken to reinforce and promote them. Tours of London were arranged for journalists from the provinces to counter an exaggerated impression of the damage inflicted on the capital, to ensure the most widespread dissemination of the fact that 'London-can-take-it', and to furnish the citizens of towns as yet untroubled by the *Luftwaffe* with a model for how they should conduct themselves when they were. The perverse glamour of blitzed London made some suicidally eager to join the exclusive club of the bombed, as Home Intelligence reported from one exasperated onlooker in Dundee: 'if only they would give us a turn, they might give London a night's rest' (qtd in Calder 1991: 128). Any falling off from this behavioural ideal – panic, cowardice, selfishness, hostility – could be discounted as an individual exception to the general rule, or else, as Angus Calder suggests, the fault of a lumbering and insensitive bureaucracy which, it was felt, offered only indifferent assistance to the heroic people.[10]

Yet as Calder has shown, there was no place in 'the Myth of the Blitz' for the continuing divisions of class, region, politics and gender which survived and were, on occasions, accentuated by the Blitz. As a result, as Tom Harrisson has observed, there has been a 'massive, largely unconscious cover-up of the more disagreeable facts of 1940–41' (Harrisson, 1990: 15). For example, Bill Brandt and Bert Hardy's photographs of Londoners seeking shelter in the Underground from German bombs, images of 'Humanity itself, in heroic repose', attained instant and widespread fame (Calder, 1991: 143). These pictures of cheerful cockneys bedding down on crowded platforms next to friends and strangers alike seemed to offer concrete evidence of the spirit of unity forged among Londoners by the Blitz. They were in fact damning testimony of a society as divided as it ever was along the age-old fault lines of class and region. The Underground shelterers represented only a tiny and specific minority of those in the central area of London seeking refuge from the bombs. As Calder notes, a 'shelter census' from November 1940 indicates that 'only 9 per cent slept in public shelters, 4 per cent in the underground railway system (though some accounts of the Blitz made it sound as if almost everyone took to the tubes); and 27 per cent in domestic shelters. In outer suburbs these proportions were even lower. The rest were in most cases either on duty or sleeping in their own homes' (Calder, 1969: 181). They were overwhelmingly from London's poorer East End which bore the brunt of the *Luftwaffe*'s early raids and where there was an acute shortage of adequate shelter, private or public: 'The steel-framed buildings in the West End notoriously provided much better protection than the nineteenth-century slums to the east' (Calder, 1969: 186).[11] The government had, at first, rejected the use of the Underground for the provision of shelter on the grounds that the railways had to be kept clear to facilitate the movement of troops, evacuees and the injured. It also feared the development of a 'deep shelter mentality' among a working class still regarded in some official circles as an unruly mob ready to panic and disintegrate into a chaotic and defeated mass when subjected to aerial assault.[12] On 12 September 1940, after five consecutive nights of bombardment, thousands of East Enders stormed the tube stations and took refuge there. The next evening, over a hundred more, led by local Communist Party members, laid siege to the Savoy Hotel demanding access to its private shelter:

> The contrast between the [Tilbury] arches [a mass public shelter] and the Tubes and the shelter provided for the occupants of the Dorchester Hotel in Park Lane was one which might well make the most myopic bureaucrat feel uncomfortable. The Dorchester had converted its Turkish baths, and there was 'a neat row of cots, spaced about two feet apart, each one covered with a lovely fluffy eiderdown. Its silks billowed and shone in the dim light in pale pinks and blues. Behind each cot hung the negligee, the dressing gown ... The pillows on which the heads lay were large and full and white ... There was a little sign pinned to one of the Turkish bath curtains. It said, "reserved for Lord Halifax"'. (Calder, 1969: 186)

It was hypocrisy to insist that 'we are all in this together' when one's chances of survival clearly depended so much on one's class and income. Families and communities may have drawn together as never before (or since) during the Blitz, but if they did they did so along the established divisions of class and region. The ideal of a nation united with the intimacy of a family was false, as Tom Harrisson notes: 'At no time in the Second World War generally and in the blitz particularly were British civilians united on anything, though they might be ready to appear so in public on certain issues' (Harrisson, 1990: 17). In this light, the promotion of official links between the Falklands Conflict and the Second World War was as apposite as it was revealing. During the fighting in the South Atlantic, as I will show, the government identified a range of communities (re)united by the challenge of war, whose apparent coherence provided models of unity for the nation as a whole, yet whose concord turned out to be more or less fabricated.

One of the catalysts of national unity at the time of Dunkirk and the Blitz was the assertion, hammered home again and again by Churchill in his war speeches, that Britain was standing alone in defence of civilised values against the forces of barbarism. Churchill's particular skill lay not only in his rhetorical power but in his recognition of the immediate impact of the war on the lives of ordinary people, in his ability to articulate for them a clear role in it, to provide them with an historical context for their actions and an ennobling narrative within which they might see and understand their role and against which they might measure their performance. As he told the House of Commons on 18 June 1940, the day after Petain had sued for peace with the Nazis:

the Battle of France is over. I expect that the Battle of Britain is about to begin. Upon this battle depends the survival of Christian Civilisation. Upon it depends our own British life, and the long continuity of our institutions and our Empire. I do not at all underrate the severity of the ordeal which lies before us, but I believe our countrymen will show themselves capable of standing up to it, and carry on in spite of it, at least as well as any other people in the world. Much will depend upon this; every man and woman will have the chance to show the finest qualities of their race, and render the highest service to their cause. (qtd in Calder, 1991: 30)

While in 1982 it was recognised that defeat at the hands of Argentina would just as surely, if less catastrophically, mark the symbolic end of empire – the continuing dream of Britain as a world power – the general public's role in rendering service to the cause and resisting the enemy was much less clear. Though dispatches from the task force often evoked and celebrated the myth of solitary defiance against the forces of barbarism so familiar from Dunkirk and the Blitz, more often than not they emphasised the task force's total isolation, even from the nation itself: 'The huge task of preparing the Royal Navy task force [*sic*] for the invasion of the Falkland Islands is complete. The 15000 men aboard the dozens of ships of the battle fleet are steeled. This tiny patch of the South Atlantic, the 200 mile total exclusion zone, often seems as busy as a summer regatta. But here the seas are bleak and deadly and there are no friendly ports within many thousands of miles. We are together but alone' (Parry, 1982: 2). Back in London, on his way home from visiting his son, gravely wounded in the Falklands and since returned to a hospital in the capital, John Lawrence was struck by how tenuous were most people's links to this war: 'As we drove home I wondered how many people in the other cars on the road had had anything at all to do with the war in the Falklands apart from seeing it on the television or in the newspapers' (Lawrence *et al.*, 1988: 69).[13]

The Falklands Conflict was, at no time, a total war of the Second World War model. At its height there were never more than 28,000 British servicemen and women and support staff directly engaged in the conflict, nor was there ever the remotest threat of any Argentine action against mainland Britain. As such, despite the Prime Minister's assertion on the day of the British reinvasion that the Falklands 'are but a heartbeat away', for the vast majority of the British population they remained half a world away, or more (*Guardian*, 22 May 1982: 1).

The government and the media set out, therefore, to involve the public in the campaign and to retain their support for it, as in the Second World War, by invoking the ideal of the nation as a family. In the first instance they stressed the close familial and cultural ties between Britain and the Falklands. As the Prime Minister pointed out in the First Emergency Parliamentary Debate, the Falkland Islanders 'are British in stock and tradition, and they wish to remain British in allegiance' (Morgan, 1982: 5).[14] Much was made in the media of the islanders' staunch loyalty to all things British, their patriotic worship of the crown, their fond regard for British icons – the Governor's official car was a maroon Hackney Cab – their love of the pub, a pint, a game of darts, and in a referred gesture of British regional rivalry, their partisan interest in the fortunes of their favourite football teams. In fighting for the Falklands, it was insisted, the task force was fighting for Britain itself, defending their freedom and defining their essential identity – a process and a prize which Jonathan Raban found painfully revealing:

> the Falklands stood anchored off the coast of South America very much as Britain stood anchored off the coast of Europe. You only had to look at the atlas to see that the identity of the Falklanders, like that of the British, was bound up in endless aggressive assertions of their differences from the continental giant across the water ... In this miniature inverted cluster, the British had hit by accident on a perfect symbol of themselves. The Falklands held a mirror up to our own islands, and it reflected, in brilliantly sharp focus, all our injured belittlement, our sense of being beleaguered, neglected and misunderstood. (Raban, 1986: 101–2).

In the opinion of *The Times'* leader writer the Falklanders were more than symbols of the British, they were our surrogates – their lot today might be ours tomorrow: 'We are an island race; and the focus of attack is one of our islands, inhabited by our islanders' (*The Times*, 5 April 1982: 9). The fate of the islanders thus not only laid bare the cultural links binding Britain and the Falklands but also united the nation in its response to their loss and its determination to reclaim them.

Each of the MPs who rose to speak on 3 April 1982, with a single exception (Ray Whitney), canvassed a similar set of themes – humiliation, wounded pride, confidence in the legitimacy of Britain's claims to the islands, hostility towards the Foreign Office, loathing of the Argentine junta and a determination to achieve ultimate victory in the South Atlantic.[15] This resulted in some curious harmonies, not least the Chairman of the 1922 Committee applauding a speech from the Leader of the Labour Party: 'There are times, Mr Speaker, in the affairs of our nation when the House should speak with a single, united voice. This is just such a time. The Leader of the Opposition spoke for us all' (Morgan, 1982: 10). Yet as Anthony Barnett has indicated, it is little wonder that the voice of the House was so united as the 'great "debate" had been a pre-selected beauty contest with only those whose patriotic features were deemed bulbous enough, allowed to display themselves before the public' (Barnett, 1982: 43). The debate counterpointed 'a succession of ultra-right-wing Tories from the South East' with 'MPs from the Celtic fringe with Falklands interests'. In Barnett's view: 'It would be hard to think of a less representative combination for the defence of British democracy' (Barnett, 1982: 41).

The unanimity of the Commons was, nevertheless, held up by the politicians themselves as a clear expression of 'the voice of the nation' on this issue, and was taken up by the media as a model for the public response to the crisis.[16] Both politicians and the media exhorted and celebrated a new spirit of national familial unity, consecrated in their profligate use of the first person plural. As Jonathan Raban observed:

> 'We' were steaming south; 'we' had declared a two-hundred-mile maritime exclusion zone around the Falkland Islands. The black face marines were 'our boys' (or, as the Prime Minister chose to refer to them, 'my boys'). A week before, no anchorman or commentator would have dreamed of risking this cosy pronoun: the state was perceived as a fragile assembly of conflicting third parties – Government and Opposition, management and unions, North and South, those in work and those out of it. But war was working its old black magic, restoring the image of the state as an extension of the self. (Raban, 1986: 137)

On the day that British troops established the beachhead at San Carlos, the BBC's *Nine O'Clock News* reported: 'The Prime Minister said today that the courage and skill of the men in the Task Force had brought a new pride to this country. Mrs Thatcher said it made us realise we are all really one family' (BBC 1 *Nine O'Clock News*, 21 May 1982: 21.00). Earlier in the campaign, when the BBC had shown itself to be more sceptical of government statements, more willing to subject them to scrutiny, and was more circumspect in its deployment of the first person plural, the Prime Minister reminded it of its duty to reflect the views of 'the vast majority of our people [who] support our task force and our boys in the South Atlantic' (Morgan, 1982: 233).[17] From 11 May the masthead of the *Sun* was augmented by the slogan, 'THE PAPER THAT SUPPORTS OUR BOYS', and as the reinvasion loomed it led the charge, albeit prematurely, with its headline of 30 April: 'IN WE GO!' (*Sun*, 30 April 1982: 1).[18]

In the first and last days of the campaign this image of national unity was both articulated and embodied in the discursive forms of the outside broadcasts that covered the departure and return of the task force ships. These employed many of the stock shots and narrative tropes established in the BBC's coverage of the Queen's Coronation in June 1953 and perfected in the media management of subsequent state occasions, other symbolic consecrations of national familial unity, most recently manifest in the broadcast of the Princess of Wales' funeral.[19] As they did at the Queen's Silver Jubilee celebrations in 1977 and the Royal Wedding in 1981, reporters moved among the crowds thronging the quays at Southampton and Portsmouth, interviewing working-class fathers and officers' wives, a brother from Glasgow, a mother from Hull, their disparate accents harmonising in a chorus of patriotic unity. The reporters' questions were carefully phrased so as to elicit expressions of support for the troops and so promote an image of national familial unity; interviewees were encouraged to comment on neither the strategic aims of the task force nor the political bungling which necessitated its dispatch, but were most commonly invited to share their feelings: 'I think everyone here's very proud of them to go out today'; 'I'd just like to say God speed lads and a safe journey back' (Warman, 1992).

In a comparison of two ITN bulletins covering the departure of the *QE 2* from Southampton, the Glasgow University Media Group noted how expressions of political or emotional dissent were edited out of one broadcast covering the departure of the ships and replaced by the single, unifying voice of the reporter, her neat, received pronunciation embodying and promoting the ideal of national unity purportedly produced by the conflict – a single, national voice for a common cause:

> The reports from the Southampton docks concentrate on the soldiers: 'without doubt', exclaims the reporter, 'it was the troops' day!' She interviews soldiers embarking on the *QE 2*, and in the early report at lunchtime she interviews two wives as well:
>
> > *Reporter*: How do you feel about him going?
> > *Wife*: Well, upset, disappointed, but it's his job, he's got to do it, so it's just one of those things really.
> > *2nd Wife*: He knows his job, so long as he keeps his head down and one hand on the lifeboat, that's good enough for me.
>
> (ITN, 12 May 1982: 13.00)

Then the report finishes with shots of soldiers waving from the ship's deck. However, by the evening the opening footage of 'the troops' day' remains, but the interviews with the wives are edited out. Instead of hearing them speak for themselves (and admit to being 'upset, disappointed') the camera focuses on their tearful faces as they wave Union Jacks on the quayside, while we hear the reporter's account of that day's emotions:

> The carnival atmosphere built up both on the quay and on the ship. The dockhead swelled with people and emotion. There was a lot of jollity and some cheeky light relief. As one well-wisher looked on, another's bra was hoisted aboard ... [The *QE 2*] slipped her moorings, leaving the crowd and the razzamatazz behind her. (ITN, 12 May 1982: 22.00)

Comparing the two bulletins, we can see the newsroom's interpretations of the event being constructed. In order to put across the final image of 'the carnival atmosphere ... jollity ... razzamatazz', the true feelings of the women left on the quay are excluded, leaving only the image of their tearful faces and brave smiles on the screen as the men sail away (GUMG, 1985: 114–15).

This image of moral and emotional unanimity was sustained not merely by silencing expressions of dissent but by actively incorporating them into the chorus of national unity. As Robin Warman of the BBC discovered when he mingled with the crowds at Portsmouth, many of those whose presence at the quayside was held up as evidence of widespread, spontaneous, popular support for the government's handling of the crisis had nothing but scorn for the politicians whose incompetence had necessitated the dispatch of the ships: 'Very sad to see that our boys gotta go down there and do something that coulda been pervented [*sic*]. It's all wrong that good Englishmen, good British stock have got to risk their lives and limb [*sic*] to get Mr Nott and Carrington out of a hole' (Warman, 1992). Indeed, the *Guardian* claimed that 'Ill-feeling towards the Government was as vociferous among the thousands who cheered the task force out of Portsmouth on the start of its voyage towards the Falkland Islands as it was towards the occupying Argentines' (10 April 1982: 2). For one woman on the quayside at Portsmouth, the crowds were not only a unified expression of support for the task force but a no less unanimous declaration of no-confidence in the government and its defence policies: 'I think we all feel the same way about this. Nott has definitely made a great mistake over this lot which proves that we do need the Navy and the dockyard men' (Warman, 1992).[20]

This ill-feeling was prompted by John Nott's 1981 Defence Review which saw the Navy's future role as concentrated in anti-Soviet and anti-submarine operations. The Defence Review, inspired, according to Simon Jenkins, 'by the most sustained attack ever mounted by the

Treasury on Defence Spending', proposed less Navy involvement beyond the NATO area, fewer surface ships and a consequent reduction in naval and dockyard support personnel (Hastings and Jenkins, 1983: 24–5). Among the casualties were many of the dock workers at Portsmouth, singled out for praise by the Prime Minister during her victory speech at Cheltenham, who had loaded, refitted and made major structural alterations to task force ships 'faster than was thought possible', yet whose skills would be surplus to the requirements of a largely sub-surface Navy (qtd in Barnett, 1982: 150).

> The wake of the last departing warship had barely settled in Portsmouth this week when civic and trade union leaders began stepping up their efforts to reverse the Government's proposed rundown of the city's historic dockyard ...
>
> Only days before, 180 of the city's dockyard workers had been handed their redundancy notices in the first phase of a planned rundown of the Portsmouth yard which will involve a further 3,000 jobs being axed over the next two years. Along with another 1,000 job losses through natural wastage, the naval base will be trimmed down to a workforce of 1,200 if the Government has its way (*Guardian*, 10 April 1982: 2).

Ironically, the dedication of the dock workers was held up as further evidence of the selfless spirit of national familial unity fostered by the crisis; as the Prime Minister saw it, these men were living symbols of 'the spirit of the South Atlantic – the real spirit of Britain' (qtd in Barnett, 1982: 150). Major General John Frost praised 'the dockyard mateys and all the other workers concerned' who 'had laboured day and night to complete their tasks' (Frost, 1983: 117). It was not, however, a selfless love of nation that had unified and motivated them, but a common fear of redundancy: the most immediate threat to their livelihoods and the well-being of their families came not from General Galtieri or the Argentinians but from the economic rationalists dictating policy to the Treasury. The speed and efficiency with which they armed and dispatched the fleet was, as such, no vote of confidence in but a gesture of defiance against the government, a shot across its bows, demonstrating and rehearsing the collective might that they could bring to bear in any outbreak of hostilities on the industrial front. Far from symbolising a new spirit of unity, the deeds and subsequent dismissal of the dock workers reflected a society riven, as ever, by the competing interests of labour and capital. Indeed, as *New Society* discovered, by the time of the Falklands crisis the dock-working community itself was fragmenting under the onslaught of economic rationalism, its logic of self-interest – personal profit before the common good – undermining the workforce's attempts to present a united front against the government's determination to run down the yard: 'We worked day and night to prepare the fleet. It wasn't patriotism it was £sd. The more overtime you work the better your redundancy money' (Roberts and Seabrook, 1982: 380). As such, despite the best efforts of the government and the media to foster an image of national unity over the Falklands, the old familiar flaws in the social fabric continued to reveal themselves. The Falklands provided no remedy for these antagonisms, merely a physical and textual locus for their ongoing enactment.

A FAMILY REGIMENT

These competing constructions of the Falklands War, as an emblem of national unity or a definitive exposure of its perennial divisions, were worked through and articulated in contrasting representations of the family and community. The official, celebratory line on the conflict identified the family as a model social unit, a source of domestic harmony, communal coherence and an ideal of social organisation. Accordingly, these official accounts made much use of the royals whose private organisation and public role made them, in the early 1980s at least, 'a family that represents the nation, in itself a symbol of national unity and social solidarity' (GUMG, 1985: 119). The Queen occupied a prominent role in these accounts in her symbolic capacity as the mother of the nation and her domestic role as an 'anxious mother' waiting like thousands of other mothers with sons serving in the South Atlantic for news from the conflict – she provided both a focus for national anxiety and a model of resolution, an ideal of personal and collective strength through whom the nation as a whole could identify with and participate in the conflict.

Yet the media's attempts to establish those ordinary families directly implicated in the war in a similar, symbolic, unifying role were far less successful. Their assumptions about the make-up, function and distribution of labour within the family implied that far from resolving the traditional inequities and divisions of British society the Falklands War had been conducted in defence if not in celebration of them.[21]

Press and TV coverage of the home front implied that when the task force sailed only women and children were left behind; indeed, as the Glasgow University Media Group noted: 'The conviction that waiting is the *women's* role is so total that "wives" seem interchangeable [with] "families" in the journalists' vocabulary: "The calls from distressed *families* for news about their men went on all night. But in the large naval estates around Portsmouth the grief is being shared by all the *wives*" (ITN, 17.45, 5.5.82)' (GUMG, 1985: 98–9). For the many men left waiting at home, fathers, brothers, sons, lovers, husbands of those who sailed with the task force, there was no place in the media's symbolic national family. Nor, for that matter, was there a place for most women. Despite the evidence of the 1980 General Household Survey which found that 'conventional family units', couples living with children, made up only 31 per cent of the national total, while households in which the woman was dependent on the man counted for a meagre 13 per cent – two thirds of married women had paid work outside the home – media coverage of the families invariably portrayed women in the home, their lives defined by their roles as wives and mothers, their identities derived from and dependent on their menfolk: 'Every report from naval married quarters includes a shot of women with children, used as "wallpaper footage"' (GUMG, 1985: 100). In one exemplary interview with 'a naval wife' the Glasgow University Media Group noted that 'the woman is not even named; instead the camera zooms in on her two-year old son as she feeds him, and the report begins: "Peter Goodfellow's father is a sailor too. He was the engineering officer aboard the frigate HMS *Antelope*. Commander Goodfellow was injured. When the news was first broken to his wife, the Navy still had no idea of the extent of his injuries. She had to wait" (BBC 1, 18.00, 4.6.82)' (GUMG, 1985: 100).

The media's depersonalisation of the families was compounded by their failure to allow the women in their stories to speak for themselves. Jean Carr, a feature writer with the *Sunday Mirror*, proposed that this may have been the result of male hegemony within the media institutions themselves; most newspapers and TV coverage treated the Falklands War mainly as a hard news story, and the gathering and reporting of such news was, at the time of the war, still a largely male preserve (Carr, 1984: xii). However, the coverage of task force families was mainly presented as human interest, and over half of the reports were conducted by women.[22] In spite of this, the women featured in the reports are rarely given the opportunity to speak, their many voices and disparate opinions summarised in and silenced by a single, authoritative (usually male) voice: 'a report on a memorial service for [HMS] *Sheffield* shows weeping widows at their pews; but the only words we hear are from the Provost, speaking about the men "who had given their lives for Queen and Country". According to the newscaster, he "summed up the feeling of the city" (ITN, 20.45, 9.5.82)' (GUMG, 1985: 108).

On closer analysis, then, this was a family which included or represented few of the nation, and in which fewer still were given a voice. Its central determining relationships, based not on love, respect or mutuality, but on authority and compliance, indicated that in time of war the media looked to the military for a model of how the private life of the nation might be most effectively ordered. During the Gulf War, for example, the royals were persistently portrayed as an extension of the military, organised like an arm of the services in readiness for their part in the fight against Saddam: 'The monarch is thought to have held her own council of war among the family and spelt out how she expects them to behave over the weeks to come. Diana has been chosen to spearhead a campaign to boost morale, holding herself ready and willing to visit hospitals should there be heavy casualties, and servicemen's families' (*Today*, 16 January 1991: 6).

Ironically, while the media promoted the military as an ideal of family organisation in time of war, the military identified the family as a model for its own organisation and relationships, promoting itself as family-centred, family-friendly, a home away from home.[23] Yet as the fighting in and around the South Atlantic escalated there were increasing complaints about the military's failure to fulfil its most basic family responsibilities, to provide the families in its charge with timely or accurate information about the welfare of their loved ones, or to furnish appropriate (if any) care for the bereaved. When Jane Keoghane's husband, Kevin, was killed in the attack on the landing ship *Sir Galahad*, she had to wait more than five days for his regiment, the Welsh Guards, to confirm his death, her ordeal intensified by the regiment's ignorance of and insensitivity to her needs:

> On Friday [11 June 1982] morning at 7.55, she was about to leave for her work as a community nurse with the local area health authority, when the camp's families' officer came to the front door with one of Jane's neighbours. The neighbour had been walking up the road when she saw the officer approaching Jane's house, intuitively guessed it was bad news and insisted on accompanying him. Jane believes, if it had not been for her, she would have been left alone after she had been told that Kevin was missing and that the official would come back to see her later. 'He didn't even sit down, he just blurted it out and I was left standing on the doorstep ... What was so awful was the complete absence of someone from the Welsh Guards who knew how to cope with the situation. As a community nurse I know how vital support systems are to families who have experienced tragedy like a bereavement and yet the Armed Forces, whose business is life and death, do not have a system that can cope with the aftermath of a war. For me this inability to know what to do, how to behave, was even more shocking from the branch of the services that prides itself on being a family regiment. I had always believed that they would take care of their own, but it is a myth, it is rubbish'. (Carr, 1984: 40–1)

Jane Keoghane was not alone in her dissatisfaction. The Glasgow University Media Group discovered 'many relatives who reported that the information [about casualties] was grossly mishandled, that the

Navy itself made the waiting much harder to bear by consistently being rude and unhelpful, and refusing to give information, and that the emergency [telephone] lines were rarely obtainable in emergencies' (GUMG, 1985: 109). Dissatisfaction broke out into open dissent on 26 May 1982, the day after HMS *Coventry* and the cargo ship *Atlantic Conveyor* had been sunk in the South Atlantic, when the Secretary of State for Defence announced the loss of the ships in parliament and on live television before he had an accurate estimate of the casualty figures or before next-of-kin had been notified. Forty women whose husbands or sons were serving with the Navy met with their local MP demanding that he raise their concerns in parliament and that he exert pressure, particularly on the Navy, to improve its information management, expedite the delivery of news, good or bad, to relatives, and demonstrate a more sympathetic response to the emotional needs of the families under its charge.[24]

These disputes and disappointments rested on fundamental differences of opinion between the military and those in its service about the structures, functioning and role of the family. For all its cuddly PR, the military has a long history of undisguised hostility towards the families under its care, as J.W.M Hichberger observes:

In the pre-Crimean Army it was virtually impossible for a soldier to retain any links with home or community. The length of service, twenty-one years, and the social disgrace attached to enlistment, made it unlikely that close family ties could be maintained. On enlisting a soldier had to swear that he was not married, and the law which held soldiers not responsible for a wife married before enlistment made the army a refuge for those fleeing domestic ties. Once in the service only six men in a hundred were permitted to marry, and then by permission of the commanding officer. These few wives were allowed because they could perform useful domestic functions and act as servants to the officers' wives. There was no restriction on the marriage of officers.

Many men formed liaisons without official sanction, and were married 'off the strength'. Military regulations virtually ordered the soldiers to abandon their women and children. No provision was made for their welfare, and low pay made it impossible for any but the most thrifty to support a wife ... The authorities were concerned to keep the men as economically independent units, living in barracks, whatever the affront to conventional moralities. (Hichberger, 1988: 160–1)

While the material conditions of service personnel and their families may have improved over the intervening years, interviews with families during and since the Falklands War indicate that the military's underlying hostility towards them, its perception of them as an unwanted burden which it would much rather be shut of, still comes through loud and clear: 'Wives and families are excess baggage and the only interest the services have in you is what your husband does. If you lose your husband you not only lose your status, but your way of life, and eventually your home if you live in married quarters' (Carr, 1984: 43). In the eyes of the contemporary military the family is regarded as more than an unavoidable nuisance, it is a focus for potential subversion in that the demands of love, loyalty and duty that it exercises over serving personnel make it a constant threat to the cohesion and efficiency of the combat unit. In an effort to negate this threat the military endeavours to draw in and subject the families under its charge to its authoritarian structures and disciplinary regime, whereupon it need no longer solicit their cooperation as it can now command their obedience: 'In the Army there are no explanations just orders, and that rule applies to the families too' (Carr, 1984: 15). The military establishes and exercises its authority, ironically, by offering a range of welfare and family services – housing, healthcare, education, pensions – in exchange for the families' compliance with a degree of military discipline and in compensation for its loss of principal rights to the serviceman's or woman's loyalty and duty, which is now owed not to the family, but to the Army, Navy or Air Force: 'In civvy street for example you can say to your husband you'd sooner he didn't do this, that or the other: but in the Army you can't, because all the time for twenty-four hours out of every twenty-four he belongs to them and not to you' (Parker, 1985: 68).

The military's primary interest in the family, then, is centred on loosening its most basic ties, interposing itself between service personnel, their partners and children in order to nullify their potential threat to the good order of the fighting force. The military, as such, continues to regard the traditional family unit as an enemy within, hostile to its structures, aims and interests, and accordingly it treats the family like any other enemy, engaging and defeating it, and then subjecting it to its authority. The family, the very emblem of social unity and national cohesion, thus served to expose the ongoing fragmentation of British society under the strain of the fighting in the Falklands. It emerged as an emotive ideological battlefield over which politicians, media pundits and the relatives of those serving in the Falklands fought for sovereignty in an effort to vindicate and promote their particular line on the war. In an entirely unexpected fashion, the family provided everybody with an opportunity to participate in the conflict.[25]

FLEECED

As it turned out, the communities under threat from and formed in response to the Argentine invasion, the Falkland Islanders, the task force and the journalists who covered their exploits, were no more harmonious or coherent than those which had united so imperfectly on the home front.

The media's determination to promote the Falklands as a model community rested in part on a direct identification between the natural features of the islands, unspoilt, pure, hardy, simple, and the implied qualities of their inhabitants. A central, operating vehicle in this process was the sheep. The sheep's associations with the pastoral in religious, literary and agricultural tradition have made it a metonym for peaceful, coherent and communal life. Yet as Theocritus and Virgil, the founding fathers of the literary pastoral, implied, the pastoral represents a moral and social ideal which is constantly threatened by evolution from within and convulsion from without, particularly those disturbances brought by war.[26] Hence the recurrent prominence of pastoral forms in the literature of conflict where, as Paul Fussell observes, it provides a means of 'both fully gauging the calamities of [war] and imaginatively protecting oneself against them. Pastoral reference, whether to literature or to actual rural localities and objects, is a way of invoking a code to hint by antithesis at the indescribable; at the same time it is a comfort in itself' (Fussell, 1975: 235). The Falkland Islands have sheep in abundance, well over half a million of them at the time of the Argentine invasion. In the absence of contemporary footage from the islands to record the effects of the Argentine takeover, references to or images of the Falklands in the British media persistently foregrounded the islands' sheep or their endless rolling pastures, which, while providing a reminder of the supposedly idealised life they had once sustained, both hinted at and implicitly condemned the 'indescribable' actions and agents of its destruction.

To the Falklanders, though, the sheep was far more than a clever literary conceit; it offered immediate and abundant evidence of their political, economic and cultural subjection to Britain. This is neatly summarised in the islands' flag, a British blue ensign with the shield on a white disc. The shield shows a white ram on a grass compartment above wavy blue and white lines bearing a depiction of a Tudor-style ship, the *Desire*, in which the English mariner John Davis purportedly 'discovered' the Falkland Islands in 1592.[27] Despite Michael Foot's reassurances during the Emergency Parliamentary Debate that '[t]here is no question in the Falkland Islands of any colonial dependence or anything of the sort', the governance of the islands was classically colonial, and the sheep was both its object and its emblem (see Figure 2), (Morgan, 1982: 8).[28] The Falkland Islands were a British Crown Colony, and as such were administered by the Colonial Office until 1966, when this office was merged with the Foreign and Commonwealth Office. The Governor at the time of the invasion, Rex

Falkland Islands : Arms

Figure 2 Fleeced – the Falkland Islands' Arms

Hunt, observed: 'Despite a population smaller than most English parishes, the Islands carried the full panoply of a colonial government' (Hunt, 1992: 52–3). In this structure, the non-elected Governor exercised effective control over the islands' cabinet, a six-man Executive Council made up of two ex-officio members, two members appointed by the Governor and two elected members from the Legislative Council. (The Legislative Council consisted of the Governor, the Chief and Financial Secretaries of the islands, and six elected members.) According to the Latin America Bureau: 'Such democracy as did exist merely allowed the local farm managers and land owners some voice in the Legislative Council, a body with little real power. The working class "kelpers" had no political party and no voice in Government' (Honeywell and Pearce, 1982: 4).[29]

The islanders' political impotence entrenched an economic subjection which was impressed upon them (if not shoved down their throats) every time they looked out of their windows, walked past a flagpole or sat down to eat. The islands' economy, like its diet and its flag, revolved around sheep – in 1976 wool had accounted for 99 per cent of all exports from the Falklands. Due to the poor quality of the pasture, the islands' wool is produced by intensive monocropping on extensive farms or ranches which, though worked and often managed by islanders, were in the early 1980s still almost exclusively owned by foreign investors – nine absentee landlords and the Falkland Islands Company, itself wholly owned by the British company Coalite. The determination of the landlords to repatriate all profits to the UK and their failure, over decades, to invest in new equipment or infrastructure further contributed to the stagnation of the islands and the hopelessness of their people. At the time of the Argentine invasion the islands possessed only seven miles of paved roadway.

Out in the countryside (or the 'camp' as it is known locally, from the Spanish *campo*) farm workers and their families lived, according to the Latin America Bureau, 'under what amounted to feudal conditions. They buy all their provisions at the company store, they eat company mutton, they live in company houses and the local farm manager living in the "Big House" has total control over the settlement' (Honeywell and Pearce, 1982: 5). Many of the journalists accompanying the task force could scarcely conceal their amazement at or their distaste for the 'feudal torpor' of life in the Falklands: was it for this that so many had died?[30]

Not surprisingly, these dispiriting conditions produced a steady flow of (generally young) people into Port Stanley in search of better opportunities, but their prospects there were no brighter. The Falkland Islands Government (FIG) and the Falkland Islands Company (FIC), the islands two main employers, had done little to develop a competent labour force, or stimulate ambition and so foster initiative among the locals, consistently appointing expatriates on short-term contracts to a majority of the senior and middle grade positions in the administration and services. Their superior salaries and overseas benefits gave them a purchasing power and a quality of life well above that of the less-educated, lower paid locals, who comprised a definable and disgruntled underclass. According to the Latin America Bureau, the Falklands economy manifested

> nearly all the traits of a classic late twentieth century dependent economy, which, were it in continental Latin America, Africa, or Asia we would definitely categorize as underdeveloped. It may not exhibit the same levels of poverty as other underdeveloped countries, but it displays the same dependence on the export of raw materials, the same lack of diversification in the economy, the same dependence on foreign capital (that is, capital entering the islands from outside), the same lack of economic and social infrastructure and the same lack of representative democratic structures. (Honeywell and Pearce, 1982: 12)

The islands also manifested many of the classic social problems of (post) colonial cultures, fragmented communities divided by economic privilege and social caste, riven by mistrust and resentment, and the wholesale breakdown of the family unit. The latter, according to Lord Shackleton and the Latin America Bureau, was directly traceable to the feudal economy of the islands: 'older children leave the islands to search for work, elderly relatives leave the settlements when they are forced to vacate their company houses at the end of their working lives, and schoolchildren must go to Port Stanley if they are to receive Secondary education' (Honeywell and Pearce, 1982: 5). The results of these structural dysfunctions are measurable in the islanders' fondness for disputation, alcohol and divorce. Marriages in the Falklands fail at a rate more than three times that of an equivalent island community in Scotland, and alcohol plays a significant role not only in sundering couples but in sending them to their graves.[31] Visiting the remote settlement of Fox Bay East, Rex Hunt found the old births and deaths register in the post office which revealed that 'a frequent cause of death among older people was alcoholism' (Hunt, 1992: 82). Despite strong local institutions and cultural traditions there was little social cohesion, as Lord Shackleton observed in his *Economic Survey of the Falkland Islands* (1976): 'the situation as regards community spirit and cohesion was perhaps well put to us by one resident when he said simply, "There is no glue"' (Shackleton, 1976: 80). The model community was, as such, a model of colonial dependence and its many ills, economic subjection, social inequality and family disunity – divisions which Argentina's invasion and Britain's recovery of the islands did little to heal. Indeed, as Bishop and Witherow note, the war served 'to multiply enmities. Falklanders who had stayed in Stanley during the occupation spoke bitterly about those who had left the islands ... But those who stayed in the capital were objects of suspicion among those in the "camp", who spoke darkly of collaboration' (Bishop and Witherow, 1982: 148).

All the brave talk about cultural bonds and familial unity between the British and the Falklanders did nothing to disguise the troops' sense of disappointment when they finally met the islanders. Robert McGowan and Jeremy Hands were with the Royal Marines when they liberated the settlement at San Carlos:

> The door of a local sheep-station labourer was tentatively knocked upon. All around Marines took up firing positions, not yet sure whether or not enemy troops were there to meet them.
>
> The sound of sleepy footsteps came from within. The door creaked open to reveal an ancient dressing gown containing the portly figure of one of the 1,800 Falklanders they had come to liberate. It was a female of the species.

She stared blearily into her garden, now infested with anxious-looking Marines. She had been waiting 49 days for this moment, yet she reacted as though it was the milkman calling for his money.

'Oh, you're back then,' was all she could muster on this historic occasion. The Marines smiled, lost for words. (McGowan and Hands, 1983: 103).

The islanders' continuing impassiveness in the face of growing losses among the task force enraged the troops. They labelled the kelpers 'Bennys', after the woolly-hatted half-wit of *Crossroads* fame, or 'BUBs' – bloody ungrateful bastards, and their derision soon turned to violence. In the absence of the Argentinians, huddled in their defensive ring around Stanley, the curmudgeonly islanders, incessantly carping about the inconveniences imposed on them by the military, provided an ideal focus for the troop's anger and aggression, an ersatz enemy on whom they could vent their fury and prepare for the engagements to come. Vincent Bramley recalled one such incident when the men of 3 Para were preparing to leave the small settlement at Teal Inlet:

With our kit packed, webbing on and bergens stacked and centralized for delivery, we sorted ourselves into marching order. Standing to one side of us was a civvie, ranting and raving at one of our SNCOs [Senior Non-Commissioned Officers] about the condition of his garden, now that trenches had replaced the neat lawn.

'Sir, the Cabbageheads [Marines] will fill them and will be staying to occupy them. Please calm down.'

The man wouldn't listen, complaining and threatening was his last wish, so he was punched square in the face and sent flying backwards onto his arse. Some of the lads who were finishing off brews spat out their tea, laughing. (Bramley, 1991: 61)

Increasingly identified with, if not as, the real enemy, the islanders were, in many respects, accorded the same treatment as the defeated Argentinians.[32] On their arrival in Port Stanley, the troops embarked on a mass campaign of souvenir hunting, the prevalence of the practice marked by the war's popularisation of three specialised terms to describe the unauthorised acquisition of booty, 'proffing', 'blagging' and 'rassing' – the latter from the naval shorthand for replenishment at sea. While Argentine and British stores were the main focus of the troops' depredations, the islanders enjoyed no special protection – their property, like that of the prisoners, was fair game to their light-fingered liberators: 'The Falklands vet, Stephen Whiteley, whose wife was killed by an artillery shell in the last days of the battle, had his collection of gold coins stolen while he was being treated in hospital' (Fox, 1982a: 278).[33]

The islanders were hardly less receptive to the troops. After the initial euphoria of their liberation had subsided, within hours of the first troops arriving in Stanley the Falklanders set about erecting physical, psychological and bureaucratic barriers to keep the newest occupying force at arm's length:

> The town was suddenly full of troops in camouflage uniforms ... The locals did not seem to care for this. There were two queues for the store, one for troops and one for the islanders. This meant islanders always got served before the soldiers ... A notice appeared in the window of the Upland Goose Hotel stating that by magistrates' order no non-residents were to enter the bar. 'I get the feeling we're not welcome here,' one Para said.
> The local sentiment against the Argentinians was beginning to spread to all outsiders. (Bishop and Witherow, 1982: 143–4)[34]

As the fact sunk in that their liberation had cost them their peace and privacy and that the troops were here to stay, the last vestiges of politeness and tolerance fell away. What this revealed was not communal regard or cultural harmony, but the hostility of bitter enemies articulated in the language of the battlefield. These enmities came to a head in the bar of the Upland Goose Hotel, where Robert McGowan and Jeremy Hands were lodging:

> Some officers had been invited in by the £20-a-bed, three-beds-to-a-room, journalistic guests, and it was clear that this was not a popular move. Des King, the landlord, had been drinking for some hours, and had been scowling from his bunker behind the bar. Now it was time to open fire. His face red with rage, he launched a salvo at point-blank range against the chiefs of 2 Para, Lieutenant-Colonel David Chaundler and his number two, Major Chris Keeble.
> 'First the fucking Argies,' he stormed, 'now you lot. When are you going to clear off and leave us in peace?'
> When one of the officers, not unnaturally, was on the point of demonstrating just how paratroopers clear enemy trenches, he was dissuaded ... The moment passed, but word got round. Some Paras wanted to level the hotel. Some Marines wanted to help them. (McGowan and Hands, 1983: 273–4)

Greater familiarity with the islands and their people did little to improve relations between the military, the media and the Falklanders, indeed, as Patrick Bishop and John Witherow wryly observed: 'If anything the case for going to war over the Falklands diminished rather than grew the more you saw of the place and its inhabitants' (Bishop and Witherow, 1982: 19). Nor did the passage of time assuage bitter memories: writing more than a year after the fighting was over, ITN's Jeremy Hands still remembered the islanders as 'a bunch of absolute arseholes' (Morrison and Tumber, 1988: 116).[35]

In April 1983, more than 500 relatives of those killed in the fighting travelled to the Falklands aboard the Cunard *Countess* to visit the graves, memorials and last known resting places of their men. They had varying motives for making the trip: 'For Lynn Gallagher it was a personal attempt to find out why the war had happened and what [her husband] Lawrence had actually died for ... Many sought confirmation of how their sons and husbands had died.' One bereaved mother felt that she 'had to go to the Falklands to face up to the reality of her son's death' (Carr, 1984: 142). What all of them shared was the need to reassure themselves that their loved ones had not given their lives in vain, that they had been fighting for something worth dying for. What they found in the South Atlantic offered them little comfort:

> To many of the passengers on the Cunard *Countess*, the islands were nothing like they had expected. Port Stanley had looked like a shanty town from the sea, and close up it was not much better. Some heard complaints from the islanders at the inconvenience of no longer being able to use Argentine hospitals, or have the option of sending their children on to higher education on what they referred to as 'the mainland' ... For Maryon Pryce's husband, Don, the journey held personal memories of his visits to the Falklands in the late sixties as an engineer on the British patrol ship, HMS *Protector*. Don remembered how he had not been allowed into the colonial club in Port Stanley, which admitted only officers and certain Falklands families. He said he noted that the same place existed and that his son [Donald, killed aboard the *Atlantic Conveyor*], not being an officer, would also have been ineligible, 'and yet he gave his life for those people to go on living like that'. (Carr, 1984: 144–5).

The islands themselves were remembered with almost universal hostility: 'The Falklands are a god-forsaken place. The islands are empty, bleak, desolate, inhospitable. I never saw a single tree' (Weston, 1989: 95). The Argentinians, bred on tales of the islands' national and mythological significance, were no more impressed than the British by what they found there. Germán Chamorro of the 7th Mechanised Infantry Regiment recalled his first, inauspicious impressions on flying into Stanley on 29 April: 'We arrived at 2 p.m. and it was fucking freezing. The place was shrouded in mist and rain. I can remember saying: "Is it for this place we came?"' (Bramley, 1994: 91).[36] One could argue that battlefields have tended to be remembered in terms of the depravities enacted on them; Edmund Blunden, with commendable reserve, recalled the Somme as 'a sad scrawl of broken earth' (Blunden, 1934: 38), while twenty years after the shambles at Gallipoli Ion Idriess' recollections were remarkably untainted by either nationalism or nostalgia: 'Of all the bastards of places this is the greatest bastard in the world' (Idriess, 1935: 55). Yet not even an overwhelming victory of the sort won by Britain in the Falklands could improve the aspect of the islands, as Sergeant Major Doherty of 3 Para ruefully observed of his arrival in Stanley: 'It's been a bloody long way to come and it's been an awful lot of trouble for a mudheap like this, hasn't it?' (McGowan and Hands, 1983: 257).

The empty landscapes on which politicians and the media from both sides had inscribed friezes from the respective nations' glorious national pasts did nothing to inspire the troops who found in the desolation of the islands only a bitter confirmation of the objective's utter worthlessness and the denial of the communal ideals which, in part, had led them there.

COMRADES IN ARMS

In the immediate aftermath of victory, out on the streets of Stanley, the paras and marines who had fought side by side to capture the hills ringing the capital were now preparing to take the fight to one another. The vanguard of the task force, 3 Commando Brigade, comprised the elite of Britain's fighting forces, among them the 2nd and 3rd Battalions of the Parachute Regiment, and 40, 42, and 45 Commandos of the Royal Marines. Their rigorous selection procedures and legendary training regimes mean that only the toughest and the best earn the right to wear the red beret of the paras or the green beret of the marines. This sort of exclusivity and the self-conscious elitism it breeds generates powerful group cohesion, underpins teamwork and ensures efficiency, confirming each member's faith in his or her own abilities and a collective confidence in the unit's pre-eminence – hence the paras' designation of all other units as 'Craphats'.

Not surprisingly, the marines and the paras have a tradition of rivalry and mutual antipathy as long as the roll call of their battle honours. While many NCOs and officers were only too happy to use this rivalry as a basis for further cementing group cohesion and fostering aggression in the run-up to the Falklands War, they greeted with unease the news that 3 Para and the Royal Marines of 40 and 42 Commando would be travelling to the South Atlantic together aboard SS *Canberra*. A purely theoretical rivalry was one thing; the physical consequences of its actual embodiment were quite another. Yet according to Patrick Bishop of the *Observer* who journeyed to the Falklands with the paras and marines aboard the *Canberra* the top brass needn't have worried: 'Apart from good natured bitching in the ship's bars about each others incompetence, glory-seeking and stupidity there was little sign of friction on the voyage out' (Bishop and Witherow, 1982: 54). Indeed, the media and some senior officers spent a good part of the journey to and from the Falklands promoting this image of once bitter rivals united, like the nation itself, in the face of a common enemy. However, it was not a version of events which found widespread support among the other ranks. One officer ('Hat' in military parlance) attempting to solemnise the new spirit of unity was speedily disabused when he addressed the men of the Parachute Regiment as they prepared to leave the Falklands:

> 'Gentlemen,' he said, 'it gives me great pleasure to thank you all for your tremendous courage throughout this campaign. It was also great to see the rift between the red and green berets buried forever more ...'
> 'Fuck off, hat,' came one shout from the back of the red berets standing bunched together.
> The abrupt insult only stalled the commander for a few seconds, then he shrugged it off with a broad grin.
> 'As I was saying, the red and green have always hated each other and it is nice ... '
> 'We still fucking hate the wankers, too!' came the next shout. (Bramley, 1991: 199)

Though mature enough to see how 'silly' the antipathy between paras and marines was, Vincent Bramley was no less effected and motivated by it: 'Mixing with the Marines was not our idea of pleasure. We had hated each other for years, and the atmosphere of rivalry was very apparent' (Bramley, 1991: 7). On occasions the rivalry broke out into violence. Dominic Gray and his fellow paras supplemented their official training with 'special missions' against their nominal comrades: 'A few of us would ambush Marines on the ship for a good punch-up ... Although we were supposed to be on the same side the rivalry between us was intense' (Bramley, 1994: 27). When there were no marines to be got at, the civilian crew were fair game: during one altercation, Gray's Corporal, Stuart McLaughlin, later killed in the fighting on Mount Longdon, beat up a crewman and then badly injured the hapless civilian's shoulder when he tried to eject him from the ship via a porthole.[37] In an effort to avoid incidents the marines and the paras were largely segregated from one another and the civilian crew on the voyage south: while they may have eaten together, they trained separately, were briefed by unit, bunked in discrete areas of the ship and, most importantly, drank in their own bars.

Yet the rivalry between units provided a constant undertone to events in the Falklands, and threatened, on occasions, to jeopardise the task force's broader aims. According to Jennings and Weale, the cracking pace set by 3 Para on their legendary tab from Port San Carlos to Teal Inlet was driven less by tactical necessity and more by unit rivalry, the desire to outstrip 45 Commando who were making for the same destination via Douglas. It was the men who suffered, and by the time they arrived at Teal Inlet they were, in Major David Collett's opinion, in no fit state to fight a battle: 'The move from San Carlos [*sic*] to Teal Inlet was a bit chaotic, to say the least. It was a bloody great free-for-all. A Company ended up stopping and going into a house and sleeping for the night ... The whole thing was chaotic, it was crazy, there were casualties going down, people going over ... It was a rush to nowhere. When we rejoined the battalion the next morning, they were in absolute shit order, to be honest' (Jennings and Weale, 1996: 101). Nevertheless the rivalries prevailed: indeed, for many men it was these, above all else, that kept them going forward. In the immediate aftermath of the battles for the hills around the capital, 2 Para and 42 Commando jockeyed for the honour of being first into Stanley. Tony Gregory of 3 Para had few illusions about who he was competing against in the Falklands: 'even though the Argies were the enemy throughout the campaign it was the Marines we were always eager to beat' (Bramley, 1994: 200). For Vincent Bramley, the bitter fighting on Mount Longdon was only a warm-up for the contest that really mattered – getting into Stanley before the marines. Within minutes of the Argentine surrender the paras were mustering new strength for the final push to the ultimate objective: 'The message [announcing the surrender] had reached everyone. I slipped off my helmet and put on my beret, which had stayed close to hand throughout. The line moved off with sudden urgency, not to move into position to kill, but to beat the Marines to Stanley. We deserved that right. We now had a different fight on our hands: entry into Stanley' (Bramley, 1991: 173).

Once in Stanley, in the chaos succeeding the Argentine surrender, there was no hope of maintaining effective segregation between paras and marines. As relief wore off, boredom and anger set in; rumours, tall-tales and half truths about the recent battles charged old rivalries with a new intensity: 'After Port Stanley fell there were many bitter accusations flying between the two units; the Paras claiming the Marines had a soft war, the Marines accusing the Paras of recklessness during the attack on Mount Longdon and throwing away soldiers' lives' (Bishop and Witherow, 1982: 56). The usual sledging all too often degenerated into brawling and the prospect of far worse among men bristling with weapons and spoiling for a fight. There was even trouble aboard the hospital ship *Uganda*, where a Royal Marine bandsman earned the displeasure of some of 3 Para's wounded by practising his trumpet through the night. The men of 3 Para decided to restore the peace and quiet by lobbing a grenade into the marine's quarters: fortunately, the intended weapon stuck in the ship's piping and the attack never eventuated, but the enmity was real enough.[38] The resulting decision to return marines and paras to the UK aboard separate vessels was, according to Ken Lukowiak of 2 Para, a prudent one: 'The powers that be realised that they would have a bloodbath on their hands that would make Goose Green look like a picnic if Paras and Marines were sent home together' (Lukowiak, 1993: 172). Vincent Bramley's account of the events on Airborne Forces Day, a traditional para celebration, aboard *Norland*, the ship carrying the men of 2 and 3 Para home, suggests that 'the powers that be' had made the right decision. An evening of drink, song and celebration was the occasion for a massive and highly destructive release of the collective tensions built up by the war as friends, acquaintances and total strangers laid into one another with fists, feet, furniture and whatever else came to hand in a 'friendly riot' that lasted all night:

> The fighting spread like wildfire across the whole room, everyone scrapping with anyone they chose. Tables, chairs, beer cans, even bodies, flew through the air in every direction. Big Jacko and I backed our way to the wall, watching and screaming with laughter at the whole scene. Two lads crashed and rolled together off a table in front of us, punching hell out of each other. Four to six others attempted to pull them apart, but ended up fighting each other. I couldn't stop laughing. Suddenly, Quincey shouted at me, 'Stop laughing,' then smacked me in the side of the head. I retaliated and Jacko tried to separate us. We rolled on the floor, punching and kicking like the other four or five hundred lads in the bar. (Bramley, 1991: 202)[39]

While the troops were happy to beat one another to a comradely pulp, they were less receptive to the journalists travelling with them, some of whom, as Ian Bruce recalled, received death threats: 'All the way through every echelon of the hierarchy of a battalion. There was hostility ... . There were death threats on board. Les Dowd [Reuters] was threatened and I was threatened: "You get in the way and we'll shoot you"' (Morrison and Tumber, 1988: 79).[40]

Yet as it turned out, the journalists had more to fear from each other.

WRITE THE GOOD FIGHT

It was not only the military's much cherished image of family unity that deteriorated into fist fights and irreconcilable animosity in the

Falklands: the journalists whose job it was to report on the fighting expended a good deal of their time and energies fighting among themselves. But this is hardly a surprise – the reporters' duty to beat the opposition and be first with the story, their professional single-mindedness, combined with some powerful personal animosities set them in competition with one another from the outset.[41] However, the enforced cohabitation of the long journey south and the professional realities this impressed upon the reporters spawned some sense of a group identity among them and on occasions subverted their traditional rivalries. Crammed together in a confined space, marooned in a sea of military uniforms with little opportunity to identify or protect a scoop, a common professional code and the exigencies of filing their copy brought about the formation of unofficial alliances and local networks. Tony Snow of the *Sun* described the genesis of an *ad hoc* pooling system aboard HMS *Invincible*:

> In ... a closed situation in a ship, it's not open competition, you've got to go and get some quotes from various seamen ... If you were one person and had to run around getting all the different quotes, by the time [you get] all those quotes and do the story and bung it through the communications system, you might not get into that day's paper. So we agreed on certain things for reaction stories ... We would all rush around, one of us would get a couple of ratings, one of us would get one of the officers, etc., and then we would come back, do the story, and, though we did separate stories, we would swap quotes from various people ... We'd have a sort of conference between each other fairly early in the morning and say 'What's on today?' ... and do a fairly early story, and then we'd cooperate during the day. (Morrison and Tumber, 1988: 62–3)

Media organisations and the MoD endeavoured to sustain and further this spirit of cooperation, but as Morrison and Tumber noted their efforts only exacerbated the existing tensions: 'By and large the pooling of copy by journalists in the field is designed to reduce pressure, but the pooling operation of the Falklands actually increased it. In effect, it was not so much a pool, as an enormous lake into which editors in London dipped. By doing so they could directly compare the performance of their man against everyone else's' (Morrison and Tumber, 1988: 60).[42] As the task force neared the islands and offensive actions began in earnest, the competition between journalists for exclusive access to and ownership of specific news events reasserted itself and most of the unofficial pooling arrangements which had sprung up were discontinued.[43] Indeed, the most impressively coordinated act of media cooperation, between the journalists aboard SS *Canberra*, was undertaken to ensure the exclusion of their colleagues from the biggest story of the war to date, the British landings on the

Falklands. Bitter that the reporters aboard HMS *Invincible* had enjoyed privileged access to the air-sea engagements which had occurred en route to the Falklands, the *Canberra* journalists colluded with the MoD Minders and the Commander of 3 Brigade to ensure that they would enjoy exclusive rights to cover the landings and that the so-called '*Invincible* Five' would be kept away from the islands for the first four days of the British assault.[44] To the troops, whose lives depended on close cooperation and effective teamwork, the journalists, squabbling over access and obstructing their colleagues, were objects of contempt, as one marine officer told Max Hastings: 'Are you surprised that we all think you're a right bunch of cunts, that here we are on the eve of the hairiest operation of the war, and all you buggers can fight about is who is going to come and report it?' (Morrison and Tumber, 1988: 82).

Questions of professional rivalry, personal loyalty and communal affiliation were complicated in the Falklands by the tensions inherent in the reporters' relationship with the military. If the professional culture and personal antipathies of Fleet Street worked to separate the journalists then, as I have already shown, the conditions of the voyage and the uncertainties of battle bonded them to the soldiers with whom they shared their respective ships and to whom they looked for companionship and protection in the chaos of combat.[45] For the journalists this seriously complicated the question of who they were serving in the Falklands – the military, the public, their employers or themselves, where their loyalties lay and with which community they identified:

> The tension implicit in the identification with the Task Force stemmed not from the question of whether an individual was or was not patriotic, but whether journalism as an impartial activity was congruent with such sentiments ...
>
> The war was supposedly about the defence of liberal democratic principles, of which the freedom of the press remains a key commitment. The war was also against the 'Argies', and patriotism was defined as support for Britain in its campaign against the enemy. In such a situation, where does the responsibility of the journalist lie: to his profession or to his country? (Morrison and Tumber, 1988: 102)

According to Morrison and Tumber, the success enjoyed in the Falklands by Max Hastings, rested on his ability to identify his own with the nation's interests and his readiness to sacrifice personal ties or professional obligations in the pursuit of private ends. Hastings presented himself not merely as an observer, but as both a proponent of and participant in the conflict.[46] Like Hemingway in the Second World War, he liked 'to take part in the action as if he was an infantry officer and then write about what had happened to him' (Knightley,

1989: 316). His enthusiasm for the cause made him a popular figure with individual units who vied for his services as a PR man.[47] This not only kept him at the centre of the news from the conflict but established a vital link between his own, the military's and the nation's advancement – Hastings was both a witness to and an emblem of the nation's resurgence. His account of the fall of Stanley is exemplary in this regard. In a telling evocation of Hemingway, who claimed to have liberated Paris with a small unit of French irregulars more than a day in advance of the main allied force, Hastings took advantage of a temporary halt in the task force's advance to be the first Briton back into Stanley. Wrapping himself in the Union Jack (!) he preceded the troops into the capital where he made straight for the nearest pub, the Upland Goose: 'Walking into the hotel was the fulfilment of a dream, a fantasy that had filled all our thoughts for almost three months. "We never doubted for a moment that the British would come," said the proprietor Desmond King. "We have just been waiting for the moment"' (Hastings and Jenkins, 1983: 350). Hastings here is no mere appendage to the task force, but it and the nation's symbolic representative, both vanguard and figurehead of its triumphal recovery of the islands, his victory the nation's victory, his actions a realisation of the nation's collective fantasy.

Hastings freely acknowledged that in pursuit of his personal interests he made use of the loyalties, obligations and access provided by both military and journalistic communities. He was eager to accompany the SAS in their assault on Mount Kent not because there was a good story to be told about their exploits there – there wasn't, the Argentinians had long since pulled out and the SAS simply occupied their abandoned positions – but because of what privileged access to the nation's most secretive, most elite and most glamorous fighting unit said about him. However, when the military's priorities diverged from his own, when his relations with them could play no role in furthering his own advancement he instantly dispensed with them. He bestowed little interest on the conflict's lesser lights, and rarely portrays himself in the company of other ranks: 'it's part of the nature of journalism: you make friends with who you can, and you get out of them what you can' (qtd in Morrison and Tumber, 1988: 69).

While he could exploit his military contacts with relative impunity, his obligations to his fellow journalists were not so easily slipped. In his readiness to use others as a means to personal promotion Hastings failed to observe some of the fundamental professional obligations he owed to his colleagues, indeed his deliberate contravention of them almost made him a belated casualty of the fighting – his finest hour was very nearly one of his last. According to Michael Nicholson of ITN, despite the intense rivalry between reporters in the field, certain inviolable professional codes remain, one of which is that one can entrust one's copy to one's colleague certain in the knowledge that it will, eventually, reach its intended destination: 'Now Max [Hastings] is a hard guy. Keith Graves [BBC] is a hard fellow, Martin Bell [BBC], John Humphries [BBC], they're all very hard workers and hard men in the field. And they don't give much. But I would give them a piece of my copy and be bloody certain that they would hand it over the other end as quickly as they could' (qtd in Morrison and Tumber, 1988: 65). Nicholson was incredulous that some of the less experienced reporters with the task force were reluctant to trust their copy to their colleagues – as it turned out, their suspicions were well-founded.

On his way to HMS *Fearless* to file the report of his triumphal entry into Stanley, Hastings was given a pooled dispatch from several other of the task force journalists who had been close on his heels describing the collapse of Argentine resistance and the fall of the capital. They asked him to pass it on to the MoD 'minders' for censorship and immediate transmission, but it never arrived. Hastings' story was a sensation, carried by almost every national, a host of provincial papers throughout Britain and major dailies the world over, leading the *Sunday Express* to claim, not implausibly, that 'only two names have dominated the Falklands War, Galtieri and Max Hastings' (21 June 1982: 1). His fellow reporters were not impressed, as Bishop and Witherow recalled: 'the fragile camaraderie which bound the hacks together during the conflict fell apart soon after we arrived in Stanley. No one had seen newspapers for weeks but when they arrived it quickly became apparent that some journalists had had better wars than others ... Max Hastings had been used everywhere, especially his account of being first into Stanley. Some of his stories had even crowded out the reports of the newspapers own man on the spot' (Bishop and Witherow, 1982: 150). Those who had entrusted him with their pooled dispatch discovered that this was not the only copy given to Max Hastings which had failed to make it back to London, as Ian Bruce of the *Glasgow Herald* remembered it: 'We discovered that a lot of the copy that we'd sent back with Max wasn't getting through ... When we [called our editors] we discovered that a fair amount had gone missing, and all of it had been entrusted to Max Hastings' (Morrison and Tumber, 1988: 154). Matters came to a head, again, in the bar of the Upland Goose where, according to one eyewitness:

> Max was sitting by the piano when Bruce started yelling at him in a loud Glaswegian accent, which translated into something like, 'Hastings, you have lost my story and now I am going to kill you,' and then he pulled out an Argentinian bayonet. Patrick Bishop's face was one of studied amusement as to where Bruce would plunge the dagger. Then Derek Hudson [*Yorkshire Post*] piped up and said, 'This

is neither the time nor the place to murder Max Hastings,' and Bruce was dragged off him. Poor Max went very white. (Harris, 1983: 143)

Hastings was suitably rewarded for his single-minded self-interest winning Journalist of the Year in the British Press Awards and Reporter of the Year in the Granada Awards; early in 1983 he was appointed editor of the *Daily Telegraph*. He emerged as one of the war's iconic figures, one of its heroes, evidently, *because* and not in spite of his disdain for the collective, familial ideals which the nation was purportedly defending in the Falklands.

Despite the government's explicit celebration of the nation's many families and the principles they embodied, its assertion that through the defence and cultivation of these families it would 'restore the essential and grander identity of the Imaginary Briton to the modern subject', the imperatives of political survival and personal self-promotion were fatally at odds with the structure, ideals and functioning of the actual families caught up in the conflict. As the conduct of the war (not to mention the conduct of contemporary domestic politics) centred and relied to an ever greater extent on the initiative and aggression of charismatic individuals disdainful of established traditions, so the family was more often and more urgently invoked as a symbol of the 'History' ostensibly recovered but actually rejected by contemporary events. The primacy of the family in images from, narratives of, reports and debates about the Falklands War thus reflected the increasing redundancy of its principles and practices in the conduct of the war and the broader political management of the nation. The family, like the 'History' it embodies, 'becomes, more urgently, the object of ceremonies of resonance and continuity when it seems actively to be threatened and opposed by an inferior present epoch – when, to put this differently, society is developing (or "receding") in a way that cuts across the grain of traditional forms of security and self-understanding' (Wright, 1985: 166). The insistent invocation of the family thus functioned as a requiem for the structures of domestic, community and national self-understanding which it embodied and whose final obsolescence was confirmed in the conduct and outcome of the war. Though little lamented, indeed barely noticed at the time, the ideals and operations of the family were, without question, the most significant casualties of the Falklands War.

4
Heroes and Survivors

I can't look at you without thinking you're dead, Phil. (Williams, 1990: 94)

FIGHTING TALK

The tensions between explicit celebration of the nation's families and the rejection in practice of their forms and principles, between the ideals of collectivism and the tangible fruits of pragmatic individualism, can be better observed and explained through an analysis of the construction and deployment of the conflict's heroic icons.

In the early weeks of the war, however, the media were less concerned with heroism than the prospects for peace. A widely accepted, if unwritten, condition of public support for the exercise of force, reaffirmed during the Gulf War, states that a government must be seen to have explored and exhausted every possible means of achieving a peaceful settlement before the people can be expected to sanction a military response. As Peter Jenkins noted in exasperation when a British landing on the Falklands was imminent: 'We may soon hear a familiar slogan of peace recruited to war service. "There is no alternative" we shall be told. That is always the story with wars. All wars have to be unavoidable. All wars have to be entirely the fault of the other side' (Jenkins, 1982: 13). Jenkins' description of how the language of peace is 'recruited' into 'war service' is a telling one in that it both exemplifies and critiques the process by which the language used to describe the pursuit of a diplomatic solution to the Falklands War ensured the failure of any such process, and thus confirmed that the conflict was, indeed, 'entirely the fault of the other side'. The peculiar geography of the Falklands Conflict guaranteed a lengthy and prominent role for diplomacy. Stanley is slightly more distant from London than Vladivostock, and far less accessible.[1] The twenty-six days between the departure of the task force's capital ships and the first naval bombardment of positions around Stanley provided the governments of Britain and Argentina with ample time in which to prepare, submit and discuss a range of diplomatic proposals. Yet the media's discursive construction of the various diplomatic initiatives suggests that it was more intent on preparing its readership for hostilities, if not promoting the cause of war, than offering a fair evaluation of the search for and the chances of peace. Their consistent representation of the progress of negotiations in terms of sport and war denied the conditions for the effective exercise of diplomacy. After all, what hope for conciliation and compromise when the language used to describe them implied that every concession was a capitulation, every attempt to strike a bargain a gutless backdown?

The search for peace was represented as a global poker game in which General Galtieri and Margaret Thatcher were playing for their political survival. For Thatcher, every move in the South Atlantic was 'a gamble' made more hazardous by Argentina's possession of a 'powerful negotiating card', the Malvinas (*Guardian*, 14 April 1982: 13). Indeed, one defence correspondent suggested after the successful recovery of South Georgia that Thatcher should cut her losses and pull out of the game while she was ahead: 'it will surely pay to settle now because if she plays again, the odds will be much worse' (Fairhall, 1982b: 15).[2] The preferred sporting parallel was with ball-games, whose adversarial dynamics and emphasis on physical contact lent themselves more naturally to descriptions of combat. British diplomats 'scored a quick goal' with UN Resolution 502, while the recapture of South Georgia transformed negotiating conditions, producing 'something of a new ball-game' (*Guardian*, 26 April 1982: 15; 27 April 1982: 2).

But it was the vocabulary of war that was most commonly plundered to furnish descriptions for the progress of diplomacy. From the outset of the dispute there were fears that as a result of the sabre rattling in the Emergency Parliamentary Debate 'the negotiating process could be sunk before it even begins' (*Guardian*, 8 April 1982: 14). Britain's success with the passing of UN Resolution 502 strengthened its position, putting at its disposal 'the panoply of formidable economic sanctions and UN pressures' (*Guardian*, 13 April 1982: 10). Despite this, the diplomatic terrain began to look ominously like the polarised battlefields of the First World War – conciliation conducted from entrenched, diametrically opposed positions across a no-man's land of mutual mistrust. 'Proposal' and 'counter-proposal' were scarcely distinguishable from attack and counter-attack, after which, as Gibbard's cartoon (from the *Guardian*, 26 April 1982 (Figure 3)) suggests, the antagonists returned to their respective trenches (physical and mental), no closer to any kind of settlement. As the task force neared the islands the diplomats were, at least discursively, conscripted, formed into search parties and sent out on the prowl for peace: 'The [peace] formula for which three mediators were again out on separate reconnaissance at first light' proved elusive, as all around them 'the diplomatic battle raged' (*Guardian*, 7 May 1982: 14; 8 May 1982: 1).[3]

Figure 3 The Diplomatic Battlefield (cartoon by Gibbard)

The final most telling interpenetration of the diplomatic by the military register came on the day before the British reinvasion of the islands when the UN Secretary General, Javier Perez de Cuellar, 'called in the Argentine and British representatives' to tell them that he had 'established a "task force" which had explored various ways in which the UN might be useful' (*Guardian*, 20 May 1982: 2). Twenty-four hours later, having talked their way to the gates of war in the language of peace, the British government scuttled the UN's conciliatory task force by using its own to launch the reinvasion of the islands. The very discourse which purportedly offered an alternative to blood-letting locked the antagonists into an unavoidable and bloody confrontation. Reversing von Clausewitz's famous dictum, policy in the Falklands War, or the language which described it, was evidently an extension of hostilities by other means.

Indeed, the transition from peace to war was, in a discursive context, virtually seamless. The same sporting lexicon which had so ably sabotaged the progress of diplomacy was deployed by the military to describe its planned assaults, plot the geography of the battlefield and allot the appropriate kudos to the victors. Soon after the recapture of South Georgia the Fleet Commander, Rear Admiral Sandy Woodward, envisioned the forthcoming realisation of the task force's dominance in metaphors drawn from boxing, football and tennis: 'South Georgia was the appetiser. Now this is the heavy punch coming up behind. My battle group is properly formed and ready to strike. This is the run-up to the big match which, in my view, should be a walkover': adding that despite their reputation for tenacity, the Argentine troops had been 'quick to throw in the towel' (Hastings and Jenkins, 1983: 155). The planning for 3 Para's attack on Mount Longdon was modelled on the tactical dispositions of Rugby Union, the various targets on the mountain described in terms of standard positions on the rugby field, 'Fly Half', 'Wing Back', 'Wing Forward', even the Battalion's start line, 'Free Kick', implying the commencement of a carefully choreographed 'set-play' (Jennings and Weale, 1996: 121–2). In the aftermath of the fighting, Land Force Commander Major General Jeremy Moore nominated Brigadier Julian Thompson as 'the man of the match' (Fox, 1982a: 297). These constructions of the war implied a simple correspondence between its moral and political dynamics and the oppositional patterns of the sports field, a reductive disposition which the very existence of a diplomatic agenda denied. They suggested, furthermore, that the war was fundamentally recreational, somehow separate from the real lives of its protagonists and the nation, a view of the fighting which, as I will show, is explicitly rejected in the form, structure and content of many of the narratives from the war.

HEROES OF OLD

As the warships bore down on the Falkland Islands and the last hopes of a peaceful resolution to the dispute slipped away, the members of the task force accrued new depths of military, political and symbolic significance, and the media focus on them, accordingly, grew more intense. It was not only the government's political fortunes and the country's sense of pride and self-worth which hung on how the troops acquitted themselves in battle, the task force also carried the burden of what Patrick Wright calls the nation's 'mythical "History"', its dreams of a return to the glories of a bygone age. '[M]ythical "History"', Wright observes:

> flows backwards because it works in a way opposite to those teleological and future-orientated conceptions in which History moves forward through time towards its goal. Contrary to this, the mythical conception of 'History' establishes a national essence which is then postulated as an immutable if not always ancient past. In this chronically and sometimes violently mournful perspective the essential stuff of history remains identical through time – even

though it is unfortunately all concentrated at an earlier point in the passage of time. Hence the passage of years becomes entropic, opening up an ever-widening gulf between 'us' in the present and what remains 'our' rightful and necessary identity in an increasingly distant past ... Only an act of heroism will reverse this trend, checking the relentless passage of time and restoring to 'us' something that 'we' in our decadence may only just still be able to recognise as 'ours'. (Wright, 1985: 176–7)

The war in the Falklands consecrated the soldier hero as both the agent of the nation's return to its 'rightful and necessary identity' and as the embodiment of that identity, a reification of the 'national essence'. The soldier focused and instigated a collective remembering of the past, reversed the tide of history, restored the pride and confidence all but eaten away by forty years of post-war decline, and so returned the people to an Edenic vision of their national past and themselves:

If the event of 'historical' significance now stands more than ever as a binding moment of public revelation rather than the making of change or a decisive event in the struggle for world development, it is not surprising that memory should also achieve a new mode alongside its customary involvement in the ordering of personal life. To an extent this is a shift from private to public, for in its newer mode memory appears as a collective and commemorative form of *anamnesis*. In Plato's conception *anamnesis* was a process through which true knowledge and understanding were derived by the recollection of 'Ideas' experienced in a transcendental realm before birth. For 'us' too it is another realm which is revealed and remembered in these auguries of the national imagination: a clear although no longer always pre-industrial world from which hope, measure, intelligibility and courage have not been banished ... While it may certainly have been betrayed, this is overwhelmingly 'our' world: 'our' birthright and inheritance, a world which 'we', exiles as we are in the Wasteland of western modernity, can recognise as our own ...

These modulations of History (of what constitutes historical significance) and memory reflect wider developments in the way British people understand their own relation to the historical process. A desire for continuity develops when the present seems actually to lack the quality, meaning and significance of History – when past and present, in other words, seem disconnected and exterior to one another. (Wright, 1985: 165–6)

The soldier's role as the living connection between the shame of the present and the glories of the past, an embodiment of the nation's collective *anamnesis*, was enhanced by the scrupulous selection of heroic individuals earning official endorsement, and then enforced by the description of their lives and deeds in narrative forms which promoted their links with celebrated figures and 'Historic' events from the national past.

The chosen narrative forms were also, in part, a natural product of the war's peculiar geography. The long voyage to the Falklands crucially shaped the conflict's discursive form, its popular representation as a journey towards personal self-affirmation and a quest for the nation's rightful and necessary identity. This narrative construction of the conflict drew on a stock array of characters, incidents and settings, popularised in the medieval romance quests of Chrétien de Troyes and Sir Thomas Malory, whose tales of Roland and King Arthur articulated and embodied moral, military and cultural ideals sacred to the nation. Paraphrasing the work of Erich Auerbach, Paul Fussell outlined the characteristic features of the generic romance quest:

> The protagonist, first of all, moves forward through successive stages involving 'miracles and dangers' towards a crucial test. Magical numbers are important and so is ritual. The landscape is 'enchanted', full of 'secret murmurings and whispers'. The setting in which 'perilous encounters' and testing take place is 'fixed and isolated', distinct from the settings of the normal world. The hero and those he confronts are adept at 'antithetical reasonings'. There are only two social strata: one is privileged and aloof, while the other, more numerous, is 'colourful but more usually comic or grotesque'. Training is all-important: when not engaged in confrontations with the enemy, whether men, giants, ogres, or dragons, the hero devotes himself to 'constant and tireless practice and proving'. Finally, those engaged in these hazardous, stylized pursuits become 'a circle of solidarity,' 'a community of the elect'. (Fussell, 1975: 135)[4]

Despite the enormous diversity in the formal responses to the Falklands War, soldiers, historians, novelists, film-makers, poets and so forth consistently draw on the discursive norms of the romance quest as a basis for their accounts of the conflict.[5] In doing so they reasserted the conventional divisions of narrative labour, enhancing the role of a select few among the 'privileged and aloof' at the expense of their more numerous but largely invisible retainers.

Major General John Frost's designation of the men who led the 2nd Battalion of the Parachute Regiment in the Falklands as a 'breed of warriors' not only described their affiliation with one of the British Army's elite units but was implicitly affirmed in the discursive associations of the forms by which he and others described them (Frost, 1983: 16). In his study of the heroic theme in Australian war writing, *Big-Noting* (1987), Robin Gerster observes that the editor of the *Official History of Australia in the War of 1914–1918*, C.E.W. Bean, '[i]n the Homeric manner ... catalogues his host of heroes, either integrating their biographical details into the main text or providing footnotes for the relevant information'. Yet whereas Bean identified 'heroes by the hundred', Homer and the historians of the Falklands War selected 'relatively few glorious figures for special attention ... and in keeping with traditional practice these men are aristocrats, the heroic chieftains' (Gerster, 1987: 68). The representation of the 'heroic chieftains' in accounts of the Falklands War closely corresponds with the Homeric pattern: their biographical details integrated into the main body of the text, the men are fixed and defined by their schools, class origins, military lineage and warrior prowess. Max Hastings offered the following introduction to 3 Para's Commanding Officer (CO), Hew Pike: 'A crisp, sharp, clever Wykehamist of thirty-nine, Pike was the son of a general, and widely regarded as a future general himself. Like most British officers of his generation, he had served in Aden, Oman and Northern Ireland, but had never been shot at by anything heavier than small arms' (Hastings and Jenkins, 1983: 114).[6] Compare this with Homer's description of Elphenor: 'offshoot of the War-god, son of Chalcodon and chieftain of the gallant Abantes. His followers were quick on their feet; they wore their hair in locks at the back; they carried ashen spears and wished for nothing better than to lunge with them and tear the corslets on their enemies' breasts' (Homer, 1957: 54). Though he cannot claim the same propinquity with the war-god, Pike's heroic status is no less apparent from his textual pedigree.

The representation of the Abantes as mindless thugs held together by their lust for violence, herd instinct and a common dress code provided a model for the media's representation of the other (subordinate) ranks in the Falklands. They were portrayed as 'emotionless efficient killers', indistinguishable from one another in their 'skinhead haircuts' and 'carefully tattered sweatshirts', who found in service life a refuge from the responsibilities of the real world: 'Sitting in a slit trench in San Carlos during an air raid I heard two marines talking about why they joined up: "I was a baker's roundsman," one said, "but I kept fucking up the orders. One day I lost £300 of cream buns so before they could give me the sack I went off and joined the marines. It's great, football twice a week, a few lectures. There's the odd yomp [march], but you usually finish up in the pub"' (Bishop and Witherow, 1982: 59–60, 61). This readiness to identify and focus on what were thought to be the common features, the caste marks, of the group can be accounted for, in part, by the reporters' ignorance about and discomfort with the other ranks. To the journalists, many of them privately schooled, university educated, largely working for metropolitan media organisations, the young working-class men who made up the bulk of the task force were an exotic, unsettling and yet strangely familiar tribe. Like anthropologists among cannibals, the journalists observed and recorded the provenance, language, customs and culture of their exotic fellow travellers. Nervous in the presence of too many knives and forks, the men 'spoke with the accents of Britain's unemployment blackspots, particularly Glasgow or Tyneside. There were surprisingly few Londoners or blacks ... All the men were fanatically clean and tidy ... They were friendly and cheerful too and courteous to a degree that was so at odds with the norm in the civilian world that we were always suspicious that our legs were being pulled' (Bishop and Witherow, 1982: 59, 61).[7] The discursive norms of the romance quest had obvious attractions for the journalists in that they offered a convenient means of dealing with potentially volatile material, the other ranks, consigning them to a minor role in the narrative as comic or grotesque, and so leaving them free to focus on the exploits of the privileged and aloof.

The representation of the other ranks as emblematic, though undifferentiated, warrior figures was most consistently effected in the Falklands through the medium of the photograph. Task force personnel featured in photographs at the time of the conflict, other than senior officers, were invariably unnamed, facilitating their construction as symbolic figures, emblems of the aims or ideals of the task force. The photograph adorning the cover of Max Hastings and Simon Jenkins' *The Battle for the Falklands* depicts a soldier squatting half in a trench on a hilltop, his rifle poking out from his position, silhouetted in the twilight. The accompanying caption enshrines the principle of anonymity as it reveals nothing about the soldier other than the unit to which he belongs and where he was when the picture was taken (Figure 4). One can deduce that it was cold when the picture was taken, as the soldier has pulled down the ear-flaps on his cap. The cap itself, as opposed to a hard hat, and as such contrary to orders, seems to be a calculated act of bravado. One of his shoulder epaulettes is flapping loose, implying the scrapes he has been through to help secure the high ground. But there is plenty of fight in him yet. He is alert, half-erect, with his rifle thrust out in front of him he looks as if he is on his way out of the trench ready to lead the advance across the hills. There is also something meditative about his pose. His head is slightly tilted to his right, at right angles to the thrust of his rifle, and his gaze seems to be fixed not on the immediate objective, but on the horizon where the sun is rising (or is it sinking?). Its very absence of identifiable detail confirms the soldier less as an individual figure and more as an icon of the ideals which made the British so successful in

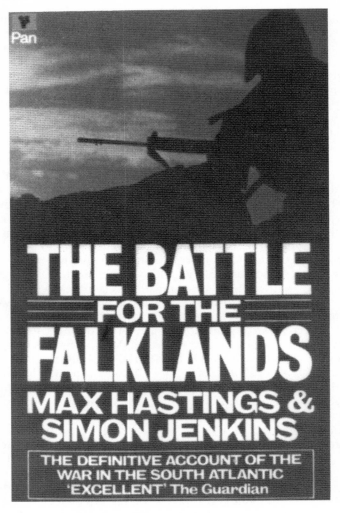

Figure 4 The Warrior Spirit (Pan paperback cover)

the Falklands – aggression, professionalism, panache and a loyalty to home and its principles.

Writing about photographs from the Second World War, Paul Fussell observed that the conditions under which most action shots were taken guaranteed the subject's anonymity, and that 'for the myth-making memory' this was 'one way of sanctifying the war. The myth requires that servicemen be depicted, at least in photographs, as virtually anonymous. Because the war was a common cause, no ordinary person has a right to appear as anything but anonymous' (Fussell, 1982: 231). The written and photographic record of the Falklands War suggests that the principle of anonymity was most energetically promoted by and among the other ranks, where it was cognate with the principles of a collective ethic centred on the mutual support of small groups willing to assist and even sacrifice their lives for one another. The centrepiece of this ethic is not an abstract ideal like the flag or the nation but the tangible communities which sustain the soldier in peace and war, his 'oppos', his platoon, the company and the regiment. Its origins lie in the tactical necessities of combat in the field, where an individual's survival depends on his effective functioning as part of a unit and where independence can hazard the lives of others. Vincent Bramley set out the credo of their ethic in his account of the battle for Mount Longdon: 'the further we went into the campaign, the less I thought of my home or family. I wasn't thinking of Queen and Country either. I thought of myself and the lads around me ... A Para team cannot work without everyone giving their best. It's the lads you fight and work for. You come second' (Bramley, 1991: 53, 61). The promotion of this collective ethic as both an operational and moral necessity not only ensured consent and enthusiasm for the campaign from among the other ranks but ensured that their contribution to it would be undervalued. This was because the principle of anonymity did not exist in opposition to but as a subordinate element in the myth of the heroic chieftain. As such, though intended to recognise and celebrate the achievements of the common soldiers and their units, the collective ethic ensured the pre-eminence of the heroic chieftains, reinforced the cultural and discursive hegemony which promoted them and maintained the anonymity of the other ranks.[8]

The most obvious beneficiary of this process was Lieutenant Colonel 'H' Jones, who emerged from the campaign as a national figure. The generous Homeric introduction bestowed on Jones by John Frost is, at first glance, as much a discursive correspondent to the public acclaim and the military honours he received as it is a depiction of the man himself:

Lieutenant-Colonel Herbert Jones was probably just the right man in the right place to lead 2 Para in the Falklands. Disliking his christian name, he always wished to be known as 'H', and he was a man who usually managed to get his own way. An Old Etonian, originally from the Devon and Dorset Regiment, he had made his mark in the Parachute Regiment as a most forceful leader. He was a keen sportsman, although his real loves were skiing and sailing rather than ball games; at any rate his hobbies served to keep him very fit. And if he was inclined to be impetuous and possibly over-ready to accept an idea before it was proven, the world is perhaps too full of the over-cautious. His one great and abiding ambition was to lead 2 Para in battle and, when he did, to lead it in the path of glory. As a CO he was most generous, kindly and thoughtful, though he could be ruthless and sometimes unforgiving when he felt that the good of his battalion was involved. He did not strive to be everybody's favourite man, but he had an innate charm that enabled him to prepare and lead his men to do their duty in the highest tradition. That he did so the world now knows. (Frost, 1983: 16)

'Glory', 'duty', 'tradition': Frost and others who wrote on the campaign confirmed Jones' credentials as a traditional heroic figure by celebrating his character and achievements in 'a fundamentally ceremonial style', using a '"raised" essentially feudal language' (Gerster, 1987: 62; Fussell, 1975: 21). Robert Fox remembered Jones as 'a chivalrous man', and on the night he wrote his report of the battle for Goose Green he consciously debated the viability of this celebratory language: 'I struggled with the word "heroic". Was it overblowing the description to call the battle heroic? Had I lost my sense of perspective? In the end I decided what was good enough for Leonidas was good enough for "H" Jones, and described his action as "heroic"' (Fox, 1982a: xiii, 203).[9] According to Paul Fussell this sort of traditional language reflected 'a static world, where the values appeared stable and where the meanings of abstractions seemed permanent and reliable', a world where 'everyone knew what glory was and what honour meant' (Fussell, 1975: 21). Frost, Fox and many other accounts of the conflict carefully construct Jones both as a metonym for this lost world of certainty and chivalry and as an embodiment of the personal and collective qualities required for its recovery and resurrection.

Yet in doing so, Frost exposes some of the social and narrative dysfunctions arising from the identification of the national interest with the interests of a privileged (and aloof) minority, the heroic chieftains. It is strongly hinted by Frost and in other accounts that the personal qualities that made Jones such an exemplary heroic chieftain were very nearly fatal to the public cause for which he was ostensibly fighting in the South Atlantic, the restoration of the Falkland Islands to British rule. Jones was 'a man who usually managed to get his own way', whose hobbies, skiing and sailing, suggested an absorption in personal rather than collective competition, implying his reluctance to subordinate his own identity and ambitions to those of the group. Jones' personal qualities, in fact, are strikingly Achillean. Describing another of the conflict's heroic chieftains, Zachary Leader identified the Achillean virtues as quickness to anger, a ferocious pride in oneself and one's unit, and a brave (even reckless) willingness to die in battle in search of a short and glorious life and an everlasting reputation.[10] Those who remembered Jones significantly memorialised him in these very terms: Frost has already referred to his ferocious pride in himself and his unit. His quickness to anger was no less pronounced: Chris Keeble, Jones' second in command, felt him to be 'intolerant in some ways – he wouldn't suffer fools', while one of Max Hastings' abiding memories of 2 Para's commander was of his 'quick temper' (Hastings and Jenkins, 1983: 269–70). Spencer Fitz-Gibbon's account of the Battle for Goose Green is strewn with first-hand testimony to Jones' explosive temper. He is variously described as 'volatile', 'a hothead', 'very abrasive', spending much of his first and final battle venting his frustration at his subordinates: 'shouting and screaming at the company commander', 'bawling', 'haranguing the intelligence officer', even 'jumping up and down in anger' (Fitz-Gibbon, 1995: 11, 20, 62, 25, 62, 12, 62 respectively).

Jones' readiness to die in battle was confirmed in the fact and circumstances of his death: he was shot and killed while single-handedly charging an Argentine defensive position at Darwin Hill where the advance on Goose Green had stalled. At the time this was interpreted as the starkest possible testimony of Jones' quality as a leader, his ability to inspire and motivate his followers and his readiness to lay down his life for the common, greater good. According to Robert Fox, the BBC Radio reporter who marched to Goose Green with 2 Para: 'It was an outstanding feat of arms ... "H" died in the style with which he had commanded his battalion, impetuous, generous and imaginative, always leading from the front ... All of us on the battlefield knew that he would not ask anyone to carry out an action that he would not do himself' (Fox, 1982a: 36, 176–7).[11] Others felt, however, that Jones' fondness for leading from the front reflected his dedication to private and not public interests, his pursuit of personal glory and an everlasting reputation at the expense of the common good. Spencer Fitz-Gibbon points out that Jones' restrictive leadership style, his determination to control rather than direct his subordinates did 'more to hinder the effective functioning of his battalion' and nearly cost it the battle, while his death was 'unnecessary, pointless, and certainly not the reason for 2 Para's eventual gaining of the upper hand' (Fitz-Gibbon, 1995: xv).[12]

The suspicion that Jones was motivated by the quest for private kudos in the Falklands is lent credence by a further Achillean echo in his character. Like Achilles, Jones was a loner who shunned the crowd; an aloof figure he is remembered by journalists and colleagues as cordial but never close. Fox recalled how he 'seemed to stand apart from the others' during the journey south (Fox, 1982a: 34). According to C.M. Bowra, Achilles conducted himself in much the same way at Troy: 'apart from Patroclus [Achilles] has no friends, and though he is on good terms with Odysseus and Aias, he is not intimate'. Achilles is aloof, Bowra claims, because he 'is the kind of hero who lives largely for himself and his own honour ... he is present at Troy presumably because it allows him to show his prowess' (Bowra, 1972: 114). Is it possible that the Falkland Islands mattered to Jones only in so far as they provided him with a stage on which he could 'lead his men in the path of glory' and so demonstrate *his* prowess? Some of his fellow task force officers certainly thought so, as Bishop noted: 'Even at the time the circumstances of H's death struck many people as extraordinary. Attacking machine gun posts is the sort of job given to a subaltern, senior NCO and a few soldiers. Some marine officers wondered whether Colonel Jones was not involved in a test of his own "bottle"' (Bishop and Witherow, 1982: 97). If he was testing the limits of his courage he did so, not as Fox suggests, out of a disregard for his own interests but from the keenest possible pursuit of them – even, if necessary, to the imperilment of the collective cause: 'Some officers suggested that H's dash up Darwin Hill was irresponsible, the renunciation of his vital task of commanding his battalion on the battlefield' (Hastings and Jenkins, 1983: 287).

In Jones' defence it should be noted that the tactical situation was more complex than these assessments imply. As Spencer Fitz-Gibbon has shown, British command tradition had, until the Falklands War, generally promoted a doctrine of restrictive control which 'results in superiors attempting to control the actions of their subordinates according to a pre-determined plan often made in great detail' (Fitz-Gibbon, 1995: xiv).[13] The battlegroup commander exercises this control by allotting specific tasks to particular units, dictating their movements on the battlefield and tying them to a rigid timing schedule. A corollary of this restrictive planning is 'a centralised style of executing command while the battle is underway' (Fitz-Gibbon, 1995: 94).[14] This leads to trouble when the realities of the battle enforce changes to the plan. In order to maintain effective control over the plan the restrictive controller will need to move forward from his HQ position, to sacrifice the overview this affords, in order to initiate and oversee any modifications to the plan. Instead of directing his subordinates the CO is increasingly drawn into an immediate leadership role. The doctrine of restrictive control thus ensures that the battlegroup commander is consistently torn between his command responsibilities and his duty to exercise effective control on the ground by taking a more direct role in the battle. The conflict between Jones' desire to set an example and lead from the front, and his responsibility to direct and command, not only reflects the seemingly irreconcilable demands of leadership facing the modern combat officer, it also embodies the dominant tension informing and shaping 'the history of the modern military establishment'. According to Morris Janowitz, this comprises:

> a struggle between heroic leaders, who embody traditionalism and glory, and military 'managers' who are concerned with the scientific and rational conduct of war. This distinction is fundamental. The military manager reflects the scientific and pragmatic dimensions of war-making; he is the professional with effective links to civilian society. The heroic leader is a perpetuation of the warrior type, the mounted officer who embodies the martial spirit and the theme of personal valour ... Military managers – in the ground, air and naval forces – are aware that they direct combat organisations. They consider themselves to be brave men, prepared to face danger. But they are mainly concerned with the most rational and economic ways of winning wars or avoiding them. They are less concerned with war as a way of life. Heroic leaders, in turn, claim that they have the proper formula for the conduct of war. They would deny that they are anti-technological. But for them the heroic traditions of fighting men, which can only be preserved by military honour, military tradition and the miliary way of life, are crucial. (Janowitz, 1960: 21, 35)

In the Falklands this tension was fleshed out not only in Jones' own inner struggles, but in his often uneasy relationship with his immediate superior, Brigadier Julian Thompson, 3 Brigade's Commanding Officer. Thompson's orders from the Land Force Commander, Major General Jeremy Moore, were to 'secure a bridgehead on East Falkland, into which reinforcements can be landed, in which an airstrip can be established and from which operations to repossess the Falkland Islands can be achieved' (Thompson, 1985: 73).[15] These orders put Thompson's task, in Gwynne Dyer's words, 'somewhere between that of a personnel manager and an air-traffic controller' and brought him into almost immediate conflict with Jones (Dyer, 1985: 137).

In response to Moore's directive that he should 'establish moral and physical domination over the enemy' Thompson ordered 2 Para to assault the Argentine garrison defending Goose Green, twenty-five kilometres south of San Carlos (Thompson, 1985: 73). However, soon after the men of 2 Para's D Company began the long march south from the beachhead on the night of 24 May worsening weather and the resultant cancellation of all helicopter sorties forced their return – no helicopters, no artillery support: no artillery support, no attack. Continuing bad weather, and his eagerness to exploit the Argentine failure to occupy Mount Kent, led Thompson to cancel the operation the next day. The garrison at Goose Green was, he contended, 'strategically irrelevant: once Stanley fell, Goose Green must go also, which was scarcely true the other way around' (Hastings and Jenkins, 1983: 265). Even Chris Keeble, the man who led 2 Para to victory at Goose Green after Jones' death conceded that '[t]o succeed in the Falklands there was little point in attacking Goose Green' (Sunday Times Insight Team, 1982: 219). Jones, 'straining at the leash' in his eagerness to get at the enemy, was 'furious', complaining that he had 'waited twenty years for this opportunity, and now some fucking Marine's cancelled it' (Frost, 1983: 45; Fox, 1982a: 177; Jennings and Weale, 1996: 97). He let it be known to journalists travelling with the task force that in his opinion the Brigadier was 'too cautious', that his reluctance to go on the offensive was sapping the men's morale and blunting their combat readiness (Fox, 1982a: 147). His views found influential support in parliament and the press.

While the loss of the *Atlantic Conveyor*, and with it most of the task force's troop carrying helicopters, on 25 May confirmed Thompson in his resolve to focus his straitened resources on the push for Stanley, it convinced many politicians and senior commanders in London that the attack on Goose Green must go ahead. In the four days since the British had established the beachhead at San Carlos on 21 May they had suffered consistent setbacks, soldiers lost, ships sunk, materiel destroyed, and yet made no discernible progress. Pressure mounted on politicians and senior officers to effect a tangible response – the task force had to be seen to be doing something. Consequently, Thompson was summoned to the satellite telephone facility at Ajax Bay where he was given direct orders from Operational Headquarters at Northwood to go ahead with the attack on Goose Green: 'I didn't want to do it but that's not new. Soldiers often have to do things they don't want to do. At the time it was clear to me that back in England there was a political need for victory, so that we could be seen to be doing something, seen to be winning. War is an extension of politics, and it is something I can live with' (Bilton and Kosminsky, 1989: 227).[16]

The attack went ahead and the politicians had their victory. The subsequent representation of that victory, the insistence that it was the brilliant planning, inspirational leadership and heroic sacrifice of 'H' Jones that had ensured the paras' success, reaffirmed the warrior hero as an icon of national pride.[17] The triumph of heroic leadership was affirmed in the subsequent distribution of official honours and driven home in later accounts of the war. Jones was awarded a posthumous Victoria Cross, the nation's highest award for gallantry, and celebrated as a national figure, a symbol of all that was admirable about the nation's conduct of the war.[18] Thompson on the other hand received a non-combat decoration, the Order of the Bath CB, retired from the Royal Marines in the mid-1980s and took up an academic post as a Research Fellow in War Studies at King's College London. His memoir of the campaign, *No Picnic*, attracted little public comment when it was published in 1985. Despite the fact that in the aftermath of victory Jeremy Moore 'heaped praise on Julian Thompson', his contribution to the war's successful outcome was consistently undervalued (Fox, 1982a: 297). The index to Robert Fox's account of the war has sixteen citations for 'Thompson, Brigadier Julian' who exercised sole command over the land campaign until Moore's arrival in the Falklands on 30 May and thereafter led 3 Brigade through the crucial battles in the hills around Stanley which precipitated the Argentine surrender on 14 June. There are twenty-four citations in the same index for 'Jones, Colonel "H"' who was dead within a week of setting foot on the islands (Fox, 1982a: 337, 335).

This discrepancy can be accounted for, in part, by the media's continuing celebration and the public's ongoing susceptibility to the mythic potency of the warrior hero. However, I believe that Jones' and Thompson's differing prominence can be more directly attributed to British domestic political concerns at the time and in the immediate aftermath of the war, and the narrative forms through which these were symbolically resolved. As I have already shown, the principles purportedly at stake in the Falklands grew out of and were defined by the Thatcher government's radical reforms at home, its determination to reconfigure the relationship between the contemporary nation and its glorious history, to fashion the future on the social and economic models of the past. By defining the war as a crusade in quest of the nation's true spirit, identifying that spirit in particular figures, promoting these figures as embodiments of and models for its recovery, all in specific, celebratory narrative forms – most notably the romance quest – the government and the media not only ensured the continuing primacy of the heroic leader in accounts of the conflict, but through the celebration of his achievements it implicitly promoted its own political agenda. Julian Thompson was therefore a victim of the political cause he so faithfully served, as the discursive norms which promoted its ends confined him, and the vast majority of the ordinary soldiers he commanded, to a supporting role in its affirming narratives.

Yet Jones was as much a liability as he was an asset to the government in that the prominence accorded him as an heroic ideal and a symbolic model for political reform consistently threatened to deconstruct the government's official line on the conflict. The fact that his indifference, even hostility, to the collective ideals of the war brought him not censure but national acclaim and official commendation suggests that the government's interest in and concern for the islands, like Jones', was proportionate with their utility to its purely selfish ends, namely their usefulness first in ensuring its survival and then promoting its domestic political goals. In and of themselves, it seems, the islands were worthless; they mattered only to the extent that they served as a symbolic surrogate for the nation, a blank screen onto which its local political concerns could be more clearly projected, defined, simplified and resolved. The war's most celebrated hero, an icon of his nation's moral and political renewal, thus served also to expose its political duplicity and moral bankruptcy.

RUMOUR CONTROL

As the task force steamed steadily southward, every day, every hour attenuated its links with the known and familiar world of home. Cut off from almost all external sources of information the troops aboard the ships, and later on the front lines, often knew less about the progress of the war than the British public. Having fought his way to Stanley where he holed up in a requisitioned house, the first news Julian Thompson had of the Argentine surrender came from the BBC: 'During the night we turned on one of our radios to the BBC World Service. We heard from 8,000 miles away about the surrender which was being conducted in a building 800 yards from where I was sitting' (Bilton and Kosminsky, 1989: 229).[19]

The news that did get through to the members of the task force, in the newspapers, videos and mail delivered by resupply vessels, offered an account of the war which seemed, by turns, sensational, trivial or just plain false, thus compounding their sense of dislocation from the real world. Max Hastings asserted that domestic accounts of the recovery of South Georgia which glossed over its many misadventures had fatally damaged the media's already fragile reputation among the troops: 'Reports published in the newspapers in London of the way in which South Georgia had been retaken were complete and absolute rubbish from beginning to end ... they did nothing to help our credibility on the spot when members of the task force were reading them' (Harris, 1983: 100).[20] The failure of task force reporters to stick even close to the facts on other occasions did little to bolster their reputation. David Tinker noted how HMS *Glamorgan*'s bombardment and raid on Pebble Island had been 'grandiosed ... out of all proportion' by a BBC crew which had been on board the ship during the operation: '(Antarctic wind, Force 9 gales, terrific disruption done, disrupted entire Argentine war effort, etc.). Mostly they sat drinking the Wardroom beer and were sick in the Heads: the weather was in fact quite good' (Tinker, 1982: 192). The troops' suspicion of the journalists gradually hardened into open contempt and an explicit rejection of their accounts of events: '"The youngest guys in the signals centre – I'm talking about kids of 19 or so – used to come and ask me why I kept giving them all this 'dross and tripe' to transmit" remembers one minder – an experience shared by most of his colleagues, both at sea and later, on the Falklands' (Harris, 1983: 36).

The patent inaccuracy of much that was written about events in the South Atlantic led the soldiers in the task force to believe, like their grandfathers before them in the First World War, 'that anything might be true except what was printed' (Bloch, 1954: 107). This scepticism returned them to 'the means of information and the mental state of olden times before journals, before news sheets, before books', occasioning 'a prodigious renewal of oral tradition, the ancient mother of myths and legends' (Bloch, 1954: 107). Rumour, innuendo and outright invention thus supplied the want of hard information within the task force (Bloch, 1954: 107). As Jennings and Weale note, once beyond reach of land 'the process of "rumour control" took hold, as everybody tried to work out from the wealth of intelligence material and gossip exactly what was going to happen' (Jennings and Weale, 1996: 66). Travelling aboard SS *Canberra*, Patrick Bishop witnessed the operations of rumour control first-hand. He recalled how, en route to Ascension Island, the mid-Atlantic resupply base,

> the ship was hit by a strange outbreak of superstition. Four days earlier we had hit a whale, killing it and staining the sea with blood, which some of the men took as a bad portent. A series of worrying coincidences followed. A story went around that a French clairvoyant had predicted that a great white whale would be sent to the bottom of the sea, plunging the world into a final war. The ship's nickname was the Great White Whale. Then it was noted that the postal number given to the *Canberra* by the British Forces Post Office was 666, which as every soldier knew from the horror movie *Omen* showing on board, was the mark of The Beast of Revelations. The story produced near panic in some quarters (Bishop and Witherow, 1982: 62)

Yet the purpose of this and the other apocryphal tales sweeping the task force was, clearly, less to provide information about the war than to mediate and exorcise common fears about it. Fear of the unknown trials to come drove many back to familiar structures for reassurance, foremost among which were the rituals of service life which afforded a talismanic defence against anxiety and superstition. 'Armies', as Richard Holmes observes, 'are ritualistic organisations', and it is the purpose of their rituals to serve 'as a precaution against disorder and a defence against the randomness of battle ... On the battlefield ritual, often in the form of the drills rammed home in peacetime training, is a raft of familiarity in an uncertain environment ... Individuals fall back on ritual, to which they sometimes attribute magical properties, as a means of defending the ego against anxiety' (Holmes, 1985: 236–8).

In the Falklands, as in the First and Second World Wars, combatants sought protection from the random misfortune of the modern battlefield in a range of amulets and ritualistic patterns of behaviour: 'A lance-corporal in 3 Para carried a St Christopher medal and touched it frequently. A private in the same battalion touched wood four times every morning, and another kept a pair of his wife's knickers in his pocket, and patted them in moments of tension. One soldier always put his left boot on first, and was sure that no harm would come to him providing that he did so' (Holmes, 1985: 239).[21]

Where soldiers turned to the rituals of drill, physical training (PT) and plain superstition for reassurance, in an effort to make sense of frightening and unfamiliar events and seek assurance of their own ultimate well-being, journalists turned to familiar narrative forms. Robert Fox, for example, put his faith in Coleridge. On various occasions in his account of the war Fox describes specific events and the behaviour of individuals in terms both determined and explicitly framed by Coleridge's *The Rime of the Ancient Mariner* (1789): 'One afternoon [Colonel] Tom Seccombe [Military Force Commander aboard *Canberra*] felt sure that a para company at firing practice on the *Canberra*'s stern was about to bring down an albatross, and, quite clearly having had enough of the Navy already on the expedition, did not want to condemn himself to a life sentence as Ancient Mariner. He ordered that all live firing practice should be curtailed for the afternoon' (Fox, 1982a: 73). The immediately succeeding description of 'all manner of living things, glinting, gliding and slithering' in the water bears an uncanny resemblance to Coleridge's description of the sea *after* the Ancient Mariner had shot the albatross and so suggests that Seccombe's precautions were in vain:

> The very deep did rot: O Christ!
> That ever this should be!
> Yea, slimy things did crawl with legs
> Upon the slimy sea. (Fox, 1982a: 73; Coleridge, 1789: 191)

In the poem, the mariner is freed from the albatross' curse only when he acknowledges the power of the Lord, repents his killing of the bird, and blesses the beauty and majesty of God's creation:

> Within the shadow of the ship
> I watched their rich attire:
> Blue, glossy green, and velvet black,
> They coiled and swam, and every track
> Was a flash of golden fire.
>
> O happy living things! no tongue
> Their beauty might declare:

A spring of love gushed from my heart,
And I blessed them unaware:
Sure my kind saint took pity on me,
And I blessed them unaware.

The self same moment I could pray;
And from my neck so free
The albatross fell off, and sank
Like lead into the sea.

(Coleridge, 1789: 198)

The second half of Fox's description of the ocean following the cancellation of firing practice balances the earlier, ill-omened account of 'glinting, gliding and slithering' things with an attempt to evoke the eerie beauty of the sea and its creatures – dolphins making the water 'boil', flying fish skimming the waves for hundreds of metres (Fox, 1982a: 70). Fox's apparently objective seascapes, like Seccombe's curtailment of firing practice, are fully significant only when they are seen in the context of Coleridge's poem. What the poem reveals is that as much as Seccombe's actions and Fox's descriptions are responses to or depictions of immediate situations, both serve, more importantly, as talismanic gestures intended to appease a greater and potentially malign power, to preserve the group from harm and ease the individual's psychological stress – palimpsestically inscribed over, they are intended as antidotes to the fate of the Ancient Mariner.[22]

Yet in the quest for personal reassurance, the writer was sometimes unwittingly conscripted into the service of propaganda, as the discursive norms in which journalists, combatants and historians sought narrative and psychological order served also to endorse, if not propound, the government's official line on the conflict. This is evident in the consistency with which differing accounts of the war describe and explain it in accordance with what Paul Fussell calls 'the mode of gross dichotomy' (Fussell, 1975: 79). Whereas in the First World War the myths and rituals which afforded the troops a degree of security and imparted a sense of meaning to fearful and chaotic events were commonly focused on threefold structures, in the Falklands, the process of ritual simplification went one step further.[23] The planning, progress and major events of the war were consistently presented and plotted through patterns of significant dualities and fixed oppositions in which the reporters found an ordered structure and a sense of security in the midst of violent and fearful events.

Apart from the more obvious, if specious polarities, between Us and Them, Good and Evil, Civilisation and Barbarity, Democracy and Tyranny, Patrick Bishop and John Witherow remarked on the fact that the Falklands was 'a remarkably two-sided war. Both sides had to rely, fundamentally, on their own soldiery and stocks of weapons, without any decisive military assistance from an outside power' (Bishop and Witherow, 1982: 17). Their subsequent account of the war is as much a product as it is the proof of this assertion. Julian Thompson's initial plan to establish a beachhead on the islands had, they noted, 'two phases' which involved the insertion of two separate sets of combat troops at two separate locations (Bishop and Witherow, 1982: 73).[24] The first offensive ground action of the campaign, 2 Para's assault on Goose Green, was planned as a 'night-day, silent-noisy battalion attack' along the parallel eastern and western flanks of the Goose Green–Darwin isthmus (Hastings and Jenkins, 1983: 274–5). On the later, epic march across East Falkland the members of 45 Commando and 3 Para walked from Port San Carlos by one of two routes, north via Douglas or south through Teal Inlet to the hills around Stanley, an ordeal described by one of two words, the marines' 'yomping' or the paras' 'tabbing'. The success of these, and all other missions in the Falklands centred on the effective operation of the 'oppo' or buddy system in which 'each soldier had a best friend upon whom he could rely and who would look after him in turn when necessary' (Bishop and Witherow, 1982: 20).[25] Yet the oppositional structures which imposed a reliable discursive form on confusing events and thereby provided writers and combatants with 'a raft of familiarity in an uncertain environment' were also the basis of the government's official version of the conflict as a straightforward struggle between the forces of Good and Evil – the structures of comfort and the language of description were thus framed within the grammar of promotion.[26]

This meant that in the process of offering, indeed through the very structures ostensibly embodying a clear and objective account of events, the government and the media were able to promote the campaign and its iconic figures. Robert Fox, for example, proffers his record of the war, *Eyewitness Falklands*, as a straightforward 'piece of reporting and observation, taken from memory, and nothing more' (Fox, 1982a: xii). Yet by framing the battle for Goose Green and 'H' Jones' death there within an ennobling context, embodied in a structure of significant dualities, in this case a recurring pattern of dawns and dusks, the book also helped establish and promote him as a national figure.

The original battle plan at Goose Green envisaged 'a six-phase assault by night and day which would lead to the capture of Darwin, the nearer of the two settlements, at dawn' (Fox, 1982a: 162). The first intimation of hostilities came, Fox recalls, 'as the light began to fade ... The sun was setting as the crash of a large explosion came from the north' (Fox, 1982a: 163). The advance began at 'dawn' and concluded with an air strike 'as the daylight began to fade' (Fox, 1982a: 168, 187). After a cold and nervous night a surrender was negotiated 'at first light', and at the conclusion of the formal ceremony, as Chris Keeble, 2 Para's acting CO, went to check up on the civilians, the moral significance of the paras' victory and the resultant return of the settlement to British rule was emblazoned across the sky in a colourful, celebratory and richly resonant counterpoint to the half light in which so much of the preceding struggle seemed to have taken place as 'a series of rainbows broke out in the autumnal sunshine' (Fox, 1982a: 190, 197).[27]

This setting provides more than a passive context for events, an appropriate chiaroscuro for the heroic deeds of the foreground. It reflects an active principle of narrative organisation, an implicit interpretation which identifies and promotes direct links between contemporary events and the moral values and historical traditions of the glorious national past. By 1914, due to their prevalence in Romantic and pre-First World War Georgian poetry, Ruskin's discussion of them in the first volume of *Modern Painters* (1843), and their significance in the literature of the Celtic Twilight, 'sunrise and sunset had become fully freighted with implicit aesthetic and moral meaning ... This exploitation of moments of waxing or waning half-light ... signals a constant reaching out towards traditional significance, very much like the system of "high" diction which dominated the early stages of the [First World] war. It reveals an attempt to make some sense of the war in relation to inherited tradition' (Fussell, 1975: 55, 57). The dawns and dusks which structure Fox's account of the Battle for Goose Green and Jones' death in it work in an identical fashion, they invite a reaching out towards and are themselves metonymic of the traditional significances, the straightforward moral polarities and historic victories of old within which these events can best be understood. The dawns and dusks thus establish the events at Goose Green, the death of Jones and his example to others as both an evocation of and a bridge back to the glorious national past.

In the preface to *Eyewitness Falklands* Jones is praised not merely as an ideal of heroic action and an inspiration to the task force and the nation as a whole, but more particularly as the instigator of and the model for Fox's own subsequent participation in the action: 'His generosity, impatience and humour were infectious and they changed almost everyone I know who was in close contact with him' (Fox, 1982a: xiii). Fox's account is, above all else, a record of that 'infection' and the changes it effected in him, the chronicle of his possession (of and) by the spirit of H Jones, his transformation from a disinterested observer to a 'hero' of the campaign and his own ultimate attainment of a place among the community of the elect – the central focus of *Eyewitness Falklands* therefore is not Jones' death but Fox's life. His celebration of Jones is, as such, essentially self-serving, one feature in a narrative strategy intended, above all else, to assure him of his own psychological and physical well-being.

Yet Fox's initial response to the conflict gave no hint that he would emerge as one of its most steadfast proponents. The rowdy, flag-waving rag-and-bone men dismantling the derelict whaling station on South Georgia were, in his view, better suited to farce than the making of history: the whole episode was '*opera buffa* ... a bizarre postscript in the chronicle of Empire in which the Marx brothers appeared to have a hand' (Fox, 1982a: 2).[28] Like most of his fellow hacks, Fox was convinced that the task force would never reach the islands, 'I thought there was a good chance that the *Canberra* would go as far as Ascension and wait there for weeks while a diplomatic settlement was achieved' (Fox, 1982a: 4).

From this perspective, the soldiers' preparations for a battle which he was sure would never come emerge as a metonym for the point-lessness of the whole campaign. Pounding the decks in their heavy boots, hoisting great logs onto their shoulders, or swinging 'like monkeys from available bulkhead and beam', bound to an endless round of Sisyphean torture, the soldiers looked to Fox less like warriors preparing for a crucial test than the fanatical devotees of some bizarre 'fitness cult' (Fox, 1982a: 8). He regarded the lectures on survival, enemy equipment and tactics as equally pointless and portrayed them as further emblems of the farcical nature of the whole campaign ('it was almost a pantomime'), zany performance pieces rather than an indispensable preparation for the 'hazardous pursuits' to come (Fox, 1982a: 67).

But as the ships moved beyond Ascension Island and Alexander Haig's shuttle diplomacy failed to produce a settlement, as PT gave place to live firing practice and air raid drills, so Fox's attitudes towards the (ongoing) lectures and the 'fitness cult' underwent a radical transfor-mation. Faced with the real prospect of a campaign, and an arduous one at that, Fox took up jogging and even joined in some of the 'gentler sessions' of PT with the troops, while the lectures he had so recently derided assumed a new relevance and in the process furnished an unexpected source of reassurance (Fox, 1982a: 8).[29] Not only did they offer potentially life-saving information – Fox conceded that they *did* provide 'some useful tips about surviving in an open boat after a helicopter had ditched' – but their ritual patterns also provided a familiar structure, a reassuring framework within which one could make sense of and so guard against the perils to come (Fox, 1982a: 67). The psychological relief, even spiritual comfort, they rendered is evident in Fox's description of their style and delivery in explicitly liturgical terms – 'litany', 'invocation', 'homilies' (Fox, 1982a: 59, 76).

While Fox, who came to mock, remained to pray at the lectures, his relationships with and treatment of the other ranks remained largely unchanged throughout his account. The specific roles allotted to them in his account and the personal characteristics attendant upon them were dictated by the discursive norms of the romance quest, where, as Erich Auerbach pointed out 'there are only two social strata: one is privileged and aloof, while the other, more numerous, is "colourful but more usually comic or grotesque"' (qtd in Fussell, 1975: 135). His representation of the other ranks as comic, grotesque or simply invisible, their roles and characters subordinate to the actions of their narrative and social superiors among the privileged and aloof, identifies them, in narratological terms, as what Greimas calls *actants*.[30] While he marched, billeted, ate and drank with the 'privileged and aloof', sketching out their individual characteristics and detailing their particular achievements in the campaign, the other ranks are most commonly defined by their rank and unit, 'one marine sergeant', 'one of the sergeants', 'a para corporal', 'a corporal', etc. (Fox, 1982a: 12, 148, 47, 12, respectively). Where names are given and the processes of individuation set in train, these are invariably negated by the other ranks' fixed, functional role in the narrative. For example, Corporal Jeremy Phillips, a sniper and one of the task force's premier marksmen, is, in the first instance, accorded individual characteristics which belie his purely subordinate role, described by Fox as 'a quiet man, an obvious loner' (Fox, 1982a: 12). Yet the discursive norms of the romance quest demand that he vacate the foreground in favour of the more complex, more active heroic chieftains, the narrative's moral and political foci, and that he take his place in the margins among the ranks of the comic grotesque, hence Fox's subsequent description of him as an 'exotic creature' who 'looked like an orang-utang in his extraordinary garb' (Fox, 1982b: 8; Fox, 1982a: 12 respectively).[31] On occasions Fox's dedicated adherence to the discursive norms of the romance quest and his consequent marginalisation of the other ranks compromised the reliability of his account. His record of the Battle for Mount Longdon, for example, contains no mention of Sergeant Ian McKay who was killed while single-handedly subduing a series of Argentine bunkers and, along with Jones, was posthumously awarded the Victoria Cross.[32] All too often, as the photographs illustrating his account show, Fox simply ignored the presence if not the existence of the ordinary soldiers around him – their's was not the anonymity of the iconic but the invisibility of the irrelevant.[33]

Fox's reductive treatment of the other ranks was a direct product of his own celebration of and identification with the 'privileged and aloof', and his aspirations towards a place among the 'community of the elect'. His progress towards this goal is marked in his gradual assumption of a more central role in the narrative arising from his adoption of an increasingly active part in the conflict. At the outset, recognising his place as an outsider, Fox aspired only to serve. However, as the ships neared the Total Exclusion Zone around the islands and severe restrictions were imposed on the transmission of news to and from the task force, as one of the battalion's chief sources of news, Fox suddenly found himself thrust into the limelight, the custodian of a valuable resource, his advice and opinions sought by some of the task force's most senior officers.[34]

At Goose Green, emboldened by his specialist knowledge of Latin culture and language, Fox made the vital step from observation to participation when he played what he portrays as an important role in the negotiations for the surrender of the Argentine garrison:

> It was quite clear from the first that the Air Force commander [Air Vice Commodore Wilson Pedrozo] was looking for an escape route of surrender with honour ... I realised that we had to sell him the idea that he had given up with great dignity ... Chris Keeble and I were left with Air Vice Commodore Pedrozo with the young Naval officer translating in bad English and myself interjecting in Italian when the lines appeared to get crossed. At one point Chris missed a step in the conversation and said: 'But I need to make sure that the civilians' safety is guaranteed. I must have that first.' The Vice Commodore said this was so, but he was worried about being seen to give up with honour. I drew Chris aside and muttered that as far as I could make out the civilians were fine, and that we should not press too hard on that point as the Argentinians might sense our concern and use the settlers as a bargaining counter. I felt that, like Italians who want to make *la bella figura* (cut a fine figure), the Argentinians wanted to save face and to have something which would enable them to say they had fought well and surrendered with honour, and this was recognised by the British. (Fox, 1982a: 193–5)

What is most striking about this record of the negotiations is that there is no mention of Fox's contribution to them in the accounts of Goose Green written by Julian Thompson, Max Hastings or Spencer Fitz-Gibbon.[35] The man who conducted the parley, Major Chris Keeble, recalled Fox only as one of the 'bewildered journalists' present there (the other was David Norris), a spectator of and not a protagonist in the proceedings (Keeble, 1985: 144).

So how can these disjunctions be accounted for? Is Fox, too intent on blowing his own trumpet, simply guilty of misrepresenting the facts? This would imply that the facts about what happened at Goose Green are fixed and known. Yet differing accounts offer varying records of the events there, selecting and foregrounding competing facts in an effort to promote varying interpretations of the battle. According to Spencer Fitz-Gibbon, the military advanced particular facts about Goose Green and ignored or discounted others in order to promote the battle as a vindication of its existing doctrine and tactics. Chris Keeble and John Frost, proud members of the Parachute Regiment, emphasised the superior leadership and fighting spirit of the paras, while differing Argentine accounts propound their tenacious defence of the settlement or the incompetence of their leaders.[36] The facts about what happened at Goose Green are evidently contingent on the nature and function of their representation. The function of Fox's account is, in part, to provide him with psychological reassurance. He endeavours to take some of the fear out of the war, to establish some semblance of order on its confused and contentious events and to assure himself of his own well-being by imposing on it a known and familiar pattern, the discursive norms of the romance quest. His avowed prominence in the battle, therefore, is not a personal vanity but a generic requirement, reflecting a desire to protect, not promote his ego. Just as so many of the facts about the Falklands War are selected and shaped by the determining political narrative of national redemption and social renewal, so Fox's record of the war and many of his facts about it are shaped by a personal narrative centred, above all else, on ensuring his psychological and physical well-being. Fox, as such, is the object as much as the agent of his account, composed by as much as he composes it.

Fox apparently attains his place within the circle of solidarity, and so affirms his status as 'the typical hero of romance ... superior in *degree* to other men and to his environment' on the night of the Argentine surrender (Frye, 1957: 33). He does so not through the successful negotiation of some symbolic feat of arms, some ritualised Test, but more appropriately through a simple act of enunciation. Just as the Falklands War has been invested with vital national significances through the implicit enunciations of narrative and historical precedence, its aims and achievements defined and affirmed in particular narrative forms and allusions, so Fox's place among the community of the elect is symbolically consecrated in a simple ritual of affirmation. Having spent the night of the surrender celebrating with Jeremy Moore and the newly liberated islanders, Fox was first on the scene when disgruntled Argentine conscripts set fire to a waterfront timber yard. The burning wood ignited discarded ammunition which threatened to engulf nearby fuel cylinders and endangered the PoWs in the area. In the absence of the military, Fox assumed control:

> I asked the [Argentine] officers to move the men because they were in danger. An Argentinian asked me if I was a British officer, and I said, 'No.' I realised they had not seen any British soldiers yet. They asked me if I was British, and I said, 'Yes.' Still the Argentinians wouldn't move with the bullets crackling and popping in the fires behind them. I was asked again if I was an officer, and finally

shouted, 'For the purposes of tonight, yes. Move your men for their own safety, you bloody fools'. (Fox, 1982a: 275)

Yet the very stimulus behind his quest for admission to the circle of solidarity suggests why he can never occupy a place within it. Where H Jones proved himself 'superior in degree to other men' by his 'brave, even reckless willingness to die in battle in search of a short and glorious life', Fox's efforts, both physical and narrative are, quite reasonably, focused on preserving his life (Frye, 1957: 33; Leader, 1988: 618). His endeavours to establish his heroic credentials are borne of his very real fears of physical and psychological harm, as such, 'the hero is one of us ... superior neither to other men nor to his environment', his behaviour governed and judged by 'the same canons of probability that we find in our own experience'. From these, Fox emerges not as 'the typical hero of romance' but as 'the hero of the low-mimetic mode, of most comedy and of realistic fiction' in which 'there is some difficulty in retaining the word "hero"' (Frye, 1957: 33–4). Excluded from the circle of solidarity Fox dedicates himself instead to establishing the reputation and celebrating the achievements of its newest star, H Jones – the man who would be Achilles has to make do with life as his faithful scribe.

HEAVEN AND HELL

If the romance quest offered Robert Fox the discursive assurance that he would come through the conflict unharmed, it offered Simon Weston the reassurance that the suffering he underwent in and as a result of the Falklands War had not been in vain. In his memoir of the campaign, *Walking Tall* (1989), Weston affirms that the war had been not the climax of but the catalyst for his heroic incarnation, for his journey to moral and, ironically, physical improvement. The appalling injuries that he suffered when Argentine planes bombed the landing ship *Sir Galahad* on which he and the 1st Battalion of the Welsh Guards were embarked sit, both physically and figuratively, at the centre of the book. There are detailed accounts of the operations to reconstruct his face and hands, all but melted in the explosions and fire aboard the ship, his deep depressions, and his attempts to refashion his life around the restrictions that his injuries imposed on him. Yet despite these details and the map of pain they plot, the book is remarkably free of bitterness because, as Weston confesses, 'I am content with what happened to me' (Weston, 1989: 177). He admits that in the light of his suffering this 'must sound strange to other people' (Weston, 1989: 177). In the context of the romance quest, however, it makes perfect sense. For all their horror, the trials which began on *Sir Galahad*'s blazing tank deck were the making, or more accurately, the remaking of Simon Weston. The work of the surgeons merely put the physical stamp on a more profound inner transformation, the genesis of 'new feelings ... new ideas' and above all a 'new spirit' (Weston, 1989: 176–7). In this regard his ordeal is presented as a metonym for the national experience of the Falklands War – his suffering and sacrifices a necessary preparation for physical rebirth, moral renewal and social redemption.

The book opens 'almost six years to the day since the troopship *Sir Galahad*, on which I was an unsuspecting passenger, had been hit by a 2,000-pound Argentinian bomb' with Weston earning his pilot's licence, soaring above the Oxfordshire countryside on his first solo flight, symbolically affirming his phoenix-like rise from the ashes of the fire and his former self, 'six years since that blazing inferno had changed my own life for ever' (Weston, 1989: 3). The image of the inferno is carefully chosen in that Weston represents his own and the nation's passage through the flames of war, from the 'hell' of *Sir Galahad*'s tank deck to the clear blue skies above Oxfordshire as a ritual purging, a form of death and resurrection (Weston, 1989: 108). Struggling off the blazing ship Weston has, quite literally, to come through the fire, to run through a wall of flame that separates the burning tank deck from the stairs which led to the upper decks 'all the way to heaven' (Weston, 1989: 109). Having passed through the wall of fire he is confronted by a 'final, harrowing image: a man, blown by the force of the explosion against the wall, and then stuck there as if he had been crucified' (Weston, 1989: 109). Weston's crucifixion, the book implies, is only beginning. Over the coming months his old self, 'the proud, swaggering young lad who left the small village of Nelson in Wales to join the Army' is, literally, peeled away layer by layer (Weston, 1989: 5). Through this ordeal he discovers new reserves of strength, a new sense of purpose in his life, in short a new self, a 'more caring and thoughtful Simon Weston' (Weston, 1989: 5).

Yet the death of the old and the birth of the new is a painful process and Weston is able to make the difficult transition only with the help of others. *Walking Tall* is as much a memorial to the sacrifice and assistance of those who helped him as it is a celebration of Weston's own determination to survive. He pays tribute to his family, the Army, and the nation as a whole, symbolically represented by the royals, acknowledging the parts each has played in his journey from death to resurrection, and noting the beneficial effects that their involvement in his struggle has had on them. The book, as such, illustrates the effective functioning and so celebrates the ideals of family, community and nation central to the official line on the conflict.

In the immediate aftermath of his injuries the only thing that kept Weston going was his determination to return to his family, and it is their love and understanding which help him through the slow process of his physical recovery. His injuries also work to knit a close family closer than ever, to heal its wounds, particularly Weston's estrangement from his sister, Helen – it is, as such, appropriate that the postscript to the book comprises a long letter from Helen celebrating this renewed sense of family unity.[37]

When not even the love and support of his family can help him through a period of deep depression it is his 'other "family"', his regiment, the Welsh Guards, who come to his aid and whisk him away to Germany for a morale-boosting break with his former colleagues which lifts him out of his despondency and furthers his gradual renewal: 'I was in Germany for nearly three weeks. When I came back I was a changed person' (Weston, 1989: 151–2).[38]

Newly motivated, Weston accepts a place on Operation Raleigh, a worldwide outward bound environmental expedition, yet until he boards the flight for New Zealand and meets the expedition's director, Colonel John Blashford-Snell, he has no idea who had nominated him for a place on the programme. Blashford-Snell reveals that the Prince of Wales had put his name forward, and continued to take a personal 'interest and concern' in his case (Weston, 1989: 160).

Weston's experiences on the road to recovery affirm the coherence and functioning at every level of the communities he had served in the Falklands and which in turn serve him so well. Family, community, nation, the book demonstrates, are not empty abstractions but living principles which augment the lives of those who put their faith in them. It is, as such, fitting that the latter chapters of his memoir record Weston's role in the service and extension of that community. On his return from New Zealand Weston helps establish a charity, Weston Spirit, dedicated to fostering 'skills in group work, leadership and community awareness' among unemployed teenagers (Weston, 1989: 164). Having benefited so much from local, professional and national communities, Weston now works to promote and extend the benefits of support and self-affirmation to others in need. It has been a long and unusually painful journey, but Weston has risen from the fires of hell and found in the Falklands the proof of his mettle, a renewed sense of self and an augmented sense of purpose – like the nation, he has been reborn in the Falklands.[39]

For others the war was less an affirming experience than a full-scale assault on the ideals for which they had fought. When they queried the conflict's aims, questioned its management or condemned its destructive effects on their lives they commonly did so by contesting its construction as a journey towards the moral and physical affirmation of the hero and his or her community thereby challenging the discursive norms of the romance quest.

In three separate accounts detailing Robert Lawrence's experiences in and after the Falklands War a range of views about the aims of the conflict, the substance of heroism and the spoils of victory are expressed through contrasting constructions of the nature and ultimate destination of the hero's journey. Lawrence, a thrusting young lieutenant in the Scots Guards was shot in the head during the battle for Tumbledown Mountain. Partially paralysed as a result of his injuries, when he expressed his dismay at his treatment by the medical profession, the South Atlantic Fund (set up to offer financial assistance to those injured in or bereaved by the war) and the military as a whole he was discarded and disowned by his regiment. Disillusioned, Lawrence left Britain for Australia in 1989. The first of these accounts appeared in Max Arthur's *Above All, Courage* (1985), a collection of interviews with twenty-nine men and one woman, all of whom served and most of whom were decorated for their actions in the Falklands War. According to Arthur, the purpose of these interviews – carefully selected from over 200 that he conducted and prefaced by the interviewee's medal citation – was both historical and celebratory: 'their words not only provide a unique chronicle of almost every facet of the Falklands Campaign, but also illustrate the indomitable spirit of the British soldier at war' (Arthur, 1985: x). No soldier embodied this spirit more completely, Arthur believed, than Robert Lawrence, and he singles him out for special mention in the preface to his book.[40] He subsequently represents the assault on an Argentine machine gun post, for which Lawrence was awarded the Military Cross, as an emblematic rites of passage, the climax of a journey from uncertainty to self-affirmation, an experience which augments and ultimately improves him: 'I got behind a rock and I threw the grenade and then I was screaming for my platoon to come on. This was probably the most fantastic thing I have ever seen in my life because they all did: every single man got up and went in' (Lawrence, 1985: 302). Yet Arthur is able to sustain this positive construction of Lawrence's experiences only by restricting the focus of his narrative to Tumbledown, by quarantining Lawrence's battle experiences from his subsequent disillusionment, gestured at here in barely a sentence.[41]

By contrast, both Charles Wood's screenplay *Tumbledown* (1987), and Robert Lawrence's own memoir, *When the Fighting Is Over* (1988) – co-authored with his father, John – spend proportionally less time on the battlefield, focusing instead on the consequences of what happened there. In *Tumbledown*, Wood contests the mythopoeic representation of the Falklands War as a celebration of heroic individualism and collective social unity by challenging the central discursive premises of the romance quest, the nature, purpose and direction of the hero's journey. What Lawrence undergoes in *Tumbledown* is not the hero's traditional progress from uncertainty and incompleteness towards moral and physical affirmation but a passage into mental and bodily torment, from arrogant self-assurance to helpless invalidity, from unthinking patriotism to scepticism and disillusionment.

Yet in spite of, indeed because of this, Wood promotes Lawrence as a hero, articulating his assault on the traditional definition of heroism through a simple structure of oppositions, rendered in Richard Eyre's BBC film in a series of stark visual contrasts. These juxtapose brief black and white shots of Lawrence as a warrior archetype with longer, full colour scenes focusing on the physical wreckage he sustained in battle – one journeying to war, a heroic figurehead perched on the prow of the southbound ship, the other fighting for continence, struggling to walk again, raging at his carers, his useless limbs and the 'cripples' around him. These images, Wood implies, are equivalent to and not exclusive of one another. Through his outraged response to his disablement, his refusal to accept the constraints it places on him, his angry confrontations with the society he served and his determined pursuit of independence and dignity, Lawrence's response to his injuries is, Wood demonstrates, no less heroic than his actions in sustaining them. Lawrence's journey then is the romance quest journey in reverse, a passage from self-assurance through self-loathing and self-doubt towards self-acceptance and ultimately pride: but his first and greatest obstacle on this journey, the screenplay makes clear, is himself.

As Wood notes in his preface, it has long been 'an accepted fact', that 'it is enough to die in battle to become a hero' (Wood, 1987: xiii). The corollary of this assumption is that, in certain contexts, it is somehow questionable to have come through a battle unscathed – an extreme view, admittedly, but one most forcefully advocated in the text by Lawrence himself during an angry outburst to the Regimental Chaplain aboard the hospital ship *Uganda*: 'Look at who is in this ward. There is not one other platoon commander, not one. Yet this is where they should be unless they are dead. I am the only platoon commander here! The others didn't do their jobs, that's why. If they had done their jobs, they would be here or dead. Where are they?' (Wood, 1987: 28).[42]

This view feeds Lawrence's conviction that his injuries, the visible citations of his valour, should afford him the consideration and gratitude of the people on whose behalf he sustained them when, in practice, they elicit only indifference, embarrassment and cruelty. Lawrence fails to see that the romance quest reading of the conflict centred on the myths of redemption and renewal has no place for, indeed is positively hostile towards, the gravely wounded. Lawrence is not only a political embarrassment he's a narrative impediment, and is treated accordingly (Figure 5). The disfigurements which, in his eyes, identify him as a hero of the nation, mark him out as an easy target for muggers, the model figures of a hostile society, and impel the military organisers of the Falkland Islands Service to confine him to

Figure 5 The Wounded (cartoon by Steve Bell)

civilian clothes and dispatch him to a remote corner of St Paul's Cathedral, quite literally to the margins of the celebratory narrative: 'Two hours. I've been sitting here two hours, Colour Sergeant. Couldn't see anything. Couldn't be seen. Couldn't wear uniform. What are they frightened of? ... It's as if we shouldn't have come back or something' (Wood, 1987: 57–8).[43]

In the face of this attempt to erase him and the other gravely injured from the official narrative of the war Lawrence refuses to go quietly, to efface himself, to reinforce the traditional invisibility of the war wounded and so sustain the romance quest myth of heroic inviolability. Instead, he confronts his society with the costs of the conflict and establishes its responsibility for them, demonstrating that any sense of shame arising from the war should not burden those who bear its wounds but those who have benefited from and will not now acknowledge them: 'Walk! Get me to walk, Benny! I'm going to march in a parade, in uniform, with medals, and show them this ... My head. I'm proud of it' (Wood, 1987: 58).[44]

If Lawrence's journey entails a progress from the self-regarding arrogance of the battlefield into the humiliating conformities of the civilian world, from self-loathing to self-love and ultimately pride, then the society he serves has an equivalent journey to make in the opposite direction, from complacency into moral doubt and physical discomfort. The war, Wood demonstrates, did not take place in a moral or geographical vacuum, it has physical, psychological and social consequences which stretch far beyond the battlefield and the men who fought there. These are most evident in those, like Lawrence, damaged by the fighting, whose return to society and the bosom of their families, it is implied, will be fraught with difficulties: 'Where were you? No good saying you weren't told I was coming. Everybody else was there. Why weren't you told? Why weren't you at Brize Norton? You must have been told. You don't bloody care. What kind of bloody woman are you?' (Wood, 1987: 34). The very qualities which ensured a British victory in the Falklands and earned Lawrence the plaudits of his society, 'violence, aggression and arrogance', are, as Zachary Leader notes, the very attributes likely to 'disrupt and alienate the community he is meant to protect' – he is thus denied and victimised by the society he served when most in need of its moral and material support (Leader, 1988: 618).

Wood attacks this 'doubleness', suggesting that the community must recognise the benefits it has reaped from the war, bear the moral costs and accept the burdens of financial and emotional care for those damaged by the fighting. Wood affirms this responsibility in simple, structural terms, through a further pattern of oppositions, sandwiching savage images from the Falklands between domestic scenes in the cosy kitchen of George and Helen Stubbs' cottage, where Robert

Lawrence and his companion Hugh Mackessac, Louise Stubbs' former boyfriend, stop in for lunch and over Shepherd's Pie and a bottle of red wine (an uncannily apposite meal, a sort of Falklands communion), Lawrence tells his story:

Int. Day. Kitchen of Stubbs House

GEORGE *comes back from showing* ROBERT *to the lavatory through a passage with military prints on the walls – huge, Victorian bravery.* HUGH *lights a cigarette ...*

Ext. Day. Mt Tumbledown

A gush of blood all over SGT MCDONALL *when he takes off* ROBERT's *beret.* CPL BAYNES *has dragged* ROBERT *from where he fell on to a slab of rock near the top of the crags. The blood has gushed in one released splash all over the front of* MCDONALL, *his arms, his face.* ROBERT *has watched it happen. There is sniper fire, which is returned, and the crump of artillery from Stanley.* ROBERT *is laid down, face up to the sky.*

(Wood, 1987: 13)

If Lawrence is, as Wood claims, a 'hero of empire', then the Stubbs have (albeit indirectly) inherited from his labour and sacrifice both material bounty – a fine Georgian cottage nestled in the Cotswolds – and the moral and psychological certitudes of imperial pre-eminence (Wood, 1987: xii). Yet while they reap the rewards of conquest they are less willing to bear any part of its costs. They refuse to let their daughter meet Lawrence and disapprove of her relationship with Hugh Mackessac, who was with Lawrence on Tumbledown, fearing that she might develop 'a penchant for killers' (Wood, 1987: 74). Indeed, the Stubbs can only enjoy their material and psychological comforts by ignoring the physical and moral brutalities on which they are founded, or by translating them into a more acceptable form. George, a conscientious objector from the Second World War collects militaria, the walls of the cottage covered in prints of what Wood calls '*huge, Victorian bravery*' (Wood, 1987: 13). Content with the sanitised postures of art, he dissociates himself from any involvement with the sharp end of war, telling Lawrence: 'Oh, I collect, but I don't *do*. Bit like the rest of the country' (Wood, 1987: 74). As long as George and the rest of the country can aestheticise and so anaesthetise war, construct it as a decorative adjunct to nationhood and not an obscene indictment of its foundations, they can ignore their complicity with its brutalities, evade the moral accounting and so pass over their duty of care for those damaged in it.

But Lawrence represents a direct assault on their complacency. Though George tries – he tells Robert that his story has been 'Fascinating' – he cannot obscure the young man's rage, paint out his paralysis, and so reduce him to another conventional study in bravery: Lawrence is alive and kicking hard, and the intensity which carried him through the fighting in the South Atlantic finally flushes George out of his defensive indifference (Wood, 1987: 74). In Lawrence's implacable determination to live on his own terms, George finds an echo of the same passionate reverence for life which kept him out of the Second World War on grounds of conscience, and is thus compelled to recognise his complicity in the wanton waste of life in the Falklands. Confronted with Lawrence's hemiplegia it is George who is left feeling incomplete, morally crippled by his having benefited from a war he now knows he should have actively opposed:

> GEORGE: I think it needed much more courage to do what he did than what I did.
> HELEN: You mean fight?
> GEORGE: No, I mean live.
>
> (Wood, 1987: 75)

In his frontal assault on the Stubbs' complacency and the more general moral apathy which it represents Lawrence achieves a more significant victory than any he attained in the South Atlantic. In asserting the nation's moral responsibility for those injured in the Falklands, insisting that they are properly cared for and satisfactorily compensated, Lawrence affirms his truly heroic stature not by his readiness to die for his country but by his determination to live in spite of it.

In Lawrence's autobiographical memoir, *When the Fighting Is Over*, the moral triumph implied in Wood's screenplay is conspicuously down-played. Lawrence and his father John avoid the tropes of a traditional, triumphant closure, focusing instead on the uncertainty of Lawrence's future, his ongoing rage at the treatment he received and his recognition that while the ideals which sustained him through the war are central to the myth of the Falklands War, there is no place in the myth for him.

Lawrence articulates his sense of betrayal and disgust, like Wood, through a strategy of narrative dissent, by undermining the romance quest hero's conventional passage to moral assurance and physical fulfilment through, in the first instance, unexpected and unsettling changes of idiom.

At its outset the memoir shows all the signs of conformity with the hero's traditional progress towards moral and physical affirmation. Looking back, Lawrence confesses that he saw his 'time in the Army as an opportunity to have a bit of a *Boy's Own* existence', and until he was wounded he did just that – night patrols in Belfast, jungle warfare training in Brunei and the glamour of ceremonial duties in London (Lawrence *et al.*, 1988: 9). The tireless practice and proving that comprised so much Army drill and training left him feeling 'totally and utterly invincible' (Lawrence *et al.*, 1988: 11).

Yet from the moment the Scots Guards set foot on the Falklands Lawrence's portrayal of succeeding events systematically debunks the archetypes of romance heroism. Until they reach the slopes of Tumbledown the guardsmen face a greater threat from their poor supply lines and the weather than they do from the enemy. Rations, slow to arrive and scarce when they do, provide little relief from the waterlogged trenches of San Carlos. Instead of honing his battle skills in preparation for the Test to come, Lawrence is flat out combating the effects of the elements, his most violent outburst a desperate attempt to save and not take life:

> Sutherland was lying in the dark in this hole full of water, and had stopped breathing. His heart had also stopped. I gave him artificial respiration and a cardiac massage to get him going again and screamed for help to try to get him out.
>
> His heart kept stopping as we carried him out and I continued giving him artificial respiration; then he threw up in my mouth. At one point I picked him up by his hair and kicked him in the back as hard as I possibly could to get him going again. (Lawrence *et al.*, 1988: 17)

When Lawrence and his men finally close with the enemy it looks, at last, as if the ideal of heroic incarnation will be realised. The battle for Tumbledown is a fierce one, and after some initial trepidation Lawrence acquits himself admirably, consistently risking his life to keep the advance going, inspiring his troops by his example, leading a dramatic charge on an Argentine machine gun post, picking off the enemy with his rifle or laying about him with his bayonet.[45] His memory of the action which won him the MC is little changed from the account he gave to Max Arthur four years earlier: 'I took off, and screamed at my men to follow me. In that instant, my one sudden thought was, are they going to follow me, or will I be left to run off on my own? But when I glanced round, there was this unbelievably fantastic sight of every man getting up and running in. I remember thinking at that moment that this was life on a knife edge. Amazing. Fantastic. Nothing would ever bother me again from then on' (Lawrence *et al.*, 1988: 30). Having attained the summit of Tumbledown, and with it realised his own ambitions of glory, Lawrence briefly celebrates his admission to the circle of solidarity by living out and bearing witness to the fantasy of his own heroic incarnation, until bombast gives place to ballistics:

I grabbed two or three people including Corporal Rennie and Sergeant McDermott, and went round the other end of the rock, and we started skirmishing down – one guy moving on while the other covered him. Again, I remember thinking that this was just like the movies ... Ian Bryden, our company second-in-command, was dashing along the top of the mountain doing all sorts of heroics. Sergeant Jackson handed his webbing and rifle to a Guardsman and went off on his own, with two grenades, to take some Argentinians out. It was all incredible stuff.

I remember seeing the lights of Stanley below us and thinking how strange it was it hadn't been blacked out. This was supposed to be a war. I turned to Guardsman McEntaggart as we went along and, for some inexplicable reason, suddenly cried out, 'Isn't this fun?'

Seconds later, it happened. I felt a blast in the back of my head that felt more as if I'd been hit by a train than by a bullet. It was a high-velocity bullet, in fact, travelling at a speed of around 3800 feet per second, and the air turbulence and shock wave travelling with it was what caused so much damage. I found this out later. At the time, all I knew was that my knees had gone and I collapsed, totally paralysed, on to the ground. (Lawrence *et al.*, 1988: 31–3).

The transition from heroic discourse to forensic analysis, from Rambo to helpless cripple all in one easy stumble signals the last narrative twitchings of the *Boy's Own* adventure, the last gasps of romance heroism. Through his injury Lawrence falls into a looking-glass world where the moral, physical and narrative certainties of the romance quest are inverted. The conventional linear progress through successive stages of heroic preparation to embodied glory is replaced by a fundamental regression to a state of infantile dependency and, once there, imprisonment in a seemingly endless cycle of therapy, tests and bureaucratic rigmarole. In a familiar landscape of institutional uniformity the protagonist makes desperate efforts to break free from the unwanted fraternity of disablement, striving only after the quotidian miracles of able-bodied dexterity. The seeds of this reversal are sown in the very moment at which Lawrence offers the ultimate confirmation of his valour, his readiness to kill, when he bayonets an Argentine soldier to death: 'I stabbed him and I stabbed him, again and again, in the mouth, in the face, in the guts, with a snapped bayonet' (Lawrence *et al.*, 1988: 32). Within hours Lawrence is on the receiving end, lying fully conscious on the operating table while the surgeon inserts a metal probe through his skull to extract the shreds of beret and bone fragments embedded in his brain.

Lawrence claims that the purpose of scenes like these and of his account generally is, in part, admonitory: 'I have a duty now, I believe, to inform my generation not only about what the fighting was like, but about what can happen to you if you get injured, in some sort of attempt to make them think twice about getting involved in another war' (Lawrence *et al.*, 1988: 193). Yet despite disillusionment at his treatment and a full-scale assault on the myth of heroic inviolability, Lawrence remains convinced that Britain's cause in the Falklands had been a just one and he continues to crave the hero's due, acclaim, acceptance and the personal affirmation these afford:

> I still believe that what I did in the Falklands War was worth doing. I still believe that what I did had to be done ... What I didn't realize, until, like so many others, I came back crippled after doing my bit for my country, was the extent to which we had been conned. Conned into believing in a set of priorities and principles that the rest of the world and British society in general no longer gave two hoots about. We had been 'their boys' fighting in the Falklands, and when the fighting was over, nobody wanted to know. (Lawrence *et al.*, 1988: 191–2)[46]

Denied a role in the narrative of national renewal his memoir and the screenplay he inspired embody his determined efforts to rewrite the Falklands myth and to inscribe himself and the other gravely wounded at its very heart.

IN THE WILDERNESS

For another member of the Scots Guards, Philip Williams, the position was quite the reverse of Lawrence's. Due to the incredible circumstances of his 'death' and 'resurrection', Williams found himself reluctantly cast as an embodied hero of the cause and so thrust into the mainstream of the Falklands myth.[47] His memoir of the campaign, *Summer Soldier* (1990), can be seen as a no less determined effort to write himself out of the war's narrative mainstream, to repudiate the role of hero and to cast himself, both literally and figuratively, back into the obscurity of the margins.

It would be hard to think of a less likely candidate for heroic incarnation than Williams. An indifferent and uncommitted soldier, he had joined the Army on a whim, more to escape the nagging of his parents and the tedium of life on the dole in Lancaster than out of any positive sense of purpose or commitment. While he enjoyed his ceremonial duties Williams was also an energetic skiver and a dedicated dope smoker. He despised the Falklands and spent the majority of his time there sheltering from the onslaughts of the weather. Driven by cold and boredom, Williams volunteered to locate casualties during the battle for Tumbledown, and while doing so suffered acute battle reaction (ABR) when a bomb exploded at his feet. Dazed and disorientated he stumbled off the mountain, wandered some miles away and in the ensuing confusion was lost by his regiment. Haunted by mirages, lapsing in and out of consciousness and sanity, he took shelter in a deserted crofter's cottage. Over the next few weeks Williams ventured further and further afield in search of food and rescue, until in mid-July he found his way to Diane and Kevin Kilmartin's farm from where he was taken to Stanley Hospital. After a few days' recuperation he was returned to his regiment at Ascension Island and flown back to the UK, seven weeks late for his own funeral.

When Williams had failed to turn up after the battle for Tumbledown the Scots Guards had listed him as missing presumed dead, notified his family accordingly and, in the absence of his body, urged them to go ahead with a memorial service in his honour. More than 300 people, relatives, friends, well-wishers, the media and an official party from the Scots Guards, gathered in a Lancaster church to witness, in the words of the local press, 'A Hero Laid to Rest' (Williams, 1990: 86). They were there, in fact, to witness the birth and not the passing of a hero. From the moment Williams went missing on Tumbledown his transformation from dope-smoking malcontent into symbolic hero was assured. As John Taylor notes: 'the acceptance of death in the national cause ... turned individual members of the Force into heroes' (Taylor, 1991: 97). Williams' transfiguration followed a familiar, ritualised pattern: initiated in the standard condolences of the official correspondence ('loss', 'sacrifice', 'cause', 'just'), solemnised in the universalising rituals of the memorial service (formal readings, traditional music, etc.), the subjects are stripped of their individual characteristics and reconstructed as both models of heroism and symbols of sacrifice to the cause – beatified as, in George Mosse's words, 'saints and martyrs' in the 'civic religion' of nationalism (Williams, 1990: 80–4; Mosse, 1990: 7). Thus was Williams transformed from a gormless teenager, 'a right little sod' who, in his parents' opinion, 'could never do anything right' into a 'son of Lancaster', 'a brave Scots Guardsman' who 'died alongside his comrades in a famous Regiment', 'giving his life in the service of his country' (Williams, 1990: 3, 9, 80, 84, 83).

But Williams was far from dead, and his resurrection, in the full glare of post-Falklands publicity, could hardly have come at a worse time for all concerned. For the Scots Guards it raised awkward questions about the thoroughness of their search for Williams and by implication the treatment of other missing and wounded in the South Atlantic. It focused attention on the indecent haste with which the media had proclaimed this awkward, inarticulate and uninspiringly ordinary teenager as a hero and thereby eroded confidence in the whole lexicon of celebration which framed the war. It bred intense speculation about the exact details of Williams' own conduct – the word desertion cropped up at regular intervals. Restored to life, Williams faced an unenviable if not impossible task, in that he had to do more than live up to a legend, he had to live *as* one – set beside his official alter-ego, the Hero Laid to Rest, he was bound to disappoint. The mythic discourse which had elevated Williams to heroic stature now crushed him beneath the weight of its unrealistic expectations. Where the Argentine gunners had failed the British media succeeded, as Williams became a casualty not of victory itself but of the discursive juggernaut which promoted its myths of individual renewal and collective redemption to the people.

Publicly commended by the Guards for his initiative and tenacity, from the moment he rejoined his regiment Williams was privately admonished for his stupidity by officers and NCOs and brutally victimised by his fellow soldiers who were resentful that his questionable conduct had implicitly impugned their own and the regiment's achievements in the Falklands.[48] Subjected to a regime of abuse Williams soon cracked. Failing to return from a fortnight's leave he took refuge in a relative's house where he was arrested by the local constabulary. While he was in police custody he suffered a nervous breakdown and when he was returned to the Scots Guards spent six months in the psychiatric wing of a military hospital before he was discharged from the Army. He failed to settle back into civilian life, and after a period of drug-addiction and various brushes with the law, culminating in a brief custodial sentence, he took to the roads and a rootless, wandering life among New Age travellers.

In *Summer Soldier* Williams' primary purpose is less to repudiate his own unwonted status as a hero – though he does that pithily enough – than it is to deconstruct the cultural and narrative grounds on which it was founded. The book is, as such, an extended assault on the forms of the romance quest and the myths of redemption they promote and sustain. It was Jeffrey Walsh's failure to pick up this metafictional focus which led him, wrongly I believe, to dismiss *Summer Soldier* as 'an angry crude book' (Walsh, 1992: 42). Angry and crude it most certainly is, yet its crudeness is no stylistic failing; it is a central structuring feature of the narrative, and an uncannily apposite response to the sanitisation of the war (both moral and graphic) orchestrated by the government and so slavishly effected by the media. *Summer Soldier* rejects the glamorised posturing which characterised both contemporary and subsequent coverage of the fighting and which helped sustain the romance quest myth of heroic inviolability, immersing itself instead in the moral, mental and physical cesspool of war. Its liberal invective, its self-consciously artless, quasi-oral form not only subvert the formalised stylistic norms of the conventional war memoir, they declare the book's distance from the personal and regimental hagiographies which dominated the conflict's literary landscape well into the late 1980s and so sustained its triumphal construction. With every curse and every homely quip, every admission of fear, incompetence and failure, Williams and his editor-cum-ghostwriter, the novelist M.S. Power, press home their assault on the discursive norms of the romance quest and their representation of the war as a sacred rite of personal and social redemption.

Unlike the hero of traditional romance, Williams has no aspirations to a place among the circle of solidarity, explicitly repudiating the proffered honour: 'I simply couldn't understand what all this hero crap was about. I just got lost, that was all. I'd been cold and hungry and shit scared. I couldn't see anything very heroic in all that' (Williams, 1990: 99). A bemused and terrified wanderer lost in a nightmare landscape, Williams presents his experiences in and his journeys within the Falklands not as a passage to moral and spiritual completeness, but as the catalyst for psychological fragmentation. Haunted by mirages, uncertain of where, even who he is, the stable self, the heroic narrative's discursive and ideological centrepiece, disintegrates:

> I was woken by soft bangings and scrapings coming from downstairs. Jesus, that frightened me ... after a bit, the noises stopped, so I clambered down from the bathroom into the loft. I stood in the doorway facing the kitchen, wondering whether to check the other rooms or get the hell out of there.
>
> Suddenly there was a shuffling sound coming from the bedrooms, and voices speaking in Spanish. Fuck me, I thought, I've only got one bloody grenade – I hope I don't have to blow myself up. Then everything went quiet again.
>
> I don't honestly know how long I stood there, it seemed like about ten minutes, but it could have been a few seconds or an hour, but the next thing I saw was this dirty looking bloke in helmet and combat clothing coming into the kitchen followed by a woman and two children ... a couple of other soldiers followed them into the kitchen, and they had rifles with fixed bayonets.
>
> All the adults seemed to be talking but their lips weren't moving. The soldier leading the group walked to within two feet of me, looked at me, turned and ordered everyone out of the croft. They trooped past me, and went out into the snow.
>
> I was pretty shattered I can tell you. I went to one of the little windows and looked out. They'd gone. I ran out and peered about for a sign of them. Nothing. There was a hillock to the left and I presumed they'd gone round behind that. It was then I noticed that the only footprints in the snow were my own. (Williams, 1990: 45–6)[49]

Williams' frank account of his incompetence, his demented wanderings and their concomitant portrait of the chaos which reigned during and after the battle for Tumbledown comprised an explicit challenge to the official account of the conflict and the conduct of British soldiers in it as a model of strategic and moral order. In an effort to contain this threat the Army dispatched a team from the Services Investigation Bureau (SIB) to elicit the details of what had happened to Williams in the Falklands and to establish some kind of discursive order over and explanation for his actions, to throw up around them the frail ramparts of narrative coherence. Yet as Williams recalled, the insubstantiality of his memories, his inability to distinguish one day or one incident from another or to impose a simple chronology on his experiences made the whole exercise as frustrating as it was fruitless: 'The main trouble was [the SIB men] wanted everything in neat, strict, military order. But nothing was in neat, strict, military order in my mind. Everything was jumbled up. Everything piled on top of one another in a heap' (Williams, 1990: 64).

Just as Williams resisted the SIB officers' determination to impose order where none existed, insisting on the authenticity of his fragmentary and jumbled memories, so in his memoir he steadfastly refuses to surrender his experiences or himself to the prefabricated narratives of personal and national affirmation. These are present in *Summer Soldier* only in the form of shattered fragments, parodic shards of or cynical allusions to latter day romance quests, the hackneyed clichés of the Hollywood war hero or the Western gunslinger, their discursive coherence and moral authority exploded, along with Williams' mental and emotional equilibrium, by events in the Falklands: 'I don't know why but for a second everything seemed to get terribly quiet. Then the shell landed close to me with a terrific explosion. I remember thinking, "God, this is a hell of a way to die," because someone had said that in some book I'd read. Then everything went black' (Williams, 1990: 37).[50]

The book's faithful adherence to the unheroic facts of Williams' experience reflects not a flight from narrative coherence *in toto*, as Jeffrey Walsh seemed to suggest, but a rejection of the dominant narrative's discursive norms and its implicit insistence that the war had redeemed the nation and improved those who took part in it. Williams' account of his time wandering lost in the Falklands draws on alternative sources of moral and discursive authority to articulate his social and political dissent.

It is no coincidence that he spends forty hungry days after his baptism of fire wandering in a wilderness blighted by war, littered with discarded weaponry and the decomposing carcasses of man and beast. After His baptism in the River Jordan, Christ spent forty days fasting in the wilderness. It was there that he encountered Satan who offered him 'all the kingdoms of the world in all their greatness' if he would only submit to his authority (Matthew 4: 8). Christ resisted the devil's temptations and, augmented by his struggle, anointed with 'the power of the Holy Spirit', he went forward to preach his father's word and to embrace the hard fate that this allotted him (Luke 4: 14). Williams too wrestled with temptation, first during his time in the physical wilderness of the Falklands and later in the emotional wilderness of his subsequent ostracism by the military and the society he had served. Like Christ, Williams' greatest struggle was to resist the temptation of the easier path: in the Falklands, the temptation to surrender to the elements and embrace physical oblivion, and on his return to Britain the temptation to put himself in the hands of the Army's PR machinery and to reap the kudos of heroism, to submit himself and his experiences to the voracious myth of national redemption, and thereby to lose his soul.[51] Christ's victory over temptation prepares and strengthens him for the physical and spiritual struggles to come: Williams' victory diminishes and all but defeats him. Indeed, as his mother remarks, with some comic prescience, on his return home: 'I can't look at you without thinking you're dead, Phil' (Williams, 1990: 94). Williams only gradually comes to accept what his mother sees intuitively, that the carefree (and careless) boy who had left for the Falklands three months earlier has gone for good, that he was, in a real sense, 'lost' in the fighting: 'I knew I had changed so much that something of me was dead. And it was something of me that I'd liked, so that made it worse' (Williams, 1990: 94–5).

Christ's suffering and death on the cross bring the hope of salvation for all; his own resurrection is a model of redemption, a reminder to the disciples and to all mankind of the means to eternal glory: 'Go throughout the whole world and preach the gospel to all mankind. Whoever believes and is baptised will be saved: whoever does not believe will be condemned' (Mark 16: 15–16). Though Williams 'died' he continues to suffer, seemingly without hope of redemption. Unlike Simon Weston, there is no stairway to salvation for him, no escape from the hell of physical and emotional torment to the heaven of inner peace. Resurrected and rebaptised in a hot bath at Stanley Hospital he is trapped and tormented in a sensory and psychological hell, doomed to constantly relive the horrors of the wilderness: 'I still couldn't believe that I was back among people. I wondered if I'd gone mad and was dreaming again ... Doors banging sounded like bombardments. Footsteps in the corridor outside like rifle fire. The rattle of metal dishes on a trolley like tanks rumbling ... And the smell of the hospital was weird after all the fresh air. For some reason the antiseptic cleanliness stank like putridness in my nose' (Williams, 1990: 59).

Worse still, he is condemned, like Christ, to preach his heretical gospel wherever he goes, to invite the scorn and suffer the blows of his society, confronting it, as he does, with truths about the war it would rather ignore. His own wretched psychological condition implicitly contests the official line on death and injury promulgated during the Falklands, that the cause justifies the cost, that the deaths and maimings in the South Atlantic are more than paid for by the individual and collective renewal engendered at home. His very existence, his all too literal resurrection, is seen not as a vindication of the conflict's redemptive ideals but as a mockery of them: ritually interred and discursively enshrined as a Hero Laid to Rest, his return from the dead and his evidently unheroic persona represent a desecration of military and civilian societies' most hallowed ceremonies, a blasphemous subversion of its holiest narratives. This perhaps explains why Williams' experiences invert the established biblical pattern of Death, Resurrection and Salvation, taking him from Death, through Resurrection and Salvation, and back to a living Death. As Williams attests, there's no peace for the undead.

Above all else, *Summer Soldier* affirms that Williams will accept no role, least of all the hero's, in any defence of the moral, military or narrative conduct of the war. In rejecting its most sacred, most social narratives, Williams symbolically repudiates the instruments of his own emotional and psychological destruction, rejecting the society which can never forgive him for coming back from the dead and telling it the truth about what he saw there. The wilderness and the obscurity it promises are infinitely preferable.

THE DISAPPEARED

While the loss of the Falklands sent admirals, editors and the great British public scrambling for their atlases, the Argentinians had no difficulty locating the islands, either geographically or culturally. The Malvinas had long occupied a central place in the mythic narrative of Argentine national identity. Ceded to the United Provinces of the Rio de La Plata when they won their independence from Spain in 1816, the emergent nation of Argentina sent its first governor to the Malvinas in 1823. His expulsion and the seizure of the islands by the British ten years later united political and religious divisions across the nation, and remained one of the few unifying issues in Argentine political or social life over the succeeding years.[52] As tangible proofs of national unity fell away, as party political differences hardened into the entrenched antipathies of class and ethnicity and the conduct of civil society became increasingly militarised, the recovery of the islands was more urgently identified as the remedy for the nation's bitter history of social and political division.[53] The physical unification of the state, it was proposed, would usher in the deeper moral and social unity that had so long eluded the nation: in and through the Malvinas, Argentina could recapture the harmony of the national past and so make itself anew. As former vice-presidential candidate Fernando de la Rua told *Gente*:

> El país no será el mismo [despues de la guerra]. La gravedad del cuadro requerirá de todos esfuerzo, actitud honradas, capacidad y sacrificio. La memoria de nuestros heroicos exige actitudes de grandeza. La economía muestra un perfíl dramático. La crisis denota bien cómo políticas ecónomicas contrarias al país pueden poner un riesgo su destino. Habra que reconstruir lo. Lo ganado en el campo de batalla no deberá perderse en los despachos de los teóricos. Es preciso terminar con las sistemas autoritarios, a instebilidad política y la no vigencia de la Constitución. Debe restituirse la democracia en plenitud. El pueblo debe ser protagonista de su destino. Ha mostrado su madurez y voluntad para alcanzarlo. (Heidel, 1982: np)

> (The country will not be the same [after the war]. The gravity of the situation requires every effort, noble attitudes, ability and sacrifice. The memory of our heroic dead demands a posture of greatness. The economy is looking perilous. The crisis serves the interests of those economic policies which may put the destiny of the country in peril. It must be rebuilt. What has been won on the field of battle must not be lost in the despatches of theory. It is necessary to end the authoritarian system, political instability and the flouting of the constitution. Democracy must be restored in full. The public must be the master of its destiny. It has shown the maturity and the will to attain it.)

Celebrating the recovery of the islands on the balcony of the Casa Rosada, General Galtieri roused the crowds thronging the Plaza de Mayo into an ecstasy of patriotic abandonment, crowds which less than seventy-two hours earlier had gathered in the same square for a violent demonstration against the junta.[54] This was the balcony from which the Peróns, Juan and Evita, had mobilised the masses, the *descamisados* (shirtless ones), with stirring speeches through the late 1940s and early 1950s, and as Galtieri worked the crowds many observers were struck by his accomplished imitation of Perón's gestural vocabulary. Next morning, the Argentine daily, *Clarín*, published a cartoon by Sabat which identified in this conscious evocation of a celebrated national past the final attainment of that elusive unity between all classes of Argentine society (Figure 6). The cartoon depicts Galtieri, Perón and the legendary tango singer Carlos Gardel arm in arm, literally, their four arms seguing into three common hands, saluting their adoring Argentine public: past and present, military and civilian, popular

Figure 6 Galtieri, Perón and Gardel (cartoon by Sabat)

hero and politician united in mutual celebration as the dream of national wholeness, territorial, political and spiritual unification, is finally realised.

This (re)discovered sense of national unity was framed, solemnised and cemented by a sacramental discourse as broad in its appeal and as socially unifying in Catholic Argentina as was the issue of the Malvinas itself. The invasion of the islands was officially represented as a crusade in defence of the true faith and in quest of the New Jerusalem of national unity.[55] Hours before the Argentine Special Forces led the initial assault on the islands their commander, Rear Admiral Carlos Busser, agreed to change the codename of the action from *Operación Azul* to *Operación Rosario*. In doing so he was not confessing to a last minute crisis of confidence in the mission, he was merely acknowledging the centrality of the crusading ideal in the war's official discursive and political construction through direct reference to the Virgin of Rosario, the patroness of Argentina, whose feast day had been established by Pope Gregory XIII in 1573 to commemorate Don John of Austria's victory over the Turks. As Jimmy Burns observed: 'Busser had no doubt that the infidel, personified by the kelpers and the seventy-odd British marines, was about to suffer an equally Virgin-sent defeat' (Burns, 1987: 68). The complex interweaving of religious and national sentiment is neatly reflected in Norberto G's account of how the news of their ultimate destination was received aboard the ship carrying him and his fellow conscripts to the islands:

> Nosotros estábamos escuchando misa y casi al final un companero de las fila de adelante gritó 'Viva la Patria' y todos, hasta el cura, empezamos a cantar el himno. Todos en el barco cantábamos el himno. En eso vemos que el cura llora y a mí, señor, le juro, se me

puso la piel de gallina. El lloraba y algunos de nosotros tambien.
(Norberto G, 1982: np)

(We were hearing mass and almost at the end a fellow from the front
rank shouted 'Long live the Fatherland!' and everybody, even the
priest, began to sing the national anthem. Everybody on the boat
was singing the national anthem. Then we saw that the priest was
weeping, and me, sir, I swear to you I had goose bumps. He was
weeping and so was almost everyone else.)

In a homily delivered to the occupying forces in the Town Hall at
Stanley on 25 April 1982, the military chaplain, Father Jorge Pincinalli,
celebrated the recovery of the islands as a triumph of Catholic
nationalism, proof that the nation's cause was just and that those who
served it were assured of special protection:

Nuestro pueblo argentino que es Católico, porque es hispánico,
porque es romano, hoy ha prorrumpido en la gesta de la reconquista
de un territorio para la Nación. Nación que tiene origen el
cristianismo. Entonces nosotros, todos los que estamos acá, tenemos
que sentirnos santamente orgullosos de pisar estas tierras; y quizá no
seamos dignos de esto. Es un gran honor, un inconmesurable honor
estar aquí. Tenemos que ver ésto como la gesta de la defensa de la
Nación para Jesucristo. Tenemos que tomar en nuestros manos el
Santo Rosario y confiar en la Santísima Virgen que siempre va a estar
con nosotros. Porque esta patria ha sido consagrada a la Virgen de
Luján. Y la Virgen de Luján y la Virgen del Rosario nos van a
proteger, tenemos que estar seguros. Y ese rosario que hoy ustedes
tienen en sus cuellos y también toman en sus manos, sepan que es
el gran instrumento. Es la gran defensa porque es la defensa del
espíritu sobre la materia. Sabemos que el espíritu es absolutamente
superior a toda materia. Por eso tenemos que confiar plenamente en
Dios, plenamente en Cristo, plenamente en la Santísima Virgen, reina
y señora de estas tierras de las Malvinas, que ya es tierra de la
Argentina. ¡Qué así sea! (Kasanzew, 1982: 160–1)[56]

(Today, our Argentine people, who are Catholic, Hispanic, Roman,
have succeeded in the reconquest of a territory for the nation. A
nation which has Christianity as its origins. So all of us who are here
have to feel miraculously proud to stand upon these lands; and
perhaps we are unworthy of this honour. It is a great honour, an
immeasurable honour to be here. We have to see this as an act in
defence of the nation for Jesus Christ. We must take the holy rosary
in our hands and trust that the holy Virgin will always be with us.
Because the fatherland has been consecrated to the Virgin of Luján.

And the Virgin of Luján and the Virgin of Rosario are going to protect us, we must be certain of that. And you must know that that rosary that you have around your necks and in your hands today is a great instrument. It is the great defence because it is the defence of the spiritual above the material. We know that the spirit is absolutely superior to all matter. Therefore we have to trust completely in God, completely in Christ, completely in the holy Virgin, queen and patroness of these lands of the Malvinas, which is now Argentine land. So be it!)

Argentina's recovery of the islands was, in Pincinalli's view, clear evidence of the power of spirit over matter, the triumph of right over might. In the impending struggle for the Malvinas, the nation, he proposed, would prove no less a source of comfort and practical support to the troops than were the rosary, the Virgin and Christ himself, in that it offered them an inspiring model for their own motivation towards and conduct in battle, an ideal of firm and decisive leadership, personal sacrifice and collective solidarity.

Yet for the young conscripts left to face the bombs, bullets and bayonets of the British, the export to the islands of the concerns and practices of Argentine domestic politics was a disaster; far from fortifying they fatally weakened the troops' resistance. The officers, NCOs and professional soldiers sent to the Malvinas, like their political masters over the preceding years of military rule, seemed more intent on making war on their own people than they were in combating the common enemies. Newly arrived in the islands, Felix Barreto found a familiar regime of chaos and brutality: 'Nobody seemed to know what do about us or to care. Major Carrizo handed over command to a lieutenant and he seemed more interested in hitting us to make us go faster than in leading us. There was no organisation by our own people' (Bramley, 1994: 71). While the worst that dissenters from the official British line on the war suffered was a beating from their former colleagues or a little abuse from the press, until the battles of 11/12 June, many of the conscripts, cold, hungry and neglected in their dugouts in the hills around Stanley, suffered more at the hands of their own leaders than they did from the enemy. Felix Barreto used to slip off Mount Longdon into Stanley every few days to help unload supply trucks and in the process steal enough food to keep himself and his friends going, until he was captured by an officer from his own side who 'marched me back up on to Longdon at gunpoint ... ordered me to lie on the ground and tied me down. I was lying there, spread-eagled and staked to the ground, wondering what was going to happen. I thought I was going to be shot. I was really depressed and frightened and cold and hungry. All I had wanted was some food' (Bramley, 1994: 74).[57]

The conduct of the war, at every level of the Argentine military, from the generals in the Casa Rosada to the corporals and conscripts in the infantry sections, demonstrated that the recovery of the Malvinas offered no magical relief from the traditional antagonisms of Argentine society, indeed, the planning and prosecution of the whole Malvinas venture betrayed a regime on the verge if not in the process of disintegration. In the Malvinas, Argentina found not a catalyst for national renewal but a return to the moral and political divisions of old, not a source of collective redemption but the very heart of the nation's darkness.

The campaign was full of uncomfortable reminders of *la guerra sucia* (the dirty war), the bitter civil conflict in which between 1976 and 1981 the military and its right-wing death squads disappeared almost 9,000 of its own citizens in the fight against 'subversion'.[58] For the conscripts, brought up in the shadow of the dirty war, the journey to the Falklands began in unsettling circumstances when they were taken from their barracks in the dead of night, hustled onto buses and hurried to airbases where they were crammed, standing-room only, onto waiting planes for a flight into the unknown – a familiar practice during the dirty war when the bodies of dissidents, living and dead, were routinely dropped into the ocean off the coast of Argentina. As Guillermo told Daniel Kon, 'no one told us officially where they were taking us. I mean, most of the soldiers were going blindly, without knowing where they were being taken. I don't know if that helps military tactics, but as a civilian, as a person, it didn't help me at all, I didn't like it at all ... many of the people with me on that trip and on the journey to Rio Gallegos had never been on a plane before in their lives. They were terrified' (Kon, 1983: 15).[59]

Once on the islands the front-line troops were confined to their positions and often kept in ignorance of where they were. It was only on the journey back to Argentina as a PoW that Guillermo learned, from his captors, that he had spent the previous eight weeks dug into the hills opposite the former Royal Marine barracks at Moody Brook: 'at the time I hadn't the slightest idea what that area was called, I didn't know where I was. When I was prisoner aboard the *Canberra*, I talked to some of the English and they showed me a very small pocket map with coloured dots marking even our positions. And those guys I talked to weren't officers, they were ordinary troops; but as soon as they had landed they had had an idea of where they were, they knew which hill was which. I, on the other hand, had no idea' (Kon, 1983: 17). The conscripts' geographical confusion is an appropriate metaphor for their narrative and political bewilderment: lauded by the government, the Church and the media as the heroes of a nation reborn, they were treated more like subversives in the divided Argentina of old, starved, beaten, staked to the ground and terrorised into submission by their uniformed commanders. Little wonder then that *la crucifixion* is a more prevalent image in the first-hand accounts of their time in the Malvinas than *la crusada*. These accounts challenge the official, evangelising narrative's depiction of the war as a means to individual and national renewal, an elevating proof of the power of spirit over matter. The conscripts write from the one place they all knew too well, from the sodden trenches, the mud, blood and gore of the battlefield. From here they expose the lie at the heart of the Malvinas campaign, that the fight for the Malvinas was not the first act in a narrative of national renewal, but the last gasp of *la guerra sucia*, not a triumphal affirmation of military rule but the ultimate confirmation of its utter failure.

Accordingly, the conscripts' accounts focus on the degradations which the conditions of the war, and the military's incompetent management of it, imposed upon them. Greeted at the airport with a reassuring 'Welcome to the Malvinas, here's your rosary', the conscripts were marched off to their positions where they set about constructing their defences against the anticipated British onslaught, and the ever-present hostility of the weather (Kon, 1983: 132). Inappropriately clothed (many of the Argentinians brought suitcases to the Malvinas, and some were issued with training shoes), infrequently supplied and inadequately rationed, the conscripts were soon reduced to dereliction and despair.[60]

Some, as Guillermo recalled, 'built caves', trenches fortified into stone sangars, and it was not long before many of the conscripts were living like cavemen (Kon, 1983: 17). Abused or abandoned by their leaders, the men forged new alliances among themselves, bypassing the military structures of regiment and unit, honouring the simple laws of supply and demand in their quest for food and fuel: 'clans started forming. Each clan was always tucked away inside its cave, living like tramps ... we were like cavemen. We made fires with odd bits of wood, we cooked in empty tin cans, we always went around with our faces and hands black from the smoke. We were tramps, we must have been a sorry sight' (Kon, 1983: 23).[61]

For those involved in the fighting, every stage in the battle for the Malvinas was marked not by the promise of redemption, but by the fear and the forms of impending extinction. Santiago Gauto spent the final hours before the British assault on Mount Longdon 'wondering if it would be my last night of life' (Bramley, 1994: 134). Like men in their graves, the conscripts huddled in their trenches awaiting the inevitable: 'That night we lay together in our holes, holding hands and praying, trying to give each other comfort and strength' (Bramley, 1994: 134). For thirty-six of Gauto's friends and colleagues from the 7th Mechanised Infantry Regiment dug into their defensive positions on Mount Longdon the night of 11 June 1982 was indeed their last as they were killed by artillery fire or the advancing men of 3 Para. For those who fought back and defended the summit of the mountain the very struggle for life was a kind of death; participating in a counter-attack on the summit, Gauto later confessed, 'was like advancing through the gates of hell itself' (Bramley, 1994: 184–5).[62] For many of those who came through the ordeal, both the conditions and consequences of their survival seemed like a mockery of their own and their society's promised rejuvenation. Horacio Benitez, shot in the head and left for dead after the battle for Wireless Ridge, was, literally, plucked from a pile of corpses and revived by a sharp-eyed sergeant. After a few weeks' recuperation he was sent back to a country which seemed entirely indifferent to events in the Malvinas:

> When I returned home my first weekend I went out with my two brothers. I was still fairly traumatised by the whole thing. We went to a bar. I expected everyone to be miserable because of what had happened, but everyone was having a lot of fun in the bar as if we had just won the World Cup. There was no trace of worry or sorrow on people's faces. In Buenos Aires it was as though nothing had happened. There had been a war down there and it went wrong and it was all over now, but no one was really interested in what had actually happened, in how many had died. People seemed even happier because the war was over. It was a party atmosphere. I had just seen what human beings can do to each other and all the sacrifices that our troops had made, but in Buenos Aires all that was worthless. No one was interested. (Bilton, 1989: 189–90)[63]

The front-line troops' direct experience of the fighting laid bare the brutal, physical truths about the war, and the false promise of either social or personal renewal through the recovery of the Malvinas. Their insight earned them the enmity of their fellow soldiers in the rear and the mistrust of their superiors. In – perhaps unconscious – mockery of their prophetic grasp of the truth about Argentina's conduct of the war, the troops in Stanley derided the filthy, ragged front-liners as 'Jews and mountaineers' (Bramley, 1994: 98). Like prophets from the wilderness, the conscripts returned to Argentina with a privileged insight into their leaders' incompetence, an insight which their leaders had good reason to fear. They endeavoured, therefore, to stifle the full extent of the disaster in the Malvinas by shrouding the troops' return to the mainland in secrecy, and secluding them from their relatives when they did come home, all the while promulgating an idealised and entirely fanciful account of the war and its outcomes.[64]

The military's attempts to conceal the true scale of the disaster in the Malvinas and what had happened to Argentina there were futile. When, on 15 June, the Argentine media announced that General Menendez and his entire garrison had surrendered to the British there was an immediate eruption of public outrage as crowds, once again, poured into the Plaza de Mayo. This time they came to bury the junta not to praise it: 'Screaming "cowards" and "sons of bitches" men and women threw coins at journalists and tried to storm the presidential palace' (Burns, 1987: 104). Within forty-eight hours General Galtieri had been removed from power, and a return to civilian rule was effected in a little over a year.[65]

In this rare show of Argentine political unanimity the war achieved, albeit temporarily, the one redemption craved by many of the disillusioned combatants interviewed soon after their repatriation. It had kindled among the public a spirit of unity like that which had sustained the conscripts during their ordeal and on which they hoped a new ideal of national identity might be founded. As Guillermo put it to Daniel Kon: 'I'd like to help keep the Argentine people united. Over there we felt that unity, and now I'm back I feel that although we lost the islands, I don't know, we could do something, we could win Argentina' (Kon, 1983: 35). It was a vain hope. Twelve years after the last shots were fired, Vincent Bramley travelled to Buenos Aires to conduct interviews with eight of *los chicos de la guerra* from the 7th Mechanised Infantry Regiment. What he found was that whatever victories might have arisen from their defeat in the Malvinas, the veterans were yet to reap any tangible benefits from them. Each of the conscripts told a tale of post-war hardship, economic disadvantage, bureaucratic indifference and official prejudice, their individual accounts harmonising on the dominant refrains of betrayal and abandonment: 'No one in authority seemed to want to know. We were having difficulties getting jobs, difficulties with the attitude of the government, difficulties with officialdom. Everything was against us. We didn't expect to be put on a pedestal, but some acknowledgment of what we had endured would have helped. Instead it was as if we didn't exist. It still is. It's all fucked' (Bramley, 1994: 228).[66]

The conscripts played a vital role in decentring power over and democratising the definition of Argentine national identity. The bungling and brutality in the South Atlantic, the junta's contempt for the men under its charge and the public more generally, made it clear that the military had forfeited – if it had ever possessed – the right to promote itself as 'the true and only valid interpreter of national interests' (Lozada *et al.*, 1982: 22).[67] Yet it is a national self-image which renders the veterans virtually invisible. The defeat in the Malvinas was a national and not purely a military humiliation and the conscripts are a constant reminder of it. The fervency with which they bore witness to this humiliation ensures their marginalisation in and by a society eager, above all else, to make a clean break with the failures of the past. As such, while Robert Lawrence demanded respect and Philip Williams craved obscurity, *los chicos de la guerra* ask only for due recognition from the society they made possible but which cannot or will not acknowledge its heroes.

5
Enemy Mine

[I]t was almost impossible to distinguish between our lot and theirs.
(Weston, 1989: 79)

THE ENEMY WITHIN

While the Argentinians were quick to recognise that the most
immediate threat to their well-being was posed by their own leaders
– 'When I came back from the war I discovered that the enemy was not
the British, but those who had taken Argentina into that situation' –
for the British, the identification of the enemy was, both morally and
discursively, a more problematic issue (Middlebrook, 1989: 290). The
final surrender of Argentine forces on 14 June 1982 gave most of the
British troops who streamed into Stanley their first close-up of the
opposition, their first chance to confront and so consider who and what
they had been combating in the preceding weeks – the opportunity to
face the real enemy. Disillusionment with the islands, disdain for the
islanders and derision for the Argentine military had, in the immediate
aftermath of the conflict, seriously complicated the question of just
what the British had been fighting for and against in the Falklands. The
generally poor performance of the Argentine forces disqualified them,
at first, from any significant role in Britain's heroic narrative of moral
triumph and national redemption. Great rewards, heroic incarnation
and collective renewal, bespoke great trials – trials which a few pitiful
conscripts sheltering under a white flag or shivering over a bowl of *maté*
hardly gestured at. Indeed, in the immediate aftermath of the fighting
the prevailing emotion among many of those who had faced up to and
fought the Argentines was not professional admiration or personal
affection but disappointment – hence the tendency among the British,
noted by Hugh McManners, 'to ridicule [the Argentinians rather] than
to portray them as odious' (McManners 1984: 45).[1] As Bishop and
Witherow noted: 'After the victory there was much talk about how well
the Argentines had fought but most of the soldiers had a fairly low
opinion of the soldiering abilities of their opponents. "Military
pygmies" was how one SAS officer described them' (Bishop and
Witherow, 1982: 20).

Contemporary reports and instant histories of the war, few of them, it should be noted, written by those who actually fought in the battles, fixed instead on the implacable hostility of the elements as a more fitting symbol of the great trials which the nation had faced and overcome in the Falklands. Locked below decks aboard HMS *Invincible*, Gareth Parry of the *Guardian* was less concerned about the Argentine military than he was about the weather, its offensive panoply described in the sort of detail usually reserved for the opposition's armoury:

The immediate prospect of battle off the Falkland Islands often seems nothing like as daunting as the possibility that some ships of the Royal Navy task force could be ordered to stand off, or into a lengthy blockade in some of the worst weather – which is already steadily deteriorating. The latest satellite reports, received directly by *Invincible* ... paints [*sic*] a grim picture of Autumn in the Antarctic, where the depth of winter comes in July. Senior officers contemplating a stand-off say the prospect would be 'almost intolerable'. South Georgia today is receiving heavy snow falls and gale force winds above thirty knots. Although the temperature is one or two degrees above freezing, the killing chill factors in the cold southerlies brings it down to 15 degrees Centigrade below ... A gale force wind blows on one day in every three ... But these seas bear little comparison with the typical 30-footers off the Falklands ... Foul weather clothing is already issued to those on board *Invincible*, in addition to the one-piece survival suits – 'once only suits' – which would help keep a man overboard alive for up to 20 minutes. Although the sea temperatures will be in the region of 4–5° Centigrade wind chill cuts it to minus 13° Centigrade. (*Guardian*, 29 April 1982: 2)

In the introduction to his memoir of the campaign, Brigadier Julian Thompson devotes more than a page to the hardships which his soldiers faced from the climate and the terrain before, almost parenthetically, acknowledging that 'when all was said and done, to win the war men had to close with and defeat the Argentine Army' (Thompson, 1985: xx). His assessment that the weather posed a greater threat to the success of the operation is further hinted at in the index to his book which has ten entries for 'Argentine Army' and thirteen for 'weather conditions' (Thompson, 1985: 191, 201). The Argentine Army in the Falklands, John Frost regretfully observed, 'was not in the same league as the German 1st Parachute Division or the 2nd SS Panzer Corps'. While some of its units fought 'stubbornly', it was only in combination with 'the weather conditions prevailing and the terrain over which our heavily laden men had to operate' that they could be regarded as having posed a real threat to the task force (Frost, 1983: 11).[2]

In most contemporary and instant accounts of the conflict there was more interest in the suddenness with which Argentine resistance collapsed than in any consideration of how they had performed in battle. This in turn led to more considered analyses of what it was that had held, or failed to hold, the competing forces together: why was it that many Argentine units had capitulated, even evaporated when they had suffered negligible losses of soldiers and equipment while their British counterparts had fought on, despite sustaining casualties of up to 50 per-cent?[3] What was it that had motivated them or precipitated their collapse? The ostensible cause of the fighting, the islands, and the antagonists' relative commitment to them evidently exercised little or no influence over the performance of the hostile armies. The members of the task force, who rarely expressed anything other than contempt for the Falklands, their people or the ideals of Queen and Country, won a resounding victory, while the Argentinians, fired by a deep attachment to *la patria* and a passionate conviction in the justice of their cause, were routed. Events in the Falklands thus supported Rudolf Binding's proposition that ideals are of little practical purpose in battle. A man, he claims, 'strikes out so that the other will not strike, he does not flee because he is fighting in an unrighteous cause, he does not attack because his cause is just, he flees because he is the weaker, he conquers because he is the stronger or because his leader has made him feel stronger. Ideals do not help him' (qtd in Holmes, 1985: 276). What makes him stronger, or believe himself to be so, is effective motivation. As Hugh McManners has observed:

> Motivation is a complicated process in which sticks and carrots are wielded simultaneously. In battles fought by small teams of men, often in complete isolation from anyone else, the sticks are not the rules and regulations of military law, but a code of behaviour already defined and accepted within each group. The leader defines, interprets and imposes this code, to which the members submit in order to remain in the group.
>
> In a hostile and dangerous environment, rejection by the group is the worst fate of all. Comfort, reassurance and protection from danger are available only from the group. For each lonely individual, earning and retaining the approval of comrades is the single most important motivating factor of all. (McManners, 1993: 80)

In Julian Thompson's view, it was the healthy functioning of just such a binding code of behaviour that kept his team together and going forward in the Falklands ensuring their supremacy over Argentine conscripts who, ill-prepared and poorly led, the victims of too many sticks and too few carrots, had been given neither the time nor the example to establish the sorts of bonds that could have held them together in the crisis of battle: 'the conscripts were not well trained and they lacked this feeling that we had – that we were all fighting for each other. They seemed to have this idea they were fighting for their flag, for their country, which is a very fragile foundation on which to base morale, because in the stress of battle it evaporates. Whereas if you're fighting for yourself, your comrades, for each other, that sustains you in the moments when you think you might be losing' (Bilton and Kosminsky, 1989: 229–30). This code of mutual surveillance-cum-mutual support has a long and venerable tradition. In the *Iliad*, Agamemnon speeds the Danaans into battle exhorting them to 'be men. Have a stout heart, and in the field fear nothing but dishonour in each other's eyes' (Homer, 1957: 106). Vincent Bramley's chief concern as he prepared himself for battle was not the presence of death or the prospect of facing the Argentinians but the possibility that he might prove unworthy of his comrades, unequal to the task of sustaining these bonds of fellowship: 'Letting the side down was my biggest fear' (Bramley, 1991: 53).[4] What Bramley and his colleagues were ultimately confronting in the Falklands then, their essential enemy, was neither the Argentine conscripts nor the weather but themselves, their own capacity for weakness and failure – the enemy was within.

DISHONOURING THE ENEMY

The media's triumphalist cheer-leading during the build-up to hostilities left little room, physical or discursive, for any such admission of frailty, less so for any sober analysis of the risks inherent in the war, or any contemplation of its physical and psychological consequences for the combatants.[5] Instead, contemporary accounts of the conflict articulated the nation's anxieties by projecting them onto or embodying them in the Argentinians. The iconic images of Argentina's defeat, Astiz capitulating on South Georgia, ragged conscripts surrendering a mountain of rifles, furious civilians rioting in the Plaza de Mayo, not only registered the utter demoralisation of the vanquished but were carefully chosen to objectify and embody what the British had most feared suffering themselves in and through the conflict in the South Atlantic, political humiliation, military collapse and public outrage – 'there, but for the Grace of God ...'.[6] In this context one can see that the various official accounts of Britain's triumph over the Argentinians serve not merely as records of the war's major events, but also (if not primarily) as extended exorcisms of the nation's deepest insecurities.

In many accounts of the war these insecurities are embodied and expressed in the form of sexual anxieties. Sex and war have been immemorially bound up in the lives of men and women, both causally in the form of sexual plunder as a corollary of military conquest, and mythologically as a continuing source of and instinctual response to both divine and human discord.[7] In 1915, deeply shaken by the First World War, Sigmund Freud proposed a socio-psychological explanation for the perennially close relationship between Venus and Mars. In *Thoughts for the Time on War and Death* (1915), he posited a connection between the 'destitution shown in moral relations externally by the states [in time of war] which in their interior relations pose as the guarantors of accepted moral usage' and a corresponding loosening of moral and sexual restraints on the home front: 'Existing taboos are not cast aside completely, but in a society at war the mechanism of sexual suppression operates at a lower level' (Freud, 1953: 7; Costello, 1985: 10). If, as Freud contended, 'Civilisation is the fruit of the renunciation of instinctual satisfaction', then the surrender to instinct implicit in war prompts an upsurge of other innate impulses, not least the sexual (Freud, 1953: 7). Twenty years later, with the Japanese in Manchuria, Mussolini preparing to invade Abyssinia and Hitler on the rise in Germany, Freud further developed his theory in the pamphlet *Why War?* (1935) in which he proposed the existence of two primary human instincts: 'those that conserve and unify, which we call "erotic" ... or else "sexual" (explicitly extending the possible connotation of "sex") and, secondly, the instincts to destroy and kill, which we assimilate as the aggressive or destructive instincts' (Freud, 1953: 90). According to Costello, these instinctual drives, which he renames 'procreation and death ... are brought into sharp conjunction by war ... the atavistic horde instinct essential to mass killing inevitably inflames the sex drive because the urge to kill and the urge to procreate are both subconsciously related as extremes of the human experience' (Costello, 1985: 139, 10). Whether one's aim in war was to kill or simply to survive, Freud's theories implied that one's motivation for either was, in the broadest sense, sexual. Accordingly, war has traditionally been regarded as the ultimate test of sexual adequacy and has thus provided a perennial focus for individual and collective anxiety.[8] Christopher Isherwood's response to the First World War is typical in this regard: 'Like most of my generation, I was obsessed by a complex of terror and longings connected with the idea "War". War in this purely neurotic sense meant The Test. The test of your courage, of your maturity, of your sexual prowess: "are you really a man?"' (Isherwood, 1947: 75–6). Half a century on, Santiago told Daniel Kon that, though excluded from the original combat lists for the Malvinas, he had fought to join *los chicos de la guerra*: 'I said: since all my friends are going, I'm going too. I didn't want them to think I was a pouf' (Kon, 1983: 63).[9]

When a nation promotes itself as macho, dominant, virile, war provides more than a focus for personal sexual anxieties, it becomes a test of its collective self-image, a crucible for the (re)casting of national identity. In the battle for the Malvinas, Argentina was not merely seeking the social and political unification of the nation but, more urgently, proof of its collective machismo. According to Reginald and Elliot: 'Argentine government, society and history together have fostered a kind of super-nationalism or *machismo* common to Central and South America, but particularly strong in Argentina' (Reginald and Elliot, 1983: 33). This was so, Jimmy Burns claimed, because of the central role occupied by the military in the social, cultural and political life of Argentina. The widespread belief that 'Argentines owed their nationhood to their military heroes' had helped to make it 'one of the world's most macho societies' (Burns, 1987: 5, 87).[10] Yet the anomalous status of the Malvinas had long implicitly challenged this prized self-image as, despite more than a century of huffing and puffing, 'the Supreme Organ of State' had failed utterly in its efforts to shift the shabby tribe of shepherds who remained in defiant occupation of the islands (Burns, 1987: 49). The Argentine political analyst Juan Plaza suggested in 1970 that the nation's inability to recover the islands betrayed a species of national impotence which symbolised and, in part, explained its failure to attain either social or political fulfilment: 'se intuye que a consciente impotencía de obtener virilmente la restitución de ése territorio da la medída de la frustración argentina como nación soberana' (Plaza, 1970: 5) (one can see that our awareness of our inability to restore that territory with due vigour gives a measure of Argentina's frustration as a sovereign nation). Argentina's recovery of the islands then was far more than a military and political coup, it was a triumphal affirmation of the nation's collective sexual identity, and a resounding vindication of its moral virtue.

Argentine coverage of the conflict established and defined its moral polarities through a process of symbolic sexualisation. The enemy's opposition to Argentine rule was accounted for by pathology not politics, held up as evidence that the British were not, as they had claimed, upholding a competing system of values, but had simply collapsed into degeneracy. In this regard Nicolas Kasanzew's description of the barracks at Moody Brook which housed the small Royal Marine detachment, Naval Party 8901, who garrisoned the islands, is both an anatomy of the enemy's depravity and a testimony to the causes of its defeat:

> Seineldin ... me mostró también el formidable armamento que había en Moody Brook. Entre él, una cantidad impresionante de sofisticado lanzacohetes portátiles que en ningún momento utilizaron los Royal Marines. Al recorrer los dependencias del cuartel, pude ver el desorden y el lujo en que vivían. Tenían dos baños de sauna, una boite y abundante provisión de vino francés. No es todo. Se les encontraron drogas. Por otra parte, todas las paredes estaban

absolutamente cubiertas de fotos pornográficas: no se podía adivinar de qué color habían estado pintadas anteriormente. Había, ademas, fotografías y videocassettes filmados en el mismo cuartel donde aparecían los marines del guarnición entregados a distintas perversiones sexuales. (Kasanzew, 1982: 11)

(Seineldin ... also showed me the formidable armaments at Moody Brook. Among them, an impressive quantity of portable surface-to-air missiles which the Royal Marines never used. On searching the outlying buildings of the barracks one was able to see the luxury and disorder in which they lived. They had two sauna baths, a club and an abundant supply of French wine. That is not all. Drugs were found. Furthermore, all of the walls were entirely covered by pornographic photographs, so that one could not tell what colour they had previously been painted. There were, besides, photographs and videos filmed in the same barracks in which marines of the garrison appeared engaged in various sexual perversions.)

Kasanzew was not only lucky to get a scoop on Moody Brook, he was fortunate to be on the islands at all, as very few Argentine and no British journalists were granted access during the brief period of Argentine rule: those *in situ* when the Argentinians arrived were swiftly deported.[11] Most correspondents dispatched to cover the crisis got no closer to the islands than Patagonia, the main staging-post for Argentine forces and tactical resupply. In Patagonia they were treated to mock battles fought by troops 'freshly groomed and uniformed' for the purpose and an official account of the war from Colonel Esteban Solis of the Argentine Fifth Army Corps, which explained its origins and progress through a symbolic dramatisation of the enemy's moral and sexual depravity: 'Journalists were treated to graphic descriptions of the British troops' alleged homosexuality and alcoholism with the intrepid Solis holding up empty bottles of beer, pornographic magazines and women's underwear' (Burns, 1987: 82–3).[12]

In Britain, the need to mobilise public support for the task force and the imperative to exorcise the humiliation of defeat and repay the Argentinians in kind led politicians and the media to an equivalent simplification of the war's complex origins, achieved through a similar strategy of sexualisation. By such means, Argentina's invasion of the islands was translated into an assault on a vital symbol of the nation's self-identity if not the keystone of its self-esteem – its (hetero)sexual integrity. Framed in this fashion, Argentina's crime was not inversion, but in the context of liberal democracy a far more heinous offence, importunacy succeeded by rape.[13] This elicited an emotive response in the press and in parliament where '[t]he very thought that our people, 1,800 people of British blood and bone could be left in the hands of such criminals', was, Sir Bernard Braine avowed in an orgasm of impotent rage, 'enough to make any normal Englishman's blood – and the blood of Scotsmen and Welshmen – boil, too' (Morgan, 1982: 16).

Yet whereas the Argentinians had regarded the enemy's apparent degeneracy as a measure of his moral depravity, British politicians and the media betrayed little interest in the moral dimensions of the Argentinians' alleged offence. For all Sir Bernard's outrage, the real focus of his anguish and that of most of his colleagues who rose to speak during the Emergency Debate was, in his own terms, the boiling of their own blood and not the shedding of others', their failure to foresee and their impotence to prevent the invasion and not the suffering of the islanders or even the moral turpitude of the enemy – it was their own reputations that concerned them: 'Whatever action is decided upon, this is a deeply depressing and distressing episode. We have failed – and failed lamentably – to defend the integrity of one of Britain's few remaining colonies ... Britain has been humiliated' (qtd in Barnett, 1982: 37). The task force was despatched, therefore, not merely to recover the islands but, in the process, to restore the nation's wounded sexual pride, or as Sir Julian Amery put it in a convenient biblical phrase, 'to wipeth stain from Britain's honour' and so 'stiffen the credibility' of its deflated leaders (qtd in Barnett, 1982: 38).

As a consequence of this double purpose, coverage of the task force on its journey south focused on its sexual as much as its military potency, each metaphorically signifying and supporting the other, and while there may have been concerns about the suitability of some of the military hardware for the task at hand, there were, as Jonathan Raban noted, no such misgivings over the adequacy or purpose of the troops' personal equipment:

> I was engrossed in the shuffle of bizarre pictures on the screen.
>   Vertical take-off fighters dithered grotesquely aloft, making the air below them boil. Marines with body-builders muscles and elaborate tattoos were doing physical jerks in an improvised gym. They were naked except for their uniform undershorts, which consisted of two Union Jacks, one fore, one aft. The crux of the frontward flags bulged with impressive genital equipment. More soldiers, their faces menacingly camouflaged with boot polish, or perhaps woad, were at bayonet practice, making horrible noises as they charged the sack.
>   ... the first objective of the voyage of the task force was to scare the invaders away from the islands by showing them bloodcurdling television pictures of what was going to happen to them when the ships arrived. This was assault by photomontage, with flags superimposed over phalluses and songs over aeroplanes, gun-muzzles and bayonets. The theme of sexual prowess and conflict was rudely

explicit: the Argentine forces and their effete supremo were going to be raped by the greater potency of the British.

... No one could now accuse the British of lacking balls: the precious objects had been exhibited on television, tastefully wrapped in the national flag. (Raban, 1986: 135–7)[14]

Clearly, the task force's goal in the South Atlantic, and the ends to which its weaponry would be put there, was not merely to achieve a military victory over Argentina but, in the process, to exorcise the nation's shame by inflicting upon the enemy a humiliation equivalent to that which it had suffered itself. To this end, the British described their military superiority over Argentina in metaphors of sexual dominance and submission. Lou Armour, one of the Royal Marines captured and expelled from the Falklands during the initial Argentine assault, expressed his determination to restore his own and help repair the nation's wounded pride in a simple, graphic image of sexual supremacy: 'We're going to go down there and "dick" that lot' (Bilton and Kosminsky, 1989: 234).

This is not to suggest that the British were intent on or ever guilty of actually sodomising the enemy; it is simply a metaphor, popular in all-male communities, to express one's power over or contempt for those weaker than oneself, a verbal ritual furnishing a lexicon of abuse more often than a physical reality.[15] British accounts of the conflict are peppered with such ritualised affirmations of the nation's military dominance: 'A few hours before the Welsh Guards were due to start an attack on a force of 250 Argentinians dug in below Mount William, one of their officers was asked what the strategy was for action. "We'll sneak up on them, open fire and give them cold steel up their arse," he replied' (Bishop and Witherow, 1982: 17–18). However, according to McGowan and Hands, one unfortunate conscript on Mount Longdon suffered the literal execution of this symbolic gesture of triumph: 'A few yards away a sergeant was barking at another young Para, saying, "What the fuck's wrong with that man?" The Para was in a trench with an Argentinian conscript who looked far from happy. The Para said: "Wouldn't get out of the trench when I told him to, Sarge, so I stuck my bayonet up his arse. He'll live"' (McGowan and Hands, 1983: 249).[16] To the macho Argentinian, sodomy was a most graphic symbol if not the ultimate expression of moral and physical disgrace. V.S. Naipaul claims that throughout Latin America buggery is regarded not as a legitimate if marginalised element of mainstream sex – 'the church considers it a heavy sin, and prostitutes hold it in horror' – but as a crude expression of power and an open gesture of contempt: 'By imposing ... what prostitutes reject, and what he knows to be a kind of sexual black mass, the Argentine *macho* ... consciously dishonours his victim' (Naipaul, 1980: 150).

Yet in the process of ritually dishonouring the Argentinians, did the British raise some uncomfortable questions about their own honour, the credibility of their own claims to (hetero)sexual legitimacy? The homosexual imagery which dominated the popular rhetoric of power and abjection, however ritualised or redundant, brought with it some unsettling truths about the military's own ambivalent relations with and attitudes towards inversion over the ages. Despite its current hostility towards overt homosexuality within its ranks, throughout history the composition of the effective fighting unit has been founded on the military's tolerance, if not active encouragement, of unusually intimate bonds among its members:

> it was recognised that the close relationships which sprang up between the members of the group had positive advantages in battle. Onasander advised that the commander should station 'brothers in rank beside their brothers, friends beside friends; and lovers beside their favourites'. The Sacred Band of Thebes was organised to make the best use of the bonds of homosexual love which the Greeks regarded as perfectly normal. The Spartan Pausanias argued that 'the most valiant army would be recruited of lovers and their favourites', because all would be too ashamed to desert. (Holmes, 1985: 294)[17]

Nor have the military's links with homosexuality been solely confined to the efficient organisation of the combat unit. Among active British pederasts prior to the First World War, 'we find soldiers specifically the focus of desire. The Other Ranks of H.M. Brigade of Guards had of course been notoriously employable as sexual objects since early in the nineteenth century, and the first German edition of Symonds's *Sexual Inversion* (Leipzig, 1896) contained an appendix, "*Soldatenliebe und Verwandtes*" (The Love of Soldiers and Related Matters), examining the pursuit of soldiers as a well-known special taste' (Fussell, 1975: 279).

In today's armed forces, however, homosexuality is a court-martial offence which can result in a dishonourable discharge, or even a term of imprisonment. The official military line is that homosexual rela-tionships are '"prejudicial to good conduct and discipline" because they [break] down the divisions between military ranks' and constitute 'a threat to the essential aggressive "manliness" of soldiers' (Costello, 1985: 156). But this is not a view uniformly shared by the soldiers themselves. According to Jennings and Weale, one case in which a member of 3 Para was discharged for active homosexuality provoked 'a certain amount of indignation within the battalion', in that the decision ignored his proficiency as a soldier – his friends regarded his homosexuality as irrelevant: '[He] was a good hard soldier ... He was a male prostitute. He got done for it, but don't get me wrong [he] was a very, very hard man' (Jennings and Weale, 1996: 37–8).

In the Falklands, the paras' opinions about and treatment of homosexuality within their own ranks were singularly ambiguous. While they were overtly hostile towards active homosexuals, as some of the gay stewards aboard SS *Canberra* found to their cost, they endorsed and operated an 'oppo' or buddy system whose most expressive gestures of mutual care and support were pointedly suggestive of that love which – more so among soldiers than the general public – dare not speak its name. When Tony Gregory fell in a river while patrolling near Estancia, his mates rushed him back to the British lines where his oppo, Paul, 'threw me into a sleeping bag and ... got in beside me and used his body heat to revive me. If he hadn't I'd have been a goner' (Bramley, 1994: 109).[18] More suggestive still were the rituals of play. Vincent Bramley recalled the celebratory piss-ups enjoyed by the paras on the voyage home, the centrepiece of which was the performance of their favourite songs: 'among them "The Zulu Warrior" and "Old MacDonald Had a Farm". The latter is performed naked on a table with a partner, simulating animal acts to the song. For example, we would sing, "And the rams were doing it there, and the rams were doing it here," while one of the partners played the ram. People might think we behaved liked homos, but while the way the lads acted and fooled about together would seem offensive to civilian eyes, it was purely an expression of camaraderie' (Bramley, 1991: 201). What these extraordinary rituals demonstrate is that the love that the soldier bears for his colleagues, whatever its form, is not a threat to or an impairment of the his 'aggressive "manliness"' but one its fundamental bases: 'A soldier fights not for Queen and Country but for those friends he loves and respects, and secondly for himself' (Bramley, 1994: x).

This, in part, helps explain the paras' response to 'Wendy', an overtly homosexual steward aboard the *Norland* who, on the return journey to England entertained the paras with their favourite songs and was, in turn, feted by the parachute battalions, presented with a red beret and made, in Ken Lukowiak's words, 'an honourable paratrooper' (Lukowiak, 1993: 173). Lukowiak claims that when he and his fellow veterans reminisce about the war, 'Wendy always gets a mention. In fact it is true to say that he now gets more of a mention than the likes of Colonel Jones VC' (Lukowiak, 1993: 173). How so? It is Wendy's symbolic status which accords him such a prominent place in the paras' recollections of the war. He embodies and objectifies the love and respect that the men felt for one another, the often unacknowledged tenderness they harboured for their oppos and friends. As such, Wendy symbolises the very basis of the paras' courage and so emerges, in a curious way, as the very image of their 'manliness':

Everyone had their own little story to tell about Wendy. My favourite is one told by one of the Battalion's SNCOs at the time: 'There I was aboard the *Norland* in San Carlos Bay, fucking Argie jets zooming above my head, the ship's been hit twice, I got some shithead on the radio screaming at me that they need more ammunition at Goose Green, we're all working like slaves to load a landing craft and I've got fucking Wendy beasting me to get a fucking move on. Fifteen fucking years I've waited for this, and when it does finally happen I've got some gay boy leaning over me telling ME to fucking hurry up because HIS boys are running out of fucking ammo'. (Lukowiak, 1993: 173)

There was, of course, never any suggestion of active sexual relations among the men in the Falklands. The difficulty for those describing and celebrating the British triumph was discursive rather than material, in that any accurate account of the bonds of comradeship that held the men together, and any honest treatment of the men's view of what they had achieved in the Falklands would compound the very anxieties that victory was intended to allay – the rhetoric of (homo)sexual domination thus subverted the celebration of the nation's renewed (hetero)sexual self-esteem.

BLACK AND WHITE

The British troops discovered in the Falklands that the kinds of fellow feeling, the species of close relationship reviled in their training and denigrated in their language, feelings objectified in and attributed to the Argentinians that they might be more readily disparaged and destroyed, were closely akin to the feelings they harboured for one another, indeed, were all but indistinguishable from the relationships that had bound them together in battle and kept them going forward to victory. They discovered, in fact, that in combating the Argentinians they were making war on themselves and the most sacred principles of their own community. In an effort to forestall demoralising and potentially damaging identification with the Argentinians, those who initially interpreted and covered the war – the government, the military, the media – as well as those who subsequently offered a more self-consciously fictionalised version of events – novelists, dramatists, screenwriters – consistently reaffirmed the enemy's status as an emblem of moral otherness, as a palpable Evil.

Ian Curteis' (unfilmed) account of the conflict's political management, *The Falklands Play* (1987), is premised on a simple structure of binaries intended to establish and reinforce what he saw as the war's straightforward moral polarities.[19] In an introduction almost half as long as the play itself, Curteis catalogues his dealings with the BBC, alleging that the national broadcaster refused to film the play because it was unapologetically 'pro-Government and pro-Mrs Thatcher' (Curteis, 1987: 32). Curteis identifies those involved in the literary battle in the same roles and relationships as those engaged in the military struggle in the South Atlantic, imposing on the debate about the play the same straightforward moral polarities which he saw embodied in the conflict. Accordingly, facing up to the might of the BBC, Curteis portrays himself very much as he had depicted Margaret Thatcher outfacing the hesitancy of her Cabinet and the might of the Argentine military: his decision to 'fight' the BBC, made during a holiday in Connemara with his wife, the novelist Joanna Trollope, is strikingly reminiscent of scenes from the play in which the Foreign Secretary, Lord Carrington, walks through the gardens at Chevening Park, Kent, accompanied by the Home Secretary, William Whitelaw, pondering his response to the Argentine invasion, and the scene in which the Prime Minister walks alone in the gardens at Chequers, wrestling with her response to the sinking of HMS *Sheffield* (Curteis, 1987: 31. See 108–9, 180–1). Carrington resigned: the Prime Minister and Ian Curteis fought on.[20]

As we see little of either the British or Argentine public in his screenplay beyond a few tellingly framed crowd shots, and nothing at all of the troops engaged in the fight for the islands, the oppositions between the two nations are embodied in and articulated through Curteis' representation of the political protagonists from the opposing sides.[21] The contrasts between them are stark, but entirely predictable in that the leading players from Britain and Argentina are presented not as fully realised figures driven by particular motivations, assisted or hindered by specific strengths or flaws, but as products and subordinates of a dominating plot, mere *acteurs* in a fable of moral antagonism.[22] The characters' primary function is semiotic, to organise the elements of the screenplay into a meaningful structure of binary oppositions.

The British, defending democracy and the rule of law, are presented as: '*vigorous, immaculately fresh and well-groomed*', '*tough and firm*', '*crisp, decisive, irrepressibly cheerful, with a dead-straight, twinkly look*', '*fresh, confident, energetic and suddenly with an indefinable aura of churchillian relish for the struggle ahead*' (Curteis, 1987: 56, 114, 130, 110 respectively). Even the Secretary of State for Defence, John Nott, whose performance during the crisis was widely criticised, speaks '*with attack and resolve, eyes flashing behind spectacles*' (Curteis, 1987: 117). These characterisations determine that the Argentinians will be as malignant and incompetent as their opponents are virtuous and efficient. As such, the moral political and social dysfunctions of the Argentine state, which the screenplay takes pains to detail – its disregard for human rights, the rule of domestic or international law, the standards of political fair play or simple moral decency – merely provide a context for and not an explanation of the junta's incompetence, brutality and malice. Accordingly, its *'most intelligent and liberal'* member, the Air Force chief Basilio Lami Dozo, spends the entire screenplay collapsed on the peripheries of the action, *'a crumpled teddy bear of a man'*: insufficiently malicious, he can occupy no effective role in the semiotic of moral extremes and so he is simply written out of the screenplay (Curteis, 1987: 61).

The source and the symbol of the junta's moral otherness is the naval chief, Admiral Jorge Anaya: *'slim, vulpine and unsmiling ... a hard man whose voice betrays no flicker of warmth or humanity'* (Curteis, 1987: 61). This description offers an implicit explanation for Anaya's determination to repossess the Malvinas by force: he does what he is, and what he is is determined by what he is not – British (Curteis, 1987: 61). General Galtieri is less the instigator than the hapless if willing dupe of the malice of others: a *'big, handsome, hard-drinking cavalry officer with hearty, drill-ground manner'* he is there less to suggest the moral bankruptcy of the Argentine state than to imply the buffoonish incompetence of its leadership (Curteis, 1987: 61). Always a couple of steps behind the wily Anaya, he lurches through the screenplay in a drink-befuddled stupor, swilling whisky from *'huge tumblers'*, stumbling into furniture, politically and socially far out of his depth (Curteis, 1987: 131). Beyond the minimal requirements of plot development, his exchanges with Anaya consistently verge on the absurd as the two men talk merely to reaffirm their place in the overall moral structure of the play, one a fool, the other a villain:

GALTIERI: Have some popcorn.
ANAYA (*screwing up his face*): How can you eat that filth!
GALTIERI: What's wrong with it? You ought to try some.
(*He crams it into his mouth, washing it down with Glenfiddich.*
ANAYA *stares out of the windows at the tree tops*) (Curteis, 1987: 62).

Not surprisingly, these symbols of vice are the custodians of a comic kingdom whose moral, political and historical shortcomings are established through a series of telling contrasts with the political and social institutions of Britain. The keynote for Curteis' representation of the Argentine state is sounded by the Home Secretary, William Whitelaw, during a conversation with his opposite number at the Foreign Office, Lord Carrington:

WHITELAW (*cheerfully*): Argentina. Where the nuts come from.
CARRINGTON (*grinning*): No, no, that's Brazil!

WHITELAW: Is it? It's all Comic Opera Land anyhow. Do you know they haven't fought *anyone* for over a hundred years, except each other?
CARRINGTON *laughs!* (Curteis, 1987: 60).

This exchange takes place after a Cabinet meeting which is presented a model of functioning democracy. Ministers, fully briefed on the threat posed to the Falkland Islands by a new Argentine junta confidently exchange their views in a disciplined and yet informal atmosphere, ruled over by the commanding presence of the Prime Minister.[23] The screenplay cuts to a no less emblematic representation of the Argentine state preceding the presidential investiture of Galtieri's predecessor, General Roberto Viola:

ARGENTINE NEWSFILM
Blare of tin trumpets, clatter of hooves, and the presidential procession swings into view in the crowded streets of Buenos Aires. Weedy cavalry in bright Ruritanian uniforms ride alongside. It is indeed close to Comic Opera Land. The crowds cheer and throw streamers. (Curteis, 1987: 60)

A land of empty ceremony and ostentation, this is a nation whose grandiose public gestures are in inverse proportion with its moral and political substance.

While Curteis' imagery may lack subtlety, his screenplay can be regarded as just one more attempt to establish the moral otherness of the Argentinians, and to play down any potential identification with them. In this it took its lead from the contemporary media coverage of the conflict which, on Fleet Street at least, with very few exceptions, endorsed a straightforwardly Manichean view of the war and its origins.[24] As Peter Stephens, a former deputy editor of the *Sun*, told Robert Harris: 'We had a black-and-white view of this war. It was us or the Argentinians. We had no dilemma about this' (Harris, 1983: 45). Another observer with few dilemmas about the war's moral landscape was the Argentine journalist and author, Eduardo Crawley. Interviewed on BBC 1's *Panorama* he set out the issues at stake in the conflict: 'the principles involved are clear. Let me put it like this. Principle number one is that one cannot tolerate the occupation of part of one's territory by a foreign power, and it is perfectly legitimate to expel the intruder; principle number two is that one cannot negotiate sovereignty under duress, namely while somebody else is occupying part of one's territory; principle number three, it is wrong to flout a resolution of the United Nations Security Council; this puts one out of international law, so to speak'. Yet despite appearances to the contrary, Crawley's lucid precis of the principles at issue in the conflict was no endorsement of Britain's moral and legal stand, but a radical deconstruction of its informing binaries, an outright rejection of its semiotic structure, in that what appeared to be grounds for antagonism were in fact a basis for consensus. The two nations were not, he pointed out, occupying positions of moral antipathy but were defending principles and beliefs that they held in common: 'Now, odd as it may seem to the British public, these are precisely Argentina's arguments' (qtd in Harris, 1983: 78).

The first-hand accounts of those who actually confronted and combated one another are full of equivalent moments of mutual recognition, when the fabricated antagonisms of politics and nationalism fall away in the face of the irresistible empathy of the troops and the inescapable likeness of the enemy. Making his goodbyes on the quay at Southampton, Simon Weston was struck, 'for some odd reason', by the similarities between the families gathered to farewell the *QE 2* and the celebrations in Argentina marking the reconquest of the islands: 'I remembered the pictures that had been broadcast on television of the crowds in the main square of Buenos Aires. It occurred to me that except for the banners and the red, white and blue streamers I'd seen on the dockside, it was almost impossible to distinguish between our lot and theirs' (Weston, 1989: 79).

When Vincent Bramley captured an injured conscript during the battle for Mount Longdon, he found that his personal responses to the enemy were more complex than the ritualised antagonisms of the training ground. His natural empathy for a frightened and wounded man threatened his ability to discharge his professional responsibilities and it was only by a conscious effort, by detaching his professional from his personal self, that he was able to perform his duty: 'The first soldier was sniffling but trying hard to control himself. I wanted to tell him that it was OK but I couldn't, for it would have shown weakness on my part. I felt for him, but my exterior had to remain controlled' (Bramley, 1991: 138).[25] In the aftermath of the fighting, free from the antagonisms of the battlefield, these natural human feelings reasserted themselves. The soldiers and media representatives who escorted the PoWs back to Argentina aboard SS *Canberra* were amazed to find how much they shared with the 'enemy', close cultural and historical ties, a common passion for sport and music, in some cases a shared language, and were both puzzled and disturbed to find that for some months past they had been doing their utmost to kill men (more often boys) who in other circumstances might have been comrades, friends, even brothers:

I went into one cabin and asked if anyone spoke English.
'I do, mate,' came the reply.
It was a real cockney accent. 'Do what, mate?' I asked, incredulously.

'I said I speak English,' he told me. And when I asked him where he learned to speak it just like us he said he had lived in Tottenham, north London, and was studying there before the war broke out. He said his name was something like Mike Savage ... he said he had what he called dual parents [*sic*] and had been studying in London up until December 1981, when he had returned to Argentina for the Christmas holidays and had been called up for conscription ... We didn't regard him as an enemy soldier, but as someone unfortunate enough to have been in the wrong place at the wrong time. (Bramley, 1994: 211)[26]

The government's efforts to down play the close ties between Britain and Argentina (not least its own long and lucrative defence links with successive Argentine regimes), to promote an image of the enemy's otherness were, as Vincent Bramley recognised, futile.[27] Far from entrenching a sense of mutual hostility the common experience of battle had forged bonds of comradeship and mutual respect that transcended the divisions of politics and nationalism. The battle for the Falklands had, in a curious sense, brought the two nations together as never before.

'STRANGE FRIENDS'

Eleven years after the fall of Stanley, Vincent Bramley travelled to Buenos Aires in the company of journalists from the now defunct British national daily, *Today*, for a first meeting between British and Argentine veterans of the battle for Mount Longdon, 'to show that the soldiers of two formerly warring nations could meet amicably without governmental interference or prompting' (Bramley, 1994: xiii). Yet to his surprise Bramley found more than conciliation there, he discovered fellowship, friendship and an uncanny sense of familiarity. Listening to the Argentine veterans describe their experiences on Longdon and their subsequent struggles in civilian life was like hearing an echo of his own and his friends' voices confessing their most intimate memories of the conflict: 'These men had stories to tell. Their war, too, was a terrible one' (Bramley, 1994: 8). Bramley determined to detail their experiences. On his return to the UK he interviewed five of his former colleagues from 3 Para, discussing their early lives, their time in the military, their preparation for and detailed experience of the Falklands and their subsequent experiences in the military and civilian life. He then went back to Buenos Aires and conducted equally probing interviews with eight Argentine veterans of the battle for Longdon, seven conscripts and one regular soldier, all of whom had served in the 7th Mechanised Infantry Regiment, later adding his own introductory, linking and interpretive commentary. The succeeding account of both sides of the battle for Mount Longdon, *Two Sides of Hell*, was published in 1994. Despite some important differences between British and Argentine memories of the war, most notably the Argentine conscripts' testimony of the abuses they suffered at the hands of their own officers and NCOs, one is most forcibly struck by the overwhelming similarities between the interviewees' responses to the various stages of the conflict – their common patriotism and pride of regiment, their disdain for the islands and the weather, love for their comrades, anguish at their losses, their courage, relief, elation and disillusionment. Bramley's editing, his free and fluid interleaving of British with Argentine accounts, further enhances the common ground that exists between their experiences. As each man recalls a specific phase of the build-up or battle, the narrative devolves into a patchwork of echoes and reaffirmations and one loses track of exactly who is talking. This is no editorial failure but an assertion and an embodiment of Bramley's central thesis, that the voices of these men are virtually interchangeable, that what binds them together is deeper and more lasting than the antagonisms that put them on opposing sides of the battlefield, and that what emerges from their experiences is not a clamour of contending voices, an extension of the conflict by other, discursive means, but a harmony of common responses to the war's significant experiences.[28]

By the end of his time in Argentina, confronted by overwhelming evidence of the similarities between British and Argentine experiences of the war, Bramley was no longer able to sustain the most basic structure of meaning, the simple oppositions between us and them, friend and foe, Brit and Argie on which his own earlier and all official accounts of the war had been premised. Not only was the enemy's voice indistinguishable from that of his comrades, but so too was his likeness. On a visit to the barracks of the 7th Mechanised Infantry Regiment, Bramley came across the Regiment's memorial to the soldiers killed in the Falklands: 'Each photo in the regimental lobby is of a soldier they lost, and every one of them is there – nearly all young men barely out of their teens. As I stared at the pictures I could see all my friends in 3 Para who had died on Longdon ... Their faces, our boys' faces – there was no difference at all really' (Bramley, 1994: 267–8). Here Bramley realises that in the Falklands he and his colleagues had been combating not moral otherness but men so much like themselves that in inflicting harm on them they were doing no less damage to themselves. Bramley thus recognises that like the defeated, he and his friends were casualties of the war, victims of their own success, victims of a hollow victory.

Not surprisingly, this was not a view of the war endorsed by the government or the media who, in different ways, had benefited and continued to profit from their promotion of a 'black and white' version

DAILY EXPRESS

JUNE 25, 1982

"I wish our all-conquering Field-Marshal could liberate the British islands from the Union junta!"

Figure 7 The Domestic Front (cartoon by Cummings)

of the war – the government re-elected, in 1983, to a further term in office in no small measure on the back of the 'Falklands Factor', while the media, revitalised by the aggressive nationalism it had so zealously promulgated, restocked the discursive armoury as the fight for national renewal moved to the domestic front. See for example the cartoon by Cummings that appeared in the *Sunday Express* on 25 June 1982 (Figure 7).[29]

In the unlikely event that either was tempted to revise its declared position on the war, the absolutism of their former pronouncements had utterly discredited the lexicon of conciliation and left little room for manoeuvre, short of humiliating retraction. Despite growing testimony through the mid to late 1980s that the war had been bloody, brutal and avoidable, and that many of those who had fought, suffered injury or lost loved ones in the fighting had since been cast off by the system they gave so much to defend, the government and the media stuck doggedly to their official, celebratory line on the conflict as a just war and a catalyst for national renewal.[30] In her speech at Cheltenham in the immediate aftermath of the fighting, Margaret Thatcher had famously claimed that victory in the Falklands proved that Britain had 'ceased to be a nation in retreat'. Eleven years later and the triumph in the South Atlantic had assumed global significance. In her Prime Ministerial memoirs she proposed that the Falklands War had not merely been a watershed in domestic politics but a key event in the most significant realignment of military, political and social power of the past half century, the collapse of communism and the end of the Cold War. In defeating Argentina Britain had reaffirmed its determination to defend democratic principles wherever the battle whatever the sacrifice and had, thereby, made a small but significant contribution to the demoralisation and eventual collapse of the Evil Empire:

> The significance of the Falklands War was enormous, both for Britain's self-confidence and for our standing in the world. Since the Suez fiasco in 1956, British foreign policy had been one long retreat. The tacit assumption made by British and foreign governments alike was that our world role was doomed steadily to diminish. We had come to be seen by both friends and enemies as a nation which lacked the will and the capacity to defend its interests in peace, let alone in war. Victory in the Falklands changed that. Everywhere I went after the war, Britain's name meant something more than it had. The war also had real importance in relations between East and West: years later I was told by a Russian general that the Soviets had been firmly convinced that we would not fight for the Falklands, and that if we did fight we would lose. We proved them wrong on both counts, and they did not forget the fact. (Thatcher, 1993: 173–4)

Despite the celerity with which Argentina returned to democratic rule, its assurances that it would seek the recovery of the Malvinas by peaceful means alone, and an increasing recognition that the combatants from either side had shared many common experiences both during and after the fighting, the government and the media continued to promote a black and white view of the causes, conduct and consequences of the war and to portray the Argentine military as an ongoing threat to the islands. Three years after the war had finished, on a return journey to the Falklands Robert Fox cautioned that 'President Alfonsín's softer line toward the military' might result in 'a real military threat to the Falklands from Argentina', a threat heightened by continuing Argentine rearmament: 'the air force in particular is now stronger and better equipped than it was in early 1982' (Fox, 1985: 327). To mark the tenth anniversary of the war Channel Four presented Denys Blakeway's two-part documentary *The Falklands War* (1992). Despite an impressive cast of those directly involved in the political, diplomatic and military conduct of the conflict, despite its pretensions to historical respectability, objectivity and definitive authenticity, the series still illustrated its coverage of Argentine politics and diplomacy with a cavalcade of Ruritanian uniforms, manikins at salute or on slow march, and the fanatical flag-waving masses forever chanting their mindless mantra, 'Ar-gen-tina! Ar-gen-tina!'[31]

In their determination to retain broader narrative and political control over popular memory of the conflict and so vindicate their maintenance of discursive hostilities, the government and the media resisted any temptation towards more widespread empathy and denied any possible recognition of or familiarity with the enemy by endeavouring to discredit the views of dissenters, where possible censoring the details of their experiences or harassing them into silence. Just prior to the screening of *Tumbledown* on 31 May 1989 and the simultaneous publication of *When the Fighting Is Over*, the *Observer* reported that the MoD had launched a 'dirty tricks' campaign against Tumbledown hero Robert Lawrence in an effort 'to denigrate the book and to cast doubts on Robert's integrity'. This campaign took the form of MoD briefings claiming the book was 'inaccurate', physical threats from Lawrence's former colleagues, even 'a letter from Lt Col Michael Whiteley, commanding officer of the Scots Guards, denying the truth of a battlefield recollection, asking [Lawrence] to write to an officer and apologise for his "mistake" and expunge the story from all future editions of the book' (Routledge, 1988: 1).[32] Vincent Bramley's memoir, *Excursion to Hell*, landed him in even bigger trouble. Bramley claimed that in writing the book his aim had been 'to give the view of the ordinary soldier, but the government did not want to know the facts of warfare as I and others like me saw it' (Bramley, 1994: xii). It obscured them by focusing instead on Bramley's allegations elsewhere in the book that British soldiers had executed Argentine PoWs.[33] These charges led to an all out assault by certain sections of the media on the overall credibility of Bramley's account, two years of 'press harassment', and an eighteen-month investigation by the Metropolitan Police's Serious and International Crimes Section culminating in July 1994 with the Director of Public Prosecution's decision not to lay charges over the incident (Bramley, 1994: xvii).[34] The media's fixation with what was a marginal issue in the book did much to bury its central message about the sheer brutality of the battle for Mount Longdon. Accordingly, three years later Bramley published *Two Sides of Hell*, written in part to 'dispel some of [the] mystery, and present more than a few hard facts' about the campaign (Bramley, 1994: x). In the book, Kevin Connery reflected on more than a decade spent trying to convince those who had taken no part in the fighting that, despite its remoteness and its relative brevity, the Falklands had been bloody and brutal, a 'war' in anybody's language: 'People say the Falklands was a conflict. It wasn't: it was out-and-out war ... In Northern Ireland I never used my bayonet, I was never required to even fix my bayonet and I never carried my bayonet on my belt. In the Falklands I carried my bayonet, I fixed my bayonet and I bayoneted somebody. That is the difference, in any soldier's book, between a conflict and a war' (Bramley, 1994: 249–50).

The gradual collapse of the official position on the war and the structure of binary oppositions which underpinned it was the result not merely of the growing number and prominence of first-hand accounts written by the men who had fought the battles, faced the enemy and seen themselves in his eyes, it was allied also to growing evidence that the government had no commitment to the values which the war had ostensibly been fought to defend and uphold. The collective ideals of family, community and race, the bonds of trust, comradeship, mutual care and support which had underpinned and supposedly been restored by the task force's success in the South Atlantic were values which it openly scorned, as was evident in its response to the miner's strike of 1984–85 in which, Arthur Marwick observed, 'Mrs Thatcher and her ministers made it conclusively clear that they felt no responsibility for the promotion of social harmony and that in pursuit of longer-term aims, they found confrontation and violence entirely acceptable' (Marwick, 1990: 342). Accordingly, the measures undertaken in the South Atlantic ostensibly to preserve social and cultural coherence were by the mid 1980s employed more and more often at home, at Orgreave, Wapping and at picket lines and demonstrations across the country to enforce the dissolution of any such coherence and the fragmentation of any sense of a genuinely collective society. By the late 1980s Britain was, Arthur Marwick claimed, 'clearly a disturbed place in which to live' (Marwick, 1990: 366).[35] The 1980s saw a drastic rolling back of the government's commitment to those institutions dedicated to the provision, defence and promotion of the family and the community, the shrinking of the welfare state, the starving of the National Health Service, the emasculation of trade unions, and a full-scale retreat from the principle of public ownership of collective assets, culminating in Margaret Thatcher's infamous assertion that 'there is no such thing as society' (qtd in Thatcher, 1993: 626).[36] These assaults on the symbolic bastions of collective values allied to the government's aggressive promotion of the enterprise culture and its attendant ethic of individualism, helped bring on the collapse of the post-war consensus which, however uncertainly, had held the nation's diverse communities together:

> Structural trends were breaking up old national loyalties and communal networks: those in authority were hastening the trends and putting nothing appropriate in the place of the loyalties and networks ... the old reference points by which individuals and groups measured their behaviour, by which their behaviour was constrained, had drastically changed. Society had been more unified under policies that deliberately sought to avoid unemployment and to sustain social benefits, policies which recognized the place of trade unions in society, and policies that upheld tolerance and

civilized behaviour as important values. Football hooligans at home saw themselves as fighting for their own particular community; football hooligans abroad, ironically, saw themselves as demonstrating British might. All this was, however distortedly, in keeping with the values of the aggressive market-place and the Falklands War. There were no longer national communal values to which all but the most desperate and alienated subscribed. Loyalty was now to the individual peer group. (Marwick, 1990: 351–2)[37]

Among the victims of this new dispensation were the veterans of the Falklands War who found the same aggression, stubborn dedication to the task and singleness of purpose which had ensured their victory in the South Atlantic now brought to bear against them in the government's adherence to the letter of the bureaucratic law, its grudging provision of benefits, and its steadfast refusal to concede moral or economic ground to the claimants when they requested assistance, compensation or recognition: 'All I get is the cold shoulder and letters full of bullshit and regulations. The government did fuck all to help me and the rest of us' (Bramley, 1994: 246).[38]

When the veterans complained about their treatment or spoke out against the government's parsimony they were slotted into the familiar structure of binaries, dismissed as troublemakers, or treated as enemies of the very system they had risked their lives to defend – Lawrence, Williams and Bramley were all, at one time or another, subject to verbal harassment, physical abuse or official investigation in an effort to silence them. It is little wonder that both British and Argentine veterans felt cheated. The ideal societies they had fought in defence of or hoped to bring into being, collective, inclusive, caring – models of their immediate military communities – had never existed. Moreover, the personal values which had sustained them in battle, mutual trust, loyalty, obedience, were exploited by their leaders to ensure that those who had sacrificed most to secure the victory would be the last to share in its spoils: 'Here is a government which slaps you on the back and says well done, wins a landslide majority at the next election with the "Falklands Factor" – the blood and sacrifice of our comrades – then kicks you up the arse as soon as your time is done. You're no use to them any more' (Bramley, 1994: 222). For all the 'hard facts' they provide about the war, it is the struggle for peace which shapes the other ranks' memoirs of the conflict. The simple polarities of the battlefield, the thrill of combat, the intensity of comradeship they so vividly convey not only celebrate these experiences in themselves but also offer a stark contrast to the dullness and self-seeking of civilian life – the unity and loyalty of the regiment a bitter indictment of the government's post-war betrayals, the empathy and understanding of colleagues a welcome relief from the indifference of the general public and the ignorance of family.[39] The veterans are adrift in the very society they brought into being. Their accounts are written out of and shaped by a sense of bitterness and disillusionment as they struggle through post-traumatic stress disorder and its attendant ills to a state in which, despite the hostility of former friends, they can live with others, live with themselves, and so make peace with the enemy within.

Conclusion
'Whither thou goest ...'

Oh! we, who have know shame, we have found release there.
(Brooke, 1915: 40)

When Spencer Fitz-Gibbon wrote *Not Mentioned in Despatches*, his exemplary exposition of 'what really happened' at Goose Green had a cautionary purpose – to ensure that 'the military lessons of the Falklands war' were not buried beneath 'the unquestioning glorification' of the nation's triumph (Fitz-Gibbon, 1995: 139, xiii, xii). In Fitz-Gibbon's view, the British Army's eagerness to promote the fighting in the South Atlantic as a ringing endorsement of its doctrine and tactics threatened to undermine its efficiency and endanger the lives of its personnel: 'if the experience of the Falklands war ... is so gravely misunderstood or misrepresented by the army establishment then what are the likely effects on the evolution of British military doctrine, and therefore on training and education, and thus ultimately on the army's future performance?' (Fitz-Gibbon, 1995: xiii). Only if the military acknowledged its mistakes, Fitz-Gibbon maintained, could it hope to profit from them.

On the domestic front in Britain, the official insistence that victory in the Falklands War was the catalyst for moral, social and national renewal had potentially catastrophic consequences. If armed confrontation is regarded as a logical and expeditious solution to the nation's problems and a potentially improving experience for those involved in it then the triumph in the Falklands has made it more likely that the nation will go to war again as combat, and its implied benefits for those participating in it, will be seen not as a means to an end but as an end in itself. The Falklands Conflict served, as such, to rehabilitate and even popularise war, to establish it not as a last resort in the face of unprovoked aggression but as a reasonable and effectual response to domestic anxieties about the national self-image and a key means of reshaping it.

Simon Featherstone notes that as a result of the 'populist nationalism provoked by the Falklands ... Several recent popular anthologies [of war poetry] ... do not give precedence to anti-war writers like Owen and Sassoon, preferring to emphasize the Englishness and self-sacrifice of minor poets'. This trend culminated soon after the Falklands War in the 'rediscovery' of Rupert Brooke, 'the disparaged poet of romantic jingoism', who 'once more became a figure of interest in the 1980s with the publication of two popular accounts of him and his circle' (Featherstone, 1995: 13).[1] Indeed, the return to romantic jingoism instigated by the fighting in the South Atlantic is perhaps most clearly revealed in the fact that in both substance and tone, Brooke's ecstatic response to the advent of the First World War serves equally well as an official soundtrack to the Falklands Conflict:

> Now, God be thanked Who has matched us with His hour,
> And caught our youth, and wakened us from sleeping,
> With hand made sure, clear eye, and sharpened power,
> To turn, as swimmers into cleanness leaping,
> Glad from a world grown old and cold and weary,
> ... Oh! we, who have known shame, we have found release there.
> (Brooke, 1915: 40)

The nationalist revival in Britain provoked by and promoted through the Falklands War provided the moral, political and discursive frame within which the nation's involvement in the Gulf War of 1990–91, and its readiness to mobilise its forces against Saddam Hussein again in early 1998 was explained and promoted.[2] The success of these ventures lay as much in the rekindling through combat of talismanic alliances from the Second World War (Anglo-US, Anglo-European) as it did in the liberation of Kuwait or the location and destruction of Iraqi chemical and biological weapons. By standing shoulder to shoulder with its closest ally, America, in the face of tyranny, the nation was reconsecrating the special relationship which underwrote its finest hours from the Second World War, redeeming its national past and so reaffirming its status as a former and future world power. This perhaps explains British Labour Prime Minister Tony Blair's elaborate toast of Bill Clinton at a recent White House banquet, where, as Martin Kettle notes: 'Blair quoted Harry Hopkins' biblical remarks to Churchill in the midst of the second world war: "Whither thou goest I will go, and whither thou lodgest I will lodge. Thy people shall be my people, and thy God my God." Then Blair continued: "And Hopkins paused, and then he said, 'Even to the end', and Churchill wept"' (Kettle, 1998: 6). And so might we all. If the nation continues to conceive of its current and future role in world affairs as an extension of its triumphs in the Second World War, to identify combat as a viable means of renewing its people and restoring its glory days then 'the end' may be all too close at hand.

In the midst of the First World War, Wilfred Owen argued that 'All a poet can do today is warn' (Owen, 1963: 31). I make no claims to be a poet, but the purposes of my own narrative are no less admonitory. This book has been an attempt to understand the discursive processes which made it possible in the Falklands War and subsequently to justify and sustain a series of perilous links between combat, national identity and the public good. The better we understand these processes the better prepared we will be to recognise them, resist them, and so secure our own and the nation's future from the fatal trajectories of the past.

Notes

INTRODUCTION

1. John Fiske calls this 'the unbeliever's use of the word' (Fiske, 1990: 88).
2. One of the central aims of *Not Mentioned in Despatches* was that of 'reducing legend to its raw data and reassembling it as history' (Fitz-Gibbon, 1995: xii).
3. My terminology here and throughout the book indicates the considerable theoretical debt I owe to Patrick Wright's *On Living in an Old Country: The National Past in Contemporary Britain* (1985).
4. See Barthes, 1973; Levi-Strauss, 1966. For a brief and useful survey of the definitions of the term see ; O'Sullivan *et al.*, 1983: 147–8 and Williams, 1983: 210–12.

CHAPTER 1

1. These articles were subsequently extended, collected and published together in book form under the title of the latter essay (Baudrillard, 1995). Originally published in *Libération* between January and March 1991, the essays attained instant notoriety; acclaimed by 'the disciples of French intellectual fashion', not merely their conclusions but their basic theoretical premises were denounced by what Christopher Norris calls the defenders of '"enlightenment" values' (Norris, 1992: 11, 12).
2. According to Norris, the popularity of the essays was evidence of a 'widespread cultural malaise for which "postmodernism" is a useful diagnostic term' (Norris, 1992: 16). The debilitating effects of this malaise are, he asserts, rooted in post-modernism's 'full-scale assault on the concepts of truth, reality and representation' (Norris, 1992: 25). One consequence of this assault, the mistaken belief that one could no longer distinguish the real from the illusory, and so no longer identify, uphold or defend the truth has, Norris laments, led to the general abandonment by intellectuals of 'any principled oppositional stand on issues of local or world politics' (Norris, 1992: 27). What Norris condemns in Baudrillard then is less the substance of his arguments than what they symbolise, the '*complicity* that exists between such forms of extreme, anti-realist or irrationalist doctrine and the crises of moral and political nerve among those whose voices should have been raised against the actions committed in their name' (Norris, 1992: 27). Norris regards political commitment not merely as a victim of epistemological

157

scepticism but as a sure remedy for it. He looks back fondly to a not-too-distant past when 'oppositional discourses possessed at least a measure of rhetorical or "performative" force, and when it still made sense for progressive intellectuals to adopt a standard-bearing role, as critics of consensus belief or purveyors of a truth hitherto concealed through the workings of ideological illusion' (Norris, 1992: 27), convinced that the return of epistemological certainty waits only on a renewal of political will.

3. See Morgan, 1982, in particular, coverage of the first emergency debate, 4–21. 'The third naval power in the world, and the second in NATO, has suffered a humiliating defeat' (Morgan, 1982: 12); 'But what a blunder, what a monumental folly, that the Falkland Islanders should be incarcerated in an Argentine gaol' (Morgan, 1982: 13); 'Let us declare and resolve that our duty now is to repossess our possessions and to rescue our own people' (Morgan, 1982: 10, *passim*).

4. See Marwick, 1990: 351–2.

5. See Orwell, 1938: 6–13, 17–18, 20–1, 32, 33–5, 51, 74, 209–12, *passim*: 'Every foreigner who served in the militia spent his first few weeks in learning to love the Spaniards and in being exasperated by certain of their characteristics' (Orwell, 1938: 11)

6. See Williams, 1991: 7–15.

7. See Bartlett, 1972. Also MacLachlan and Reid, 1994, 68–72.

8. See Cunningham, 1988, 49–52.

9. See Orwell, 1938: 216, 227, for his declaration of intent and his confession of his own partiality: 'It will never be possible to get a completely accurate and unbiased account of the Barcelona fighting, because the necessary records do not exist. Future historians will have nothing to go upon except a mass of accusations and party propaganda. I myself have little data beyond what I saw with my own eyes and what I have learned from other eyewitnesses whom I believe to be reliable. I can, however, contradict some of the more flagrant lies and help to get the affair into some kind of perspective' (Orwell, 1938: 216); 'I have tried to write objectively about the Barcelona fighting, though, obviously, no one can be completely objective on a question of this kind. One is practically obliged to take sides, and it must be clear enough which side I am on. Again, I must inevitably have made mistakes of fact, not only here but in other parts of this narrative. It is very difficult to write accurately about the Spanish war, because of the lack of non-propagandist documents. I warn everyone against my bias, and I warn everyone against my mistakes. Still, I have done my best to be honest' (Orwell, 1938: 227).

10. 'In our time', Orwell wrote in 1946, 'it is broadly true that political writing is bad writing'. This is because 'political speech and writing are largely the defence of the indefensible. Things like the continuance of British rule in India, the Russian purges and deportations, the dropping of the atom bombs on Japan, can indeed be defended, but only by arguments which are too brutal for most people to face, and which do not square with the professed aims of political parties. Thus political language has

to consist largely of euphemism, question-begging and sheer cloudy vagueness' (Orwell, 1957: 153).

11. For an account of the PSUC's assault on and ultimate destruction of the POUM see Carr, 1977: 170–7. *Homage to Catalonia*, in particular 188–248 was, in no small part, a spirited defence of the POUM 'from a sea of "the most appalling lies"' yet it 'met with no response from the English left. The *New Statesman* would not print his articles; Gollancz refused to publish his classic *Homage to Catalonia*. When it was published by Secker and Warburg it sold "damn all"' (Carr, 1977: 176–7).

12. See Orwell, 1938: 220.

13. For the official line on the conflict see CoI, 1982; FCO, 1982; MoD, 1982; Secretary of State for Defence, 1982. Ana Baron, London correspondent for the Argentine magazine, *Gente*, described 'la versión oficial' of the British recovery of South Georgia (Baron, 1982: np). There is no single, monolithic official narrative, but a community of agreement about the causes of the war (Argentine aggression, Argentine diplomatic intransigence), its progress (the smooth functioning of the well-oiled British military machine, the plotting of a superior strategy successfully carried through thanks to better British tactics and training despite the enemy's numerical advantage), and its consequences (national renewal, the resurrection of national pride and the nation's re-emergence on the world stage as a force to be reckoned with). Each of these are enlarged upon, in various forms and at varying length, in a range of instant histories, regimental accounts and personal memoirs from the campaign which I will examine over the succeeding chapters.

14. See Routledge, 1988: 1; Williams, 1990: 112–17.

15. Media policy on the war and its consequences have been exhaustively studied. See Adams, 1986; Foster, 1992; GUMG, 1985; Harris, 1983; HCDC, 1982; Mercer *et al.*, 1987; Morrison and Tumber, 1988.

CHAPTER 2

1. Robert Harris described the editorial in terms of the space it occupied: '68 column inches, more than 5 and a half feet, of authoritative prose rolling inexorably to its majestic conclusion' (Harris, 1983: 38).

2. For a serious, if synoptic analysis of these heady days see Clarke, 1996: 207–15.

3. Clarke proposes an alternative approach to twentieth-century British history:

> The history of twentieth-century Britain ... threatens to become a history of decline, centred on the question: where did it all go wrong? This vision is understandable but myopic. For it implies a sort of history that is now often regarded as old fashioned – one in which international rivalry, whether of a military, political or economic kind, is taken as the all-embracing theme ... There is room for more than one perspective on the history of the British people in the

twentieth century. What is needed is an account which makes sense of the political and economic changes that transformed Britain, but one which also pauses to piece together other, diverse aspects of the experience of the three entire generations who lived through this era of unexampled change. This story cannot simply be told as one of decline. Though the laurels of international leadership passed to others during the twentieth century, Britain still had its moments of glory, not all of them illusory; and Britons nourished hopes, not all of them misguided, that a condescending posterity should not dismiss but try to understand. (Clarke, 1996: 3, 5)

4. As Margaret Thatcher herself noted: 'I had great regard for the Victorians for many reasons – not least their civic spirit to which the increase in voluntary and charitable societies and the great buildings and endowments of our cities pay eloquent tribute. I never felt uneasy about praising "Victorian values" or – the phrase I originally used – "Victorian virtues" not least because they were by no means just Victorian' (Thatcher, 1993: 627).

5. See Winchester, 1983: 21–31. For the Argentinians, of course, the situation was reversed in that while the media was able to provide extensive coverage of the reconquest of the islands, coverage of the final stages of the battle for the Falklands, the defeat and surrender of their forces, came almost exclusively from British sources. See 'La Guerra Que No Vimos', *Gente*, June 1982, No. 883.

6. Elsewhere, the Governor claimed that the small settlement at Roy Cove 'could have been a small hamlet in Lorna Doone country' (Hunt, 1992: 91). As *The Times* pointed out: 'When British territory is invaded, it is not just an invasion of our land, but of our whole spirit' (*The Times*: 5 April 1982).

7. For more details on the classical pastoral see Marinelli, 1971, and Barrell, 1972.

8. Anthony Barnett identifies such a cultural persistence in what he wryly terms the 'country-cottage fetish and allotment consciousness of the English' (Barnett, 1982: 102).

9. I owe this point to Taylor, 1991: 71–8. See also Gray, 1997: 12, for a discussion of how Thatcherism's transformation of Britain destroyed the very ideal of the nation it had hoped to preserve.

10. As David White fetchingly put it: 'There is some corner in the English mind that is forever Ambridge' (qtd in Wiener, 1981: 78).

11. This, in turn, reflects a subtle but significant evolution in the use of pastoral imagery in the context of war. 'English ruralism', Simon Featherstone notes, has traditionally 'acted as a counterpoint to imperialist nationalism' (Featherstone, 1995: 29). In the context of the Falklands War, instead of counterpointing 'imperialist nationalism' rural imagery stimulated and provided a rallying point for its renewal, for the rekindling of what the Prime Minister in her speech at Cheltenham called 'that spirit which had fired [the nation] for generations past'.

The enemies within were represented by the unions who were portrayed as stubbornly refusing to embrace 'the new mood of the nation' and so preventing its return to the glories of the past:

> If the lessons of the South Atlantic are to be learned, then they have to be learned by us all. No one can afford to be left out. Success depends upon all of us – different in qualities, but equally valuable.
> During this past week, I have read again a little known speech of Winston Churchill, made just after the last war. This is what he said:–

> We must find the means and the method of working together not only in times of war, and mortal anguish, but in times of peace, with all its bewilderments and clamour and clatter of tongues.

> Thirty-six years on, perhaps we are beginning to re-learn the truth which Churchill so clearly taught us.
> We saw the signs when, this week, the NUR came to understand that its strike on the railways and on the Underground just didn't fit – didn't match the spirit of these times. And yet on Tuesday, 8 men, the leaders of ASLEF, misunderstanding the new mood of the nation, set out to bring the railways to a halt ... this tiny group decided to use its undoubted power for what? – to delay Britain's recovery, which all our people long to see. (qtd in Barnett, 1982: 151–2)

12. Ideological here in Williams' definition of it as 'the set of ideas which arise from a given set of material interests' (Williams, 1983: 156).
13. For more on Tom Smith's incredulous response to the 'cup of tea picture' see Morrison and Tumber, 1988: 181.
14. For more on this see Harris, 1983: 56–7.
15. Baudrillard's observations about the effects of instant TV coverage during the Gulf War are particularly germane in this context. See Baudrillard, 1995: 46–50.
16. There is a dizzying array of material on the news, I have found the following particularly useful: Chibnall, 1977; GUMG, 1976; GUMG, 1980; Hall *et al.*,1978; Hartley, 1982; Windschuttle, 1988: 261–80.
17. For more on hegemony see Fiske, 1990: 176–8; Hartley, 1982: 58–62; Thwaites *et al.*, 1994: 157–9; Turner, 1990: 210–15; Williams, 1983: 144–6.
18. For an account of the process by which the media were grudgingly accorded places on the voyage see Adams, 1986: 5–6; Harris, 1983: 15–25. For the Navy's initial plans for the management of information and how these altered see HCDC, 1982: Vol. I, ch. 3.
19. See McCullin and Chester, 1990: 254–8; Morrison and Tumber, 1988: 5–6.
20. This accorded with the view widespread among the task force reporters that the Falklands War was 'very much a home story' (Morrison and Tumber, 1988: 16). See also Morrison and Tumber, 1988: 7–10, 11, 16, 20.

21. Robert Fox's identification with the military was, if anything, closer. He was at pains to point out that when he talked about 'we' in his reports he was not describing '"we, Britain"', but '"we, the soldiers"' (Morrison and Tumber, 1988: 107).

22. McDonald had formerly been in charge of the ministry's pay and recruitment section.

23. For a more detailed analysis of the tension between a demand for news, the need for security and the resulting accommodations, including censorship, see Adams, 1986: 17–19; Foster, 1992; Mercer *et al.*, 1987: 175–96; Morrison and Tumber, 1988: 189–226; Young, 1992.

24. All news was henceforth promulgated in an official daily communique, delivered usually by McDonald himself, in his trademark, punctilious monotone. Keith Waterhouse described him as 'the only man in the world who speaks in braille' (qtd in Harris, 1983: 103).

25. Had the Argentinians seen the story it seems unlikely that they would have taken it seriously. Italo Piaggi, the Commander of the Argentine garrison at Goose Green, told Martin Middlebrook that on the night before the battle for Goose Green when the BBC inadvertently alerted the Argentinians to the impending attack he heard and dismissed the broadcast: 'I did not take it too seriously; I thought it was more a psychological action because it would be crazy for them to announce an actual move. I made no changes because of that broadcast' (qtd in Middlebrook, 1989: 180).

26. These complaints included the military Directors of Public Relations' dismay at the failure of the MoD to publicise the heroic efforts among industry and elsewhere on the domestic scene: 'great opportunities were missed for the positive projection of single-minded energy and determination by the British people in their support of the task force' (Harris, 1983: 105–6). The military DPRs claimed that McDonald kept them in the dark and so prevented them from doing their jobs. There were complaints about failings in the censorship system which allowed sensitive information to find its way back to the UK, most notably Mike Nicholson's identification of HMS *Conqueror* as the submarine which sank the *Belgrano*. Subsequently, there were disputes over what form the second screen of censorship in London should take, how it should run and who should operate it. See Harris, 1983: 105–9.

27. Martin Cleaver of the Press Association told Morrison and Tumber that there were pictures of 'gore and red meat' which the PA had, and the ministry released, but editors chose not to use. See Morrison and Tumber, 1988: 182.

28. The MoD claimed that its information policy was founded on 'the overriding dictates of national and operational security and the protection of the lives of our servicemen and servicewomen' (HCDC, 1982: Vol. II, ch. 1, para 2). On 8 April 1982 the MoD sent a signal to task force ships telling correspondents to 'feel free to file their stories and material'. It identified ten areas which the journalists should avoid in order to guarantee 'responsible reporting', which were:

1. operational plans, which would enable a potential enemy to deduce details of intentions.
2. speculation about possible courses of action.
3. state of readiness and detailed operational capability of individual units or formations.
4. location, employment and operational movements of individual units or formations, particularly specialist units.
5. particulars of current tactics and techniques.
6. operational capabilities of all types of equipment.
7. stocks of equipment and other details of logistics.
8. information about intelligence on Argentinian dispositions or capabilities.
9. communications.
10. equipment or other defects. (Mercer *et al.*, 1987: 156).

29. See Morrison and Tumber, 1988: 178.
30. For more on the process of transmitting film see Morrison and Tumber, 1988: 17. Through the period of the whole campaign only 202 photographs were transmitted from the task force back to the MoD (Morrison and Tumber, 1988: 179).
31. For more on the career of the *General Belgrano* see Brown, 1989: 41; Dobson *et al.*, 1982: 151; Gavshon and Rice 1984: 97–8.
32. Harris' advice was to 'keep the runways out of order so that our enemy, if he's worth calling that, can't use them' (BBC 1 News: 2 May 1982 17.50).

CHAPTER 3

1. Travelling around the coast of Britain at the time of the Falklands War, Paul Theroux was struck by the readiness with which people moved from news or talk of the Falklands to more congenial reminiscence about the Second World War, a more distant but altogether more authentic, more intimate conflict; it was as if anxiety about the adequacy of the response to a test of the nation's essential identity engendered a sort of nostalgic pilgrimage to its last known resting place, half in lamentation, half in hope of inspiration:

   The next day I heard two tattling ladies talking about the Falklands. It was being said that the British had become jingoistic because of the war, and that a certain swagger was now evident. It was true of the writing in many newspapers, but it was seldom true of the talk I heard. Most people were like Mrs Mullion and Miss Custis at the Britannia in Combe Martin, who, after some decent platitudes, wandered from talk of the Falklands to extensive reminiscing about the Second World War.
   'After all, the Germans were occupying France, but life went on as normal,' Mrs Mullion said.

'Well, this is just it,' Miss Custis said. 'You've got to carry on. No sense packing up.'

'We were in Taunton then.'

'Were you? We were in Cullompton', Miss Custis said. 'Mutterton, actually.'

'Rationing seemed to go on for ages!' Mrs Mullion said.

'I still remember when chocolate went off the ration. And then people bought it all. And then it went on the ration again!'

They had begun to cheer themselves up in this way.

'More tea?' Mrs Mullion said.

'Lovely,' Miss Custis said. (Theroux, 1983: 136)

2. During the Gulf War, for example, the public was exhorted to take an active role in the conflict through the unlikely agency of shopping. Dismayed by a perceived lack of commitment to the operations in the Gulf from Britain's nominal allies in the European Community, the *Daily Star* transposed the polarities of the battlefield to the shops and markets of Britain, and encouraged its readers to '*be* historical', to strike a blow against the 'spineless frogs' and cowardly Belgians by declaring war on their produce: 'Today when you go shopping, boycott that Italian spaghetti, the French bread, German sausages, Portuguese sardines, oranges, olives and all the rest of that foreign muck. Be proud to buy British. And don't think of booking a holiday abroad. STAY HOME' (*Daily Star*, 17 January 1991: 8). Thus were the deadened routines of daily life, sitting in front of the television and not cooking the spaghetti, translated into active participation in the great events of the day.

3. Lloyd George told Churchill that he 'must not allow himself to be converted into an air-raid shelter to keep the splinters from hitting his colleagues' (qtd in Calder, 1991: 23).

4. See Clarke, 1996: 193.

5. The royal family has traditionally served as a symbol of this national/familial unity; accordingly, in time of war, its structures and the behaviour of its individual members has assumed a deeper, representative significance – the King and Queen refusing, like most other Londoners, during the Second World War to abandon their home despite the Blitz; the Queen anxiously waiting with other mothers for the safe return of her son, Prince Andrew, from the South Atlantic; the royal family organised like a domestic arm of the military machine during Operation Desert Storm, each of its members designated a specific task on the home front.

6. In this regard it comes close to Benedict Anderson's definition of the nation as 'an imagined political community ... it is *imagined* because the members of even the smallest nation will never know most of their fellow-members, meet them, or even hear of them, yet in the minds of each lives the image of their communion ... it is imagined as a *community*, because, regardless of the actual inequality and exploitation that may prevail in each, the nation is always conceived as a deep, horizontal comradeship' (Anderson, 1983: 6–7).

7. 'The blitz (a word abbreviated from the German *blitzkrieg*) is generally accepted as beginning in Britain with the first big aerial bombardment of London on 9 September 1940 and thereafter concentrating on that target until a switch to the provinces, via Coventry, on 14 November, and concluding with a record assault back on London 10 May 1941 and a final night over Birmingham on 16 May' (Harrisson, 1990: 14–15).

8. As Calder notes, the Home Intelligence reports were compiled from summaries of the press, reports from postal and telephone censorship, police duty rooms, BBC Listener research, reports from W.H. Smith which owned a large chain of newsagencies in city centres and at railway stations whose managers supplied information about conversations and gossip concerning the war, reports from the managers of the large chain of Granada cinemas, and information from Citizens' Advice Bureaux, Women's Royal Voluntary Service units, and other community organisations (Calder, 1991, 121).

9. A script most memorably, if not most typically, played out by Greer Garson and Walter Pigeon in William Wyler's 1942 MGM blockbuster *Mrs Miniver*. As the Luftwaffe's bombs rain down around their home in Kent the Minivers sit in their Anderson shelter at the bottom of the garden, she knitting, he smoking his pipe and reading a book – even stepping outdoors at one point to admire the fireworks over London: 'fine barrage tonight darling'. The film played a vital role in bringing America into the war: Churchill thought very highly of it, claiming that it was worth more than a destroyer to the nation's war effort.

10. See Calder 1991: 125. 'The occupation of the London Underground by shelterers becomes a heroic assertion of popular rights against a legacy of inept bureaucracy and Tory rule' (Calder, 1991: 47).

11. See Calder, 1969: 179–81.

12. This was the response to mass bombardment predicted by the most influential theorist of mass demoralisation, the Italian General Guilo Douhet in his manifesto for the aerial bombardment of civilian populations, *Il dominio dell' aria* (1921). Angus Calder refers to a 'craven populace invented by the official imagination' which, it was feared 'would contract out of the war effort and immerse itself more or less permanently in the womb-like security' provided by the government (Calder, 1969: 179). Hence the determination to eschew deep shelters and rely on the Anderson shelter as the centrepiece of its domestic shelter programme. Nonetheless, fear of a breakdown in working-class morale remained widespread. Harold Nicolson noted in his diary entry for 17 September 1940: 'Everybody is worried about the feeling in the East End, where there is much bitterness. It is said that even the King and Queen were booed the other day when they visited the destroyed areas. Clem [Davies, Liberal MP for Montgomeryshire, and leader of the Liberal Party 1945–46] says that if only the Germans had had the sense not to bomb west of London Bridge there might have been a revolution in this country' (Nicolson, 1967: 114–15). Angus Calder offers a judicious assessment of the response of the East End to the Blitz and why, while

there was anger and even despair among the people, there was neither revolt nor panic (Calder, 1969: 164–7).

13. Newly returned from the fighting, Vincent Bramley of the Parachute Regiment was driven to rage by a similar sense of how uninvolved, if not uninterested, the broader population was in what had happened in the South Atlantic:

> There was traffic on the roads, shops, people walking about doing their own thing. It all seemed unreal. After only three months away it was a shock to see civilization again. The odd thing was, I felt anger. Anger at everyone for doing their own thing. It was as if something in my head was urging me to shout at them as they walked along the streets, 'Hey, you lot, licking your fucking ice-creams, there's a fucking lot of injured guys over there. Friends have been killed, but all you're interested in is yourselves'. (Bramley, 1991: 208)

The situation in Argentina was much the same. Horacio Benitez, wounded in the battle for Wireless Ridge and returned to the mainland aboard a hospital ship found life in Buenos Aires unconcerned by events so close at hand: 'In Buenos Aires it was as though nothing had happened. There had been a war down there and it went wrong and it was all over now, but no one was really interested in what had actually happened, in how many had died' (Bilton and Kosminsky, 1989: 189–90).

14. Though the British Nationality Bill of 1981 had proposed that they be stripped of their right of abode in the UK, and made purely subjects and not citizens of the country.

15. The only man who spoke out of turn was Ray Whitney, see Morgan, 1982: 14.

16. The statistical evidence does not back this up. Morrison and Tumber's quantitative analysis of responses to a range of questions about British policy over the Falklands revealed that around 50 per cent of the population believed that the Argentinians 'had at least some legitimate right to the Falklands' (Morrison and Tumber, 1988: 286–7).

17. Peter Snow had outraged politicians, MoD officials and certain members of the public when, on Sunday 2 May's edition of *Newsnight*, in his efforts to produce a clear picture of events from a variety of sources he observed: 'Until the British are demonstrated either to be deceiving us or to be concealing losses from us we can only tend to give a lot more credence to their version of events.' Sir Frank Cooper was deeply dismayed: 'Peter was behaving as if he were a disinterested referee', while John Page, Conservative MP for Harrow, was considerably more moved finding the BBC's 'unacceptably even handed' approach 'totally offensive and almost treasonable' (qtd in Harris, 1983: 72).

18. This was resurrected and emended nine years later during the Gulf War as 'THE PAPER THAT SUPPORTS OUR BOYS AND GIRLS'.

19. Peter Clarke claimed: 'In a television age, the BBC made its reputation all over again in its coverage of major national events, which reinforced its image as the most august of public corporations and the voice of the establishment. The Queen's Coronation in June 1953 showed the way. Here was a pageant of national renewal, spoken of as inaugurating a new Elizabethan age, presented for the first time as a television spectacular ... It showed how the monarchy could be projected through the new medium, with a smooth voice-over from the doyen of commentators, Richard Dimbleby, who became little less than a national institution himself' (Clarke, 1996: 251–2).

20. 'If this had happened in eight months time we wouldn't have had a Navy to send thanks to Mr John Nott's Defence Cuts, so really he should resign immediately' (Warman, 1992).

21. Media coverage of the families directly implicated in the war was consistently drawn in opposing, if not hostile, directions. It endeavoured to *personalise* the families so that they were recognisably 'like us' and we could readily identify with them; yet in order to maintain their effective functioning as vehicles for collective involvement in the conflict, their role as emotional ciphers, it was vital that they remained anonymous, that they were *depersonalised* by the media representation of them. Accordingly, in the process of forging and promoting an image of the nation drawing together like a family in the face of the fighting, the media's construction, coverage and treatment of the actual families caught up in this process exposed both its speciousness and the causes of its failure.

22. As the Glasgow University Media Group noted: 'Over half the reports on families at home were done by women reporters, who covered only a small minority of the diplomatic, political news, and only one military story (on the Red Cross "safe" zone in Port Stanley)' (GUMG, 1985: 99).

23. Not only does this offer a positive image to potential recruits in a competitive job market, it also ensures that once recruited those soldiers, sailors and airmen are likely to better perform their duties (particularly in time of war) freed from anxieties about the welfare of their families.

24. See Morgan, 1982: 233 for a record of the MPs questions, and GUMG, 1985: 109–11 for the TV treatment of the wives' demonstration.

25. According to Jean Carr, the military's instinctual paternalism, its certainty that the families under its charge would (and should) bow to its authority and comply with its directions reflects its inability to acknowledge or adapt to the expectations and demands of a post-conscription generation to whom the services represent a stable though usually temporary job, a career move, not a *raison d'être*: See Carr, 1984: 6.

26. See, for example, Virgil's first *Eclogue*, 'The Dispossessed', where Meliboeus laments his expulsion from his farm resulting from Civil War:

> meanwhile the rest of us are off; some to foregather with the Africans and share their thirst; others to Scythia, and out to where the Oxus rolls the chalk along; others to join the Britons, cut off as they are by the whole width of the world. Ah, will the day come, after many years,

when I shall see a place that I can call my home, see turf piled high on my poor cottage roof, and in due time survey with pride the modest crop that is my little realm?

Is some blaspheming soldier to own these acres I have broken up and tilled so well – a foreigner, to reap these splendid fields of corn? Look at the misery to which we have sunk since Romans took to fighting one another. To think we have sown, for men like that to reap! Yes, Meliboeus, now graft your pears; now plant a row of vines!

Forward, my goats, forward, the flock that used to be my pride. Never again, stretched out in some green hollow, shall I spy you far away, dangling on the rocky hillside where the brambles grow. There will be no songs from me, my goats, and I shall lead you no more to crop the flowering clover and the bitter willow shoots. (Virgil, 1961: 32)

27. See Devereux, 1992: 87. Until 1948, the animal in the crest was a bull: the increasing monocropping of wool led to the amendment.

28. The UN certainly didn't see it this way. In 1965, the United Nations' 'General Assembly Resolution 2065 (XX): Question of the Falkland Islands (Malvinas)' invited Britain and Argentina 'to proceed without delay with the negotiations recommended by the Special Committee on the situation with regard to the Implementation of the Declaration of the Granting of Independence to Colonial Countries and Peoples with a view to finding a peaceful solution to the problem' (Reginald and Elliot, 1983: 146). See also 'UN General Assembly Resolution 1514 (XV): Declaration on the Granting of Independence to Colonial Countries and Peoples' (Reginald and Elliot, 1983: 144).

29. According to Lord Shackleton, as a result of the colonial system of government: 'Apart from the right to vote for the small group of people who make up the legislative council (dominated, at least numerically, by farm-owners and managers) [the ordinary Falklanders] have no real opportunity to influence decisions on public affairs' (Shackleton, 1976: 81).

30. See also Bishop and Witherow, 1982: 147.

31. *Gente*'s Alfredo Serra claimed that 'las islas (pocos lo saben) tienen el mayor índice de divorcios del mundo' (Serra, 1982: np) (the islands (how few know it) have the highest incidence of divorce in the world). The article as a whole offers a somewhat parodic portrait of colonial degeneracy through the (imaginary?) figure of Archibald Ellskilling.

32. See Bramley, 1991: 195 for his account of a hostile encounter with some of the local kelpers when he and his colleagues made it clear that they held them accountable for the dispute.

33. See Bramley, 1991: 179 for an account of the surrender of an Argentine helicopter and the looting of the machine and its crew.

34. Concerning the 'magistrates' orders' McGowan and Hands recalled: 'One landlord, full of that truth serum called Scotch, broke down in an emotional fit of honesty a little later and confessed, "It's not really an official ban. We all got together and decided to keep them out. We were worried they would wreck our pubs"' (McGowan and Hands, 1983:

269).

35. Even Ewen Southby Tailyour, a Royal Marines Major with an ency-
clopaedic knowledge of the islands' coastline and an avowed affection
for the islanders, conceded that they were, for the most part, 'a drunken,
decadent, immoral and indolent collection of dropouts' (qtd in Hastings
and Jenkins, 1983: 38).

36. For the emptiness and hostility of the islands see also: Bramley, 1991,
38; Bramley, 1994: 109; McGowan and Hands, 1983: 9; Williams,
1990: 28.

37. For more on this see Jennings and Weale, 1996: 77–8.

38. See Jennings and Weale, 1996: 174.

39. There was also considerable friction between the paras and the Scots
battalion who ran into each other at Ascension Island as the paras
headed home and the Scots headed for garrison duties on the Falklands.
See Bramley, 1991: 205.

40. For more on the death threats see Morrison and Tumber, 1988: 79–80.

41. For the journalists' professional priorities see Morrison and Tumber,
1988: 59–75. John Shirley gave a synopsis of some of the ill-feeling
simmering between the journalists, most of which seemed to centre on
Max Hastings. See Morrison and Tumber, 1988: 66–7. Dr Morgan
O'Connell, a psychiatrist who travelled to the Falklands as part of the
medical team, told Robert Fox that psychiatric casualties would significantly out-number physical wounds and that 'the most vulnerable
group is the press. You are all individuals, and work against each other,
so you cannot support yourselves as a team' (Fox, 1982a: 17).

42. For more on pooling practices see Morrison and Tumber, 1988: 60–2,
69–70, 72–3.

43. See Morrison and Tumber, 1988: 63–5. Ian Bruce thought otherwise,
claiming that rivalry gave place to cooperation. See Morrison and
Tumber, 1988: 73.

44. The *Invincible* Five were Alfred McIlroy, Gareth Parry, Mick Seamark, Tony
Snow and John Witherow. For a more detailed account of the plotting
among the *Canberra* journalists and the response of the *Invincible* Five
see Harris, 1983: 120–30; Morrison and Tumber, 1988: 43–58.

45. See Chapter 2, 32–3. See also Gareth Parry of the *Guardian*'s declaration
of his 'terrific kind of admiration' for the troops (Morrison and Tumber,
1982: 26).

46. The explicit purpose of Hastings' reports, to further the war effort, was
closely akin to much Argentine coverage of the conflict. Jimmy Burns,
for example, held up José Gómez Fuentes' reports as a model of Argentine
indifference to the truth, yet the rationale of his reports is virtually
indistinguishable from Hastings': 'If there is a war in my country, I will
give information which unites the country and I will omit everything
which does not. Now this is called disinformation. What's that? I don't
understand' (qtd in Burns, 1987: 82). Regarding his reports as his
contribution to a successful military outcome in the Falklands, Hastings
tailored them to that end: 'When one was writing one's copy one
thought: beyond telling everybody what the men around me are doing,

what can one say that is most likely to be most helpful to winning this war' (qtd in Harris, 1983: 135). On those occasions when his professional duty to give an honest account of 'what the men around me are doing' clashed with his personal commitment to be 'helpful to winning this war', when an accurate record of events might have impeded the progress of the cause or the advancement of his own interests, Hastings put personal and national promotion above his professional responsibility to inform. See Morrison and Tumber, 1988: 113.

47. Having lost twenty men in an accident early in the campaign, the SAS decided that they needed more publicity, so that the work of the soldiers who had been killed in the helicopter accident might be better appreciated. See Fox, 1982a: 220–1. Morrison and Tumber claimed that the military was only too ready to use the media to improve its profile or advance its causes and that there was substantial competition between ships and units for press coverage. See Morrison and Tumber, 1988: 23. On 1 June 1982 an SAS patrol took Hastings with them when they seized the summit of Mount Kent. (See Morrison and Tumber, 1988: 82 for Hastings' account of the ill-feeling that his presence on the exercise caused between himself, John Shirley, Patrick Bishop and Kim Sabido. The latter had been denied a place on the venture to Mount Kent by 42 Commando, the main attack force to whom they were attached. See Vaux, 1986: 102.) From its forward slopes, with Stanley in sight, Hastings used the mobile satellite facilities provided by the SAS to transmit a glowing account of their exploits back to their HQ in Hereford from where it was passed on to the MoD for censorship and distribution to the media.

CHAPTER 4

1. As the Latin America Bureau noted: 'Prior to the recent conflict, the islands' main link with the outside world was by way of the weekly flight operated by LADE, the Argentine government's air service. Carrying passengers, mail and general cargo, LADE's short haul aircraft operated a service to Comodoro Rivadavia in southern Argentina. The Port Stanley airstrip was not capable of accommodating intercontinental flights. Since the Falkland Island Company withdrew its monthly sea link with Montevideo in 1971, it has been replaced by a sea link direct to Britain. The Dutch ship *AES*, chartered by the company, makes the five-week trip from Gravesend to Port Stanley four times a year' (Honeywell and Pearce, 1982: 3).

2. Fifteen years after the final shots were fired the sporting metaphors persisted in descriptions of the war's diplomatic manoeuvres. In *Green-Eyed Boys*, an eyewitness account of the Battle for Mount Longdon, Jennings and Weale described the members of 3 Para as 'very small pawns in a very large game of international diplomatic chess' (Jennings and Weale, 1996: 64).

3. Michael Charlton's history of Falklands diplomacy was, appropriately, titled *The Little Platoon: Diplomacy and the Falklands Dispute* (1989).
4. See Auerbach, 1953: 107–24.
5. Addressing a conference of Scottish Conservatives only days after British forces had established a beachhead on the Falklands, the Prime Minister described Argentina's invasion of the islands in just these terms, as 'one of those insidious tests which throughout history evil has used to undermine the resolve of the good. The world wondered would the good and true respond? And the good and true did' (*Guardian*, 17 May 1982: 2). Her representation of the conflict as a moral crusade not only refined the delicate shadings of its historical, legal and political complexities into the stark polarities of a fable, it also underpinned the persistent promotion of the war's 'privileged and aloof' above their faithful but largely invisible retainers.
6. See also Adkin, 1992: 22–3; Fox, 1982a: 21, 27–8, 34–6, 74, 295–6, *passim*; Frost, 1983: 84; Hastings and Jenkins, 1983: 106–7, 114, 137–8, 269–70, *passim*.
7. For more on the other ranks' fear of knives and forks see Bishop and Witherow, 1982: 23.
8. For more on this see Foster, 1993: 19–27.
9. Extending the medieval metaphor, Major John Kiszely of the Scots Guards described Jones' death as 'like a gauntlet being thrown down to other officers' (Kiszely, 1985: 299), while to Hugh McManners of the Royal Artillery, Jones' Regiment, 2 Para, was 'our "mailed fist"' (McManners, 1984: 150).
10. See Leader, 1988: 618.
11. Jones' citation for the Victoria Cross insists that his actions were the catalyst for the collapse of Argentine resistance: 'The devastating display of courage by Colonel Jones had completely undermined their will to fight further' (qtd in Frost, 1983: 166). Adkin perpetuated the fiction: 'It was his plan, his example, and finally his sacrifice, that gave 2 Para their will to win' (Adkin, 1992: 13). Spencer Fitz-Gibbon demurs; not only was Jones' plan 'sometimes a hindrance to 2 Para', but he claimed to 'have found no evidence to say that H's sacrifice inspired anybody' (Fitz-Gibbon, 1995: xv, 133).
12. For more on Jones' intrusive command style see Fitz-Gibbon, 1995: 95.
13. Fitz-Gibbon identifies an opposed model of tactical command which he calls '*directive command*' (Fitz-Gibbon, 1995: xiv).
14. 'Directive command rests on an understanding that combat is inherently chaotic; that it cannot be tamed, but that the chaos can be exploited by the more flexible and quick-reacting command system. It implies a system in which orders are given in the form of *directives*. A directive is an order which indicates an end-state to be achieved, but which leaves the method of its achievement to the imagination and on-the-spot judgement of the subordinate commander. This allows subordinates the freedom to act appropriately in response to unfolding events – whatever surprises may occur during the fighting – while still providing

the guidance necessary to prevent diversification of effort' (Fitz-Gibbon, 1995: xiv).

15. For the full text of Moore's orders see Thompson, 1985: 73–4.
16. The history of the mission is a little more complicated than this. See Adkin, 1992: 68–79; Frost, 1983: 39–46; Thompson, 1985: 74–82.
17. As Spencer Fitz-Gibbon points out, it also endorsed a range of dubious command practices and long since discredited tactics. Fitz-Gibbon feared that the military's eagerness to eulogise Jones might lead it to overlook the important lessons to be taken from his failure at Goose Green, that the shortcomings of restrictive control might be turned into a vindication of its practices: 'When historians, journalist-authors and the writers of post-operations reports retrospectively tidy up the battlefield and give an impression that what was meant to work actually did work, this tends to lead to the obvious but possibly false conclusion that the command theory was vindicated in practice' (Fitz-Gibbon, 1995: xiv). His analysis of the assault on Burntside House provides a fine example of such tidying up and the resultant 'manufacture of military myths':

> Hastings and Jenkins (p276) write of A Company as they approached Burntside House: 'They were still 500 yards short when the enemy dug in around it opened fire.' Nobody consulted in this study suggests that the enemy began firing when A Company were still so far away. Had they done, it would have called for a considerable tactical effort to close with the enemy over such a long distance of open country under fire. And the occupants of the house at the time, together with several of the commanders involved in attacking it, deny that the enemy were either dug-in or around the house.
>
> Martin Middlebrook has A Company execute a deft flanking attack with considerable direct-fire support (*Task Force* p258): '3 Platoon went to ground and put down very heavy fire on the house; 1 and 2 Platoons moved around, shooting as they came.'
>
> Which may describe Platoon battle-drills, but not this particular battle! And Bishop and Witherow write (p92): 'The Argentinians defended hard, but the three-to-one imbalance and the Paras' superior firepower overwhelmed them. Most of the Argentinian defenders were killed or wounded in the attack.'
>
> The highest estimate of Argentinian dead as a result of this engagement I have heard is two or three.
>
> The effects that such stories help to produce are very important. A Company's task is made to look a difficult one when it was in fact practically a walkover. Their achievement in the battle is therefore made to look the more astounding. And as a result, if a more critical officer argues that the British army ought to reform its tactical training, it is easy for the more complacent to point to the magnificent results in the Falklands campaign – of which this episode is only one small example. (Fitz-Gibbon, 1995: 29)

18. See, for example, the *Daily Star* of 31 May 1982, '"H" is for Hero', or the same paper's 15 June edition which prominently features a picture of Jones in a front-page photomontage headlined: 'They did not die in vain'. See also Taylor, 1991: 99–100 for more on this.

19. See also Lawrence *et al.*, 1988: 17; McManners, 1984: 202; Smith, 1984: 236.

20. The SAS patrol set down on the island's Fortuna Glacier had to be withdrawn in the face of adverse weather conditions. Two Wessex helicopters crashed in their efforts to extract them, and they were only evacuated thanks to the brilliant flying of Lieutenant Commander Ian Stanley in a third helicopter. Next day, 23 April, fifteen SAS men in five Gemini inflatables set off from HMS *Antrim* for Grass Island: two of the boats suffered engine failure and though the other three made their target they had to be withdrawn later in the day when ice splinters, driven by the howling gale, punctured the inflatable cells in their craft. For a full account of the mission see Perkins, 1986; Hastings and Jenkins, 1983: 151–5; Sunday Times Insight Team, 1982: 142–8.

21. In his study of combat and identity in the First World War, *No Man's Land* (1979), Eric Leed noted: 'The sheer scale of technologically administered violence seemed to force the regression of combatants to forms of thought and action that were magical, irrational and mystic. Magic', he suggested, 'is an appropriate resort in situations where the basis of survival could not be guaranteed by any available technology' (Leed, 1979: 128). Paul Fussell notes that in the First World War: 'no front-line soldier or officer was without his amulet, and every tunic pocket became a reliquary' (Fussell, 1975: 114). See also Charlwood, 1956: 144–5 for an insight into the elaborate superstitions operating in Bomber Command during the Second World War.

22. As Steve Hughes, 2 Para's Medical Officer noted: 'There was always the superstition, almost a religion among the soldiers, that offending against some moral or higher code would bring retribution. They thought that people who behaved outside what they regarded as the norm became somehow marked, and that something would happen to them. They perceived a definite dividing line between good and bad on the battlefield' (qtd in McManners, 1993: 350).

23. See Fussell, 1975: 125–31.

24. 3 Para and 42 Commando were landed at Port San Carlos; 2 Para and 40 Commando at San Carlos. 45 Commando was also landed to secure helicopter landing facilities and a military hospital at the old Ajax Bay refrigeration plant.

25. For the effectiveness of this system see Bishop and Witherow, 1982: 20. Other notable binaries included a system of pairs governing the soldiers' rationing. On the march they carried sufficient rations for two days, and when they stopped to eat they had a choice of two ration packs. See Fox, 1982a: 89 for details of the meals. For more on rations see Hanrahan and Fox, 1982: 113–14.

26. These physical dualities embody what Claude Levi-Strauss called 'the logic of the concrete', transposing the abstract polarities which underpinned

the government's response to the conflict into a pattern of straightfor-ward physical binaries. For more detail on the logic of the concrete see Levi-Strauss, 1966.

27. For the sunrise/sunset imagery surrounding the death of 'H' Jones see Fox, 1982a: 170, 173, 174, 182.

28. Better still, Osvaldo Niella, Captain of the *Bahía Buen Suceso*, the ship which transported to South Georgia the men who provided the flashpoint for the dispute, Constantino Davidoff's scrap metal workers, suggested that the disputes which led to the war could all be traced back to the tango. As he told Martin Middlebrook:

> Yes, the workers fixed up a flagpole, only an improvised one three or four metres high, and put up an Argentine flag. It was nothing to do with me. The men seemed very pleased to be there. They would be making good money; also, one feels a bit more patriotic when one is away from home, particularly when one has arrived in a place which you feel belongs to your country. They were working hard during the day and had a bit of a party at night, with some drink and tango music under the flagpole. (qtd in Middlebrook 1989: 9)

See also Foster, 1990: 139–50.

29. Bishop and Witherow note that after the Exocet attack on HMS *Sheffield*, lectures on survival assumed 'a new urgency'. See Bishop and Witherow, 1982: 67–8.

30. See Hawkes, 1977: 88–9; Rimmon-Kenan, 1983: 29–42.

31. Similarly, Patrick Bishop's initial designation of Phillips as 'One of the most impressive members of 3 Para' is succeeded by a description of his 'brown muscular face' and 'powerful simian body' (Bishop and Witherow, 1982: 60). Compare these reductive representations of Phillips with Vincent Bramley's detailed study of his experiences in and his life after the Falklands in *Two Sides of Hell* (1994), where, for the first time, the man emerges as more than a function of the narrative and social agendas of others, as the agent and not merely the object of action. See Bramley, 1994: 44–7, 245–8.

32. See Fox, 1982a: 249–50. McKay does get a brief mention in the postscript (Fox, 1982a: 321–2).

33. Photographs from the war largely maintained the anonymity of the other ranks. See photo 37 in Adkin, 1992: 247. According to John Taylor, 'the transition from nameless to named, or invisible to seen ... was a business fraught with military and political implications'. Ordinarily the common soldiers could make this transition only by 'the acceptance of death in the national cause', whereupon they 'moved from being the nameless members of a team to a place of invincibility when their names were entered in the Roll of Honour' (Taylor, 1991: 97). See Jennings and Weale, 1996: 120 – the top photograph opposite shows the members of 3 Para's Anti-Tank platoon at Teal Inlet, yet names only those who were later killed on Mount Longdon.

34. See Fox, 1982a: 83, 132.

35. Adkin does mention Fox's role (Adkin, 1992: 265–6), though this is hardly surprising as he uses Fox's account as one of the key sources for his information about the battle. Italo Piaggi notes that 'dos periodistas' were present at the surrender but gives neither of them a role in negotiating the details (Speranza and Cittadini, 1997: 155–6).

36. See Bramley, 1994: *passim*; Fitz-Gibbon, 1995: 127–31, *passim*; Frost, 1983: 59–95; Keeble, 1985: 139–44; Speranza, 1997: 156–7. As Italo Piaggi told Graciela Speranza, after he surrendered to 2 Para's Chris Keeble:

> Keeble expresó sus felicitaciones por la resistencia opuesta por las fuerzas argentinas y me confesó ahí mismo que había sufrido doscientos cincuenta bajas durante el ataque. Me dijo textualmente: 'Yo pensaba desayunar el 28 a la mañana en Goose Green, pero ustedes nos obligaron a combatir 24 horas más de lo previsto'. (Speranza, 1997: 156)

> (Chris Keeble expressed his admiration at the resistance put up by the Argentine forces and confessed to me at the same time that he had sustained 250 casualties during the assault. He told me parenthetically: 'I had intended to have breakfast in Goose Green on the morning of the 28th but you obliged me to fight for 24 hours more than I had foreseen'.)

For Argentine views on the high command's incompetence see Speranza and Cittadini, 1997: 183.

37. See Weston, 1989: 185–7.

38. It wasn't only his regiment that came up trumps: the Guards Association of Australasia invited Weston to Australia for an all-expenses-paid goodwill visit, and it was during this trip that he was first conscious of the new man emerging from the wreckage of the old: 'For the first time since I'd been injured, I began to relax on my own and to enjoy meeting new people at gatherings. I had begun to realize that I could face up to others on my own terms and be me Simon – not just a burned face' (Weston, 1989: 159).

39. The war was, ultimately, the salvation of Ken Lukowiak's life. Though post-traumatic stress disorder resulting from his experiences there precipitated the breakdown of his marriage, the collapse of his subsequent relationships, drug dependency and a prison term, his salvation comes from writing about their cause: 'Why was I the way I was, with my constant mood changes, my sudden outbursts of violence, my lonely moments of depression? Then I picked up a pen. I wrote these words: "The shelling had stopped. We got to our feet and continued to move forward." My writings, which have now grown into this book, had begun' (Lukowiak, 1993: x).

40. 'I was especially moved by the bravery of Bob Lawrence and his astonishing determination to overcome the severe injuries he sustained' (Arthur, 1985: x).

41. 'I had to fight hard when I came back to England for everything that I wanted' (Lawrence, 1985: 305).

42. Philip Williams noted how this point was driven home during his training with the Scots Guards: 'we were getting lectures on the past glories of our regiment, and supposedly being impressed by the battle honours gained at the Somme and El Alamein. The lecturer kept stressing the number of Guards who'd been killed and it struck me then that to be dead was much better than coming back alive' (Williams, 1990: 18).

43. See Wood, 1987: 54–7, 72.

44. See Wood, 1987: 46–7; 50, 67. See also Lawrence *et al.* 1988: 'I felt I'd done my job for the system, and if only the system would do its job as well as I had done mine, with the same degree of sacrifice, I would be looked after an awful lot better' (93).

45. For Lawrence's account of his part in the battle see Lawrence *et al.* 1988: 23–33.

46. 'When thousands of fighting troops suddenly march into your house to tell you, with the barrel of a gun stuck up your nose, that you must no longer speak English, but Spanish, you have a right to be defended by any civilized nation' (Lawrence *et al.*, 1988: 192).

47. Paul Greengrass' 1988 film loosely based on Williams' experiences was appropriately titled *Resurrected*.

48. See Williams, 1990: 112–16.

49. The influence of *Robinson Crusoe* (1719) is clear here. In Defoe's novel it is the cannibal's footprint that exposes how fragile are the physical and psychological defences that Crusoe has erected against the irruptions of nature. Here, through the symbol of the footprint, the destabilising influence is traced to Williams himself – the enemy is within.

50. See Williams, 1990: 35, 39, 44, *passim*.

51. 'I couldn't feel a thing, numb all over. You can't imagine how comfortable that was, just feeling nothing. I really felt like staying there, and I don't know what made me change my mind': 'It's been arranged that you have regular visits from a military PR from Preston. He'll handle the press for you, so you'll have nothing to worry about. Just remember, say nothing to anyone unless the PR approves. Nothing, understand?' (Williams, 1990: 47, 71).

52. For an accessible account of the early history of the islands see Honeywell and Pearce, 1982: 23–36. For details on the disputes about title to the islands see Beck, 1983: 6–24; Bologna, 1983: 39–48; Goebel, 1982; Gustafson, 1988; Myhre, 1983: 25–8.

53. For more on this see Crawley, 1984; Makin, 1983: 49–68; Potash, 1980.

54. See Burns, 1987: 49, for an account of the demonstration.

55. For an analysis of Catholic nationalism in Argentina see Burns, 1987: 68–73.

56. During the war the Catholic Weekly, *Esquiu*, featured on its cover a picture of 'a map of Argentina surrounded by a rosary and the slogan, "We have a powerful weapon"' (Burns, 1987: 70). See also the *Financial Times*, 12 May 1982.

57. See Bramley, 1994: 71–6, 84, 99–100, *passim*; Kon, 1983: 65, 66, 73–6. Had Argentina's professional soldiers put as much energy into repulsing the British as they did into pursuing and persecuting their own conscripts, had they defended their line as steadfastly as they guarded their status and privileges, then the battle for Stanley might have proved far tougher. The maltreatment of the conscripts by their officers remains a continuing source of fierce debate in Argentina after the war. See 'El Soldado fue estaqueado', *La Voz*, 4 March 1984, np.

58. In a profile of Mario Benjamín Menendez, Galtieri's appointee as the military governor of las Islas Malvinas, Augustín Bottinelli drew explicit parallels between Menendez's role in the dirty war, particularly his defeat of the ERP (Ejercito Revolucionario Popular, Popular Revolutionary Army) in Tucuman Province in 1975 and his current position in the Malvinas:

> Era 1975 y aquel coronel estaba viviendo una guerra cruel, dura, sin leyes. Una guerra contra un enemigo capaz de cualquier recurso, de cualquier trampa ... Hoy, Mario Benjamín Menendez es general y está en otro frente, en otra batalla. Ahora, como dicen los militares, frente a una guerra más convencional, pero tan o más difícil que aquella. (Bottinelli, 1982: 62).

> (It was 1975 and that colonel was living through a cruel war, hard, without laws. A war against an enemy capable of any action, any trick ... Today, Mario Benjamín Menendez is a general and this is another front in another battle. Now, as the military say, he is heading a more conventional war, but no more difficult for that.)

For more details on the dirty war and the fate of the disappeared see CONANEP, 1986; Crawley, 1984: 421–39; Graham-Yooll, 1981; Simpson and Bennett, 1985. For one man's testimony of his own disappearance see Timerman, 1982.

59. Mansilla Fidel recalled his own departure for the islands:

> Nadie nos había dicho que ibamos a la guerra. Un día cuando nos dirigiamos a 'Rancho' ... nos hacen ir al pañol, donde nos entregan el casco, la mochila, carpa, fusíl, cargadores, y luego de ello, sí, nos dejan ir al rancho. Luego nos dicen que hebamos a realizar un simulacro y nos cargan en un Avion Hércules, en el mismo se cargaron Jeeps, camiones, cañones, municiones, y otro tipo de armamento. Recién cuando estabamos en pleno vuelo, nos dicen que ibamos con destino a las Islas Malvinas, a algunas se les escaparon unas lágrimas, la mayoria éstabamos muy nerviosos. (Fidel, 1995: 8)

> (Nobody told us that we were going to war. One day when we were on our way to the canteen they made us go to the square where they gave us a helmet, a rucksack, tent, rifles, charges and then, yes, they let us go to the canteen. Then they told us that we were going on an

exercise, and they loaded us into a Hercules, in the same one they loaded jeeps, trucks, artillery, shells and other kinds of weapons. Newly settled on the plane they told us that our destination would be the Malvinas, and some shed tears – the majority were very apprehensive.)

60. See Bramley 1994: 11 for an account of some of the inadequate equipment issued to the Argentine conscripts. It should be noted, however, that Argentine boots were considered far superior to the British DMS (Direct Moulded Soul) variety, 'made of compressed cardboard and leather', which were hopeless at keeping out the wet (Bramley, 1991: 48). See also Kevin Connery on 'the useless DMS boots' (qtd in Bramley, 1994: 152). British troops often stripped Argentine corpses of their boots, a practice which, on occasions, as Stephen Newland of the Royal Marines recalled, had unexpected consequences: 'In the middle of all this shit flying around, Tony Koleszar, my LMG (light machine gun) gunner, decided he needed a new pair of boots. As he was moving forward, he spotted this trench with this dead spic in it and because they looked the right size, Tony got in and started taking the bloke's boots off. All of a sudden, the geezer sat up! Tony had instant heart failure. Somebody put the spic away; I don't know whether Tony did, but he scrubbed round the boots – he didn't fancy them after that!' (Newland, 1984: 258).
61. See also Bramley, 1994: 75.
62. See also Kevin Connery's testimony in Bramley, 1994: 131.
63. See Bramley, 1991: 208 for a similar response from the author on his return to Britain.
64. See Bramley, 1994: 253, 255.
65. See Burns, 1987: 101–35 for a detailed account of the transition process.
66. For a parallel British view see Bramley, 1994: 46–8.
67. For the origins of the military's central place in Argentine politics and society see Burns, 1987: 1–11; Makin, 1983: 49–68; and Potash, 1980. Writing in *Clarín* eight years after the war had finished, Roberto Russell noted: 'El intento agónico de recomposición del orden autoritario mediante la invasión de las islas Malvinas produjo contrariamente a lo pensado por sus promotores, la fractura definitiva de la autocracia' (Fernandez, 1990: 23) (The agonised attempt to restore authoritarian order through the invasion of the Malvinas produced the opposite of what its authors had intended, the final fracture of autocracy).

CHAPTER 5

1. This tendency had its origins in the view, widespread among the military experts who appeared on news and current affairs programmes, that the Argentine forces would be a pushover. Brian Perrett claimed that the Argentine Navy was 'essentially a coastal defence force': Admiral Antoine Sanguinetti of the French Navy was less flattering, declaring that 'the

Argentine navy was fit only for scrap', prophetically adding that '[i]t would only need two torpedoes for the Argentine navy to be sent packing' (Perrett, 1982: 49; *Guardian*, 17 April 1982: 2). If anything, their Army was accorded less respect. The 29 April edition of the current affairs programme *TV Eye* featured a discussion between Rear Admiral Martin Wemyss, Air Vice Marshal Stewart Menaul and Lieutenant Colonel Colin Mitchell which, among other topics, assessed the likely performance of the Argentine Army:

> They're national service boys, ten thousand, who aren't even a formation ... They are very untrained, they've never seen a shot fired in anger, none of their officers have ... I should think the morale of the Argentines in the Falklands is absolute zero now ...
> And I should think the appearance of ten Royal Marines will be enough to make them have this dysentery we've heard about in the newspapers ...
> They don't know where we're coming. They don't know where we're going to land, they don't know what we're going to do. I think they're in complete confusion. (qtd in Adams, 1986: 89)

2. The soldiers who fought and defeated the Argentinians were generally far less dismissive. Robert Lawrence claimed to have been told by 'some Paras who had been at Goose Green and Darwin' that the Argentine resistance was flimsy:

> 'get within two hundred metres of them and they'll run away. And if you hit a machine-gun sangar with an anti-tank weapon, it will stop.'
> ... The troops we were to face at Tumbledown, however, were extremely well-trained and well-equipped marines in their mid-twenties, who had had recent fighting experience in the Argentinian civil war. They had had years of aggression. (Lawrence *et al.*, 1988: 24)

3. 3 Para suffered more than 50 per cent casualties in the battle for Mount Longdon.

4. Secluded in his cabin on the night before he sailed for the Falklands, Kevin Connery's fears were centred squarely on himself, on his ability to live up to his own and his colleagues expectations of him. See Bramley, 1994: 16.

5. Peter Jenkins and David Fairhall counselled caution in the *Guardian*, to no effect, and when Ray Whitney attempted to do likewise during the First Emergency Parliamentary Debate he was accused of 'defeatism' and, according to Anthony Barnett, 'subjected throughout to an intense and furious barrage of heckling and disruption from his own [Conservative] side of the gangway' (Barnett, 1982: 40). For an edited version of Whitney's speech, minus the interjections, see Morgan, 1982: 14.

6. For a detailed and lengthy expression of these particular concerns and the '[s]orrow, shame and anger' they occasioned (Morgan, 1982: 33), see

Morgan, 1982: 4–21, 26–70. See also Lord Whitelaw: 'I think what was in our minds was: We have to do something, and if we don't send a Task Force, what else shall we do? Parliament was going to meet on Saturday, we were going to have a very hostile House of Commons, a hostile Press and many criticisms of what had happened. And if we hadn't reacted very sharply then we probably wouldn't have survived as a government' (Bilton and Kosminsky, 1989: 295). For Margaret Thatcher's responsiveness to public opinion see Thatcher, 1993: 181. For the humiliation of surrender see Lou Armour in Bilton and Kosminsky, 1989: 233.

Over the weeks the search for a political scapegoat shifted onto the BBC whose 'even-handed' coverage of events drew a hostile response from MPs. See Harris, 1983: 73–91, in particular his account of the grilling given to George Howard (Chairman of the BBC) and Alasdair Milne (Director General Designate of the BBC) by the Tory Media Committee, Harris, 1983: 84–5.

7. The *Iliad* offers an obvious example. Women are prized trophies of conquest, and many of the Greek's woes stem from Agamemnon's decision to strip Achilles of the woman he was awarded as 'a tribute from the ranks', Briseis (Homer, 1957: 27). See also Homer, 1957: 23–8. Hector visualises Andromache's fate at the fall of Troy, 'dragged off in tears by some Achaean man-at-arms to slavery' (Homer, 1957: 129). The origins of the siege of Troy lie in sexual discord, Paris' abduction of Helen from Menelaus, and before that the dispute between the three goddesses, Hera, Aphrodite and Athena, over the Apple of Discord, resolved in the Judgment of Paris (Zimmerman, 1964: 143).

More recently there has been a wide array of studies of women, sex and war, most notably Bethke-Elshtain, 1987; Squier *et al.*, 1992.

8. Among Australian soldiers and writers of the Second World War, '[r]obust sexuality in alliance with combat experience … is seen as the trademark of true manhood' (Gerster, 1987: 184).

9. The status of war as the ultimate affirmation of masculinity has long been used to pressure the uncertain or the unwilling into military service, and as Robin Gerster points out, some of the most ardent proponents of this moral blackmail have been women, particularly during the First World War when:

the pressure on men to do their masculine duty was immense, and often emanated from the women themselves. The coercive methods of women's recruiting groups ranged from the sending of white feathers to those considered fit for battle, to poems which none-too-subtly challenged the masculinity of the 'shirker'. A poem entitled 'The Test' asks of the man who is 'fearful of the bayonet's stabbing bite' …

> 'Will she who is worth the winning,
> She who is yet to be won,
> Take to her marble bosom, one who has turned
> from a gun?'   (Gerster, 1987: 50)

10. The systemic nature of Argentine machismo is evident in the law of *patria potestad*, which, until it was repealed in 1985, was 'perhaps the most acute expression for many years of the male dominance of society and the subjugation of women. The *patria* gave exclusive rights to a father over a child's education, travel and finances, effectively separating the wife from any control over her own life and that of her family' (Burns, 1987: 187). For a more savage review of Argentine machismo ('a society spewing on itself') see Naipaul, 1980: 148–51. See also Fox, *Antarctica and the South Atlantic*: 'The claim to the Falklands, the islands of the "Andean Loop", of the Scotia Sea and the Antarctic Peninsula form part of the "machismo" of Argentine nationalism, the virile image of a youthful and increasingly powerful South American state' (Fox, 1985: 326).

11. See Winchester, 1983: 29–31.

12. Burns notes that 'during the fight against subversion ... the military often dismissed political dissidence as a symbol of sexual degeneracy' (Burns, 1987: 83).

13. Francis Pym commended the fortitude of the kelpers in the face of their ordeal: 'The Falkland Islanders have reacted with courage and dignity to the rape of their islands' (Morgan, 1982: 29). On the islands themselves John Smith took a similar view of events: 'The town has been raped brutally and without warning' (Smith, 1984: 38). Cecilio Morales, writing in *The Washington Post*, could scarcely believe the British line: 'one would think that the fair Britannia was a vestal virgin whose flower had just been lost to savage rapists' (Morales, 1982: 7).

14. Both historical and more overtly fictional treatments of the war betray a macabre fascination with soldiers who sustain injuries to the groin. In Walter Winward's *Rainbow Soldiers* (1985) the comparative quality of the opposing armies is signified by their relative virility. (The British cover of the book has an illustration of a soldier seated on a rock, smoking, his rifle protruding from between his legs.) While the sexual exploits of the various members of 3 Platoon, D Company are extensively detailed the Argentine conscripts' military inadequacy is implied in their sexual immaturity: 'Was this who they were expected to fight? He didn't look old enough to get a hard on' (Winward, 1985: 302). For the platoon's sexual exploits see Winward, 1985: 183–4, 243, *passim*. The defeat or disablement of both British and Argentine soldiers is correspondingly registered in the extinguishing of their sexual prowess. In 3 Platoon's climactic assault on the Argentinian's defensive positions one of its members, Davey Binns, is 'ripped from crotch to armpit' by a mortar shell, while another, Non-Legless Jones, is wounded 'with a bullet in the groin' (Winward, 1985: 416, 445). Stung by their losses, the platoon advances up Wireless Ridge threatening the enemy with immediate emasculation: 'those friggin' Argies had better watch their balls' (Winward, 1985: 447). One Argentine soldier unable to do so was Beto Jordan-Arditti who, having trodden on a mine, has, like Goering, no balls left to keep an eye on: 'the Argentine anti-personnel mine beneath them exploded as one of them stepped on it and blasted the three to smithereens, hurling Beto, as metal entered his groin and abdomen,

sideways, where he landed on a second mine that finished the job'
   (Winward, 1985: 434). See also Kon, 1983: 185.
15. 'In most armies, "hazing" contains some element of sexual innuendo to
   personalize the insults – based on male-dominated heterosexuality. US
   Army training in particular emphasizes masculinity and macho ideals –
   far more than British Army training (which puts more emphasis on
   self-reliance and initiative), although both stress what might be called
   "supermasculinity"' (McManners, 1993: 114). See also Abbot, 1981:
   78–80 for a startling account of life in modern America's penal system
   where the physical realities of sexual domination more often replace the
   purely verbal formulae.
16. For similar images and episodes see McGowan and Hands, 1983: 110–11,
   169.
17. John Costello notes: 'the very success of the classic Greek "phalanx"
   depended on the front-rank and rear-rank men who called each other
   "comrades in arms". As one British general observed, "Being what they
   were, they were probably found in one another's arms more often than
   would accord with modern ideas of military discipline"' (Costello, 1985:
   159). For other accounts of the uses of homosexual bonds within the
   military see Rowse, 1977.
18. In an effort to ensure the survival of as many men as possible, everybody
   was taught basic first-aid on the voyage south, more specifically, as
   Hugh McManners recalled, the techniques of 'external heart-massage,
   mouth to mouth resuscitation and putting up drips, either intravenous
   or intra-rectal, introducing a new cry onto the modern battlefield:
   "Medic, Medic ... shove it up my arse for goodness sake!"' (McManners,
   1984: 15–16).
19. After submitting an early draft of the play, Peter Goodchild, the BBC's
   Head of Plays, came to see him to express his reservations about and
   propose certain amendments to the script:

   > These were his points:
   > (a) He felt 'unhappy' at those parts of the script that referred to what
   >   I have called the Prime Minister's private and instinctive self: for
   >   instance, her writing in her own hand to the relations of all
   >   servicemen killed during the fighting; her weeping quietly on the
   >   loss of the *Sheffield*; her showing private grief of any sort. He had
   >   no objection to the bellicose Iron Lady of the public scenes.
   > (b) He felt equally 'unhappy' at those speeches in the script that
   >   described the Falklands Conflict as being fought to resist
   >   aggression, and thereby in a long tradition of such resistance
   >   that we, as a nation, have manifested again and again since the
   >   sixteenth century.
   > (c) He 'suggested' that I might consider rewriting some war-cabinet
   >   scenes to show Ministers taking into account what he called 'the
   >   coming election' when making military and political decisions
   >   during the crisis, and tailoring those decisions to the object of

winning that election. It was, he said, naive of me not to imagine that such things might have happened.

(d) He 'suggested' that I might write in a good deal more opposition to the Government's policies of sending the Task Force and fighting a hot war than I already had – in Parliament, in the press and country.

(e) He suggested that more explanation of Galtieri's frequent drunkenness might usefully be added. (Curteis, 1987: 25–6)

When Curteis refused to make the proposed changes, the BBC axed the play. The BBC denied, with equal vehemence, that its cancellation of the production was in any way politically motivated. Michael Grade, then Director of Programmes, claimed that the production had been abandoned because of the 'laughably poor quality of the script'. Indeed, far from impugning the Prime Minister, Grade claimed that the cancellation of the script had been made in her best interests: 'I respect the Prime Minister. All the alterations we proposed to Curteis had been *to protect Mrs Thatcher!*' (Curteis, 1987: 44). In a letter to the *Sunday Telegraph*, Bill Cotton, Managing Director of BBC Television, concurred with Grade: 'The Falklands Play ... was referred to Director of Programmes, Michael Grade, and myself, to read in July 1986. It was the first draft of the script seen by the BBC. We separately concluded that the script was, as a drama, not yet good enough for the investment of the £1 million necessary to finance such a production. That was a proper professional decision, one of the dozens made each year in assessing the potential, readiness and cost of major drama projects' (*Sunday Telegraph*, 22 February 1987: 12).

In the face of this straightforward attack on the quality of his work, Curteis spends much of his introduction questioning the BBC's qualifications for making such a decision, dividing those involved in the controversy over the play into two opposed camps: the elect, fellow travellers on the Tory right wing who recognise the essential quality of Curteis' work, and the philistines, to whom a play is no more than a platform for propaganda, a sheaf of papers or a purely commercial proposition. It is the timeless dichotomy between the Cultured and the Barbarians, between Us and Them, and it underpins Curteis' attempt to impose on the debate about the play the same simple moral oppositions which he saw manifested in the conflict itself.

20. This carefully constructed position on the fight for the play was ruthlessly deconstructed by Malcolm Deas in one of the very few independent reviews of the play, published in the *Times Literary Supplement*, in which he suggested that: 'A close reading of the script might lead one to conclude that for reasons of taste as well as of timing, [the filming of the play] was cancelled on pressure from Conservative Central Office' (Deas, 1987: 512).

21. The Argentine public are, by turns, '*surging masses*' or a '*mob*' (Curteis, 1987: 127, 81 respectively). They are fickle, hysterical, atavistic, as extreme in their support for the regime as they are violent in their later

opposition to it. The British, on the other hand, are seen collectively only once, farewelling the capital ships at Portsmouth, '*singing, swaying well-wishers waving the Union Jack*', united in their convictions, resolute in their support and restrained in its expression, a vision of moral, social and psychological balance (Curteis, 1987: 113–14). Yet significantly, this same image of the quayside crowds at Portsmouth was identified by Morrison and Tumber as a beloved set-piece used by the government and the media to suggest an untenably 'broad national support' for the dispatch and aims of the task force. See Morrison and Tumber, 1988: 305.

22. See Rimmon-Kenan, 1983: 34–5.
23. See Curteis, 1987: 58–60.
24. The *Guardian* and the *Financial Times* were the only notable dissenters from the official supportive line.
25. It was only by switching off and letting his training take over that Kevin Connery could deny his common humanity, his identification with the enemy, and so sustain the momentum of attack in the bitter hand-to-hand fighting on Mount Longdon. Indeed, Connery's response to the Argentinian seems calculated as much to silence as it is to kill him, to deny the common bonds of family and culture that bind him to this man, and so retain the professional detachment that enables him to do his job. See Bramley, 1994: 153.
26. See also Bramley, 1991: 193, *passim*; Fox, 1982a: 287, 291.
27. See the response of the Under Secretary of State for the Armed Forces (Jerry Wiggin) to written questions about existing links between Argentina, the British military and the defence industry (Morgan, 1982: 71–2). See also tables detailing UK military equipment sales to Argentina in Honeywell and Pearce, 1982: 131–2.
28. See Bramley, 1994: 88, 89, 96, 97, 131, 184–5, 205, 208, 209, 226, *passim*.
29. See Marwick, 1990: 282–3. See also Cummings' cartoon, 'Our all conquering Field Marshal ... ', *Sunday Express*, 26 June 1982.
30. The revisionist view of the war began with Gavshon and Rice, 1984, which offered a forensic analysis of the government's decision to sink the Argentine cruiser, *General Belgrano*, and the consequences of that order. Two further books pursued the government over the Belgrano affair, Dalyell, 1983 (later followed by two more books on the same subject) and Gould, 1984; Carr, 1984, detailed the government's indifference towards the emotional and material needs of the task force families during and after the war; Bilton and Kosminsky, 1989, a companion piece to their 1987 documentary *The Falklands War – The Untold Story* (Yorkshire Television, 1987), was the first text originating in England to give the ordinary Argentine combatants and their families a voice, and to directly address the difficulties suffered by veterans of the war adjusting to ordinary life.
31. Jennifer Selway, reviewing the series for the *Observer*, thought that it offered new, historical perspectives on the war and described it as 'cool and analytical' (*Observer*, 12 January 1992: 59).

32. There had been a similar row a little over a year earlier concerning the decision not to proceed with Ian Curteis' *The Falklands Play*. See Curteis, 1987: 17–52 for his version of the BBC 'conspiracy' to foist its left-wing views on the nation and deny it access to the true, heroic account of the conflict: 'This was not shallow jingoism, but the dramatic rising to the surface once more of values and issues that we on these islands have cared most profoundly about down the centuries, and on which our civilized freedom rests' (Curteis, 1987: 15).

33. See Bramley, 1991: 144 for the original allegations. Jennings offer a more detailed account of the alleged events, and the subsequent investigations, Jennings and Weale, 1996: 163–5, 189–91.

34. See Jennings and Weale, 1996: 177–9 for an account of the 'battle' fought out between newspapers for and against the investigation: 'In essence, those opposed to it – spearheaded by the *Daily Mail* – argued that no public interest was served by conducting an expensive investigation into isolated incidents that had happened in exceptional circumstances more than a decade before; those in favour – led by *Today* and the *Independent* – believed that honour and justice demanded a resolution of the allegations'. In the event, after an eighteen-month enquiry, Barbara Mills QC, the Director of Public Prosecutions, decided that 'the evidence is not such as to afford a realistic prospect of conviction of any person for a criminal offence' (Jennings and Weale, 1996: 179, 180).

35. Peter Clarke claimed that over the period of the Thatcher government '[b]y any test, from statistical surveys of relative incomes to the striking reappearance of beggars on the street, Britain became a more unequal society' (Clarke, 1996: 400).

36. For a more detailed consideration of the policies and effects of Thatcherism there is now a bewildering array of sources. See Clarke, 1996: 358–400; Hall and Jacques, 1983; Jenkins, 1987; Marwick, 1990: 278–396; Young, 1989. Gray points out that Thatcherism destroyed the very ideal of Britain it was ostensibly committed to preserving:

> Thatcher was possessed by a vision of a country whose institutions had been ruthlessly reshaped but whose character remained miraculously unaltered. Markets were injected into hospitals and universities, council tenants were chivvied into buying their homes, public services were scorned as feckless repositories of unthinking compassion, and job insecurity was intensified for a host of occupations and professions. No corner of British life was left undisturbed.
>
> Despite all the social dislocations that these policies produced, the conservatives imagined Britain would still somehow be the place mocked in the post-war Ealing films, a nation of stoical conformists bicycling impassively around changeless village greens.
>
> This picture may have had a faint semblance of reality in the Britain of the 1950s and 1960s that had been moulded into something approaching one nation by the reforming Labour government of 1945. By the time Major left office, it was little more than a confection

of the Tory media. In combination with vast changes in the world economy, Conservative policies had undone the social and family structures that underpinned pre-Thatcher Britain. (Gray, 1997: 12)

37. In 1994, Paul Addison added a new postscript to his history of British domestic politics through the Second World War, *The Road to 1945*:

Whatever Mrs Thatcher's intentions when she arrived at Number Ten, I did not imagine that any government had the power to repeal the post-war settlement. I was wrong, of course, society had changed. If I were writing *The Road to 1945* today, my account would be overshadowed by the knowledge that the brave new world of Attlee, Beveridge and Keynes was never the enduring structure it appeared to be. It was more like a Ministry of Works prefab, intended for some deserving young couple at the end of the war. Mr and Mrs Tebbitt (let us say) were extremely grateful for it at the time, and later on it was used by the council to provide emergency accommodation for the homeless. But finally it was bulldozed away in spite of many pleas to preserve it as a memorial to a more civilised era: and with it there departed the essential wartime vision of a society in which the state maintained a framework of social justice for all. (Addison 1994: 280)

38. See also Bramley, 1994: 221–2, 245, *passim*; Lawrence *et al.*, 1988: 75–6, 94–5, 118–19, *passim*. For a parallel Argentine view see Bramley, 1994: 228.
39. See also Bramley, 1991: 208–12; Bramley, 1994: 237–40, 247, 248, *passim*; Williams, 1990: 72ff.

CONCLUSION

1. Donald Davie claimed that during the Falklands War there was a renewed 'recognition, by the nation at large, of martial valour as indeed a value, and one that we have giggled about for too long' (Davie, 1983: 1).
2. Not least in the organisation of press and public relations. According to Lieutenant-Commander Arthur A. Humphries, a 'public affairs specialist' with the US Navy: 'the Falklands War shows us how to make certain that government policy is not undermined by the way a war is reported' (qtd in MacArthur, 1992: 138). According to MacArthur, Humphries' 'basic recommendations for military public relations ... may well have served as a partial blueprint for Operation Desert Storm' (MacArthur, 1992: 139). For more information on how the lessons from the Falklands War were taken up and used in the Gulf, see MacArthur, 1992.

Works Cited

Abbot, Jack (1981) *In the Belly of the Beast* (New York: Random House).

Adams, Valerie (1986) *The Media and the Falklands War* (London: Macmillan).

Addison, Paul (1994) *The Road to 1945*, revised edition (London: Pimlico).

Adkin, Mark (1992) *Goose Green. A Battle is Fought to be Won* (Barnsley: Pen and Sword).

Anderson, Benedict (1983) *Imagined Communities*, revised edition [1991] (London: Verso).

Arthur, Max (1985) *Above All, Courage. The Falklands Front Line: First-hand Accounts* (London: Sidgwick and Jackson).

Auerbach, Erich (1953) *Mimesis: The Representation of Reality in Western Literature*, translated by Willard Trask (Princeton: Princeton University Press).

Aulich, James (ed.) (1992) *Framing the Falklands: Nationhood, Culture and Identity* (Milton Keynes: Open University Press).

Barnett, Anthony (1982) *Iron Britannia* (London: Allison and Busby).

Baron, Ana (1982) 'Las Mentiras de los Ingleses', *Gente*, 29 April 1982, No. 875.

Barrell, John (1972) *The Idea of Landscape and the Sense of Place: An Approach to the Poetry of John Clare* (Cambridge: Cambridge University Press).

Barthes, Roland (1973) *Mythologies*, translated by Annette Lavers (London: Paladin).

Bartlett, Frederick (1972) *Remembering: A Study in Experimental and Social Psychology* (Cambridge: Cambridge University Press).

Baudrillard, Jean (1995) *The Gulf War Did Not Take Place*, published in French 1991, translated with an introduction by Paul Patton (Sydney: Power Publications).

Beck, Peter (1983) 'The Anglo-Argentine Dispute over Title to the Falkland Islands: Changing British Perceptions on Sovereignty Since 1910', *Millennium: Journal of International Studies*, Vol. 12, No. 1.

Bell, Steve (1983) *The IF ... Chronicles* (London: Methuen).

Bethke-Elshtain, Jean (1987) *Women and War* (Brighton: The Harvester Press).

Bilton, Michael and Peter Kosminsky (1989) *Speaking Out: Untold Stories from the Falklands War* (London: Andre Deutsch).

Bishop, Patrick and John Witherow (1982) *The Winter War: The Falklands* (London: Quartet).

Blakeway, Denys (1992) *The Falklands War* (London: Channel 4).

Bloch, Mark (1954) *The Historian's Craft*, translated by Peter Putnam (Manchester: Manchester University Press).

Blunden, Edmund (1934) *The Mind's Eye* (London: Jonathan Cape).

Bologna, Alfredo Bruno (1983) 'Argentine Claims to the Malvinas Under International Law', *Millennium: Journal of International Studies*, Vol. 12, No. 1.

Bottinelli, Agustín (1982) 'La Otra Guerra del General Menendez', 29 April 1982, No. 875.

Bowra, C.M. (1972) *Homer* (London: Duckworth).

Bramley, Vincent (1991) *Excursion to Hell. Mount Longdon: A Universal Story of Battle* (London: Bloomsbury).

Bramley, Vincent (1994) *Two Sides of Hell* (London: Bloomsbury).

Brooke, Rupert (1915) 'Peace', *Men Who March Away: Poems of the First World War*, edited with an introduction by I.M. Parsons (London: Chatto and Windus [1965]).

Brown, David (1989) *The Royal Navy and the Falklands War* (London: Arrow).

Burns, Jimmy (1987) *The Land That Lost its Heroes: Argentina, the Falklands and Alfonsín* (London: Bloomsbury).

Calder, Angus (1969) *The People's War; Britain 1939–45* (London: Jonathan Cape).

Calder, Angus (1991) *The Myth of the Blitz* (London: Jonathan Cape).

Calvocoressi, Peter (1978) *The British Experience 1945–75* (London: Bodley Head).

Carr, Jean (1984) *Another Story: Women and the Falklands War* (London: Hamish Hamilton).

Carr, Raymond (1977) *The Spanish Tragedy: The Civil War in Perspective* (London: Weidenfeld and Nicolson).

Charlton, Michael (1989) *The Little Platoon: Diplomacy and the Falklands Dispute* (London: Blackwell).

Charlwood, Don (1956) *No Moon Tonight* (Ringwood: Penguin).

Chibnall, Steve (1977) *Law and Order News: An Analysis of Crime Reporting in the British Press* (London: Tavistock).

Clarke, Peter (1996) *Hope and Glory: Britain 1900–1990* (London: Penguin).

Cockerill, Michael (1982) 'Whitehall and the Media War', *The Listener*, 21 October 1982.

COI (Central Office of Information) (1982) *Britain and the Falklands Crisis* (London: HMSO).

Coleridge, Samuel Taylor (1789) *The Rime of the Ancient Mariner*, *Poetical Works*, ed. E.H. Coleridge (London: Oxford Paperbacks, 1969).

CONANEP (1986) *Nunca Mas: A Report by Argentina's National Commission on Disappeared People* (London: Faber).

Costello, John (1985) *Love, Sex and War: Changing Values 1939–45* (London: Pan).

Crawley, Eduardo (1984) *A House Divided: Argentina 1880–1980* (London: Hurst).

Crick, Bernard (1992) *George Orwell: A Life*, new edition (London: Penguin).

Cunningham, Valentine (1988) *British Writers of the Thirties* (Oxford: Oxford University Press).

Curteis, Ian (1987) *The Falklands Play: A Television Play* (London: Hutchinson).

Dalyell, Tam (1983) *One Man's Falklands* (London: Cecil Woolf).

Davie, Donald (1983) 'Editorial', *PN Review*, 34, 10 (2).

Deas, Malcolm (1987) 'Between the Acts', review of *The Land that Lost its Heroes* by Jimmy Burns and *The Falklands Play* by Ian Curteis, *Times Literary Supplement*, 15 May 1987.

Defoe, Daniel (1965) *Robinson Crusoe* (London: Penguin).

Devereux, Eve (1992) *Book of World Flags* (London: New Burlington Books).

Dobson, Christopher, John Miller and Ronald Payne (1982) *The Falklands Conflict* (London: Coronet).

Donnelly, Peter (ed.) (1979) *Mrs Milburn's Diaries. An Englishwoman's Day-to-Day Reflections 1939–45* (London: Futura).

Dyer, Gwynne (1985) *War* (London: Bodley Head).

Ezard, John (1995) 'The Harsh Toll of Joybells', *Guardian Weekly*, 7 May 1995.

Fairhall, David (1982a) 'The Next Round Won't Be Plain Sailing', *Guardian*, 28 April 1982.

Fairhall, David (1982b) 'Battle Options in the South Atlantic Strategy', *Guardian*, 26 April 1982.

FCO (Foreign and Commonwealth Office) (1982) *The Falkland Islands: The Facts* (London: HMSO).

Featherstone, Simon (1995) *War Poetry: An Introductory Reader* (London: Routledge).

Fernandez, Roxana (1990) 'La Cuenta Regresiva', *Clarín*, 24 March 1990.

Fidel, Mansilla (1995) 'Las Malvinas Testimonios', *Periodico Gaucho Rivero*, November 1995.

Fiske, John (1990) *Introduction to Communication Studies*, second edition (London: Routledge).

Fitz-Gibbon, Spencer (1995) *Not Mentioned in Despatches: The History and Mythology of the Battle for Goose Green* (Cambridge: Lutterworth).

Foster, Kevin (1990) 'The Falklands War: Irony as Exposure and Coverup', *Troops Versus Tropes: War and Literature*, ed. Evelyn J. Hinz (Winnipeg: Mosaic).

Foster, Kevin (1992) 'The Falklands War: A Critical View of Information Policy', *Defence and the Media in Time of Limited War*, ed. Peter R. Young (London: Frank Cass).

Foster, Kevin (1993) 'Heroism and Hegemony in the Falklands War', *Meridian*, Vol. 12, No. 1.

Fox, Robert (1982a) *Eyewitness Falklands: A Personal Account of the Falklands Campaign* (London: Methuen).

Fox, Robert (1982b) 'On Board S.S. *Canberra*', *The Listener*, 22 April 1982.

Fox, Robert (1985) *Antarctica and the South Atlantic: Discovery, Development and Dispute* (London: BBC).

Freud, Sigmund (1953) *Civilisation, War and Death*, ed. John Rickman (London: Hogarth Press).

Frost, Major General John (1983) *2 Para Falklands: The Battalion at War* (London: Sphere).

Frye, Northrop (1957) *Anatomy of Criticism: Four Essays* (Princeton: Princeton University Press).

Fussell, Paul (1975) *The Great War and Modern Memory* (New York: Oxford University Press).

Fussell, Paul (1982) 'The War in Black and White', *The Boy Scout's Handbook and Other Observations* (Oxford: Oxford University Press).

G, Norberto (1982) 'Estoy Orgulloso, Señor, Quería Venir', *Gente*, 8 April 1982, No. 872.

Gavshon, Arthur and Desmond Rice (1984) *The Sinking of the Belgrano* (London: New English Library).

Gerster, Robin (1987) *Big-Noting: The Heroic Theme in Australian War Writing* (Melbourne: Melbourne University Press).

Goebel, Julius (1982) *The Struggle for the Falkland Islands*, ed. J.C. Metford (New Haven: Yale University Press).

Gould, Diana (1984) *On the Spot: The Sinking of the Belgrano* (London: Cecil Woolf).

Graham-Yooll, Andrew (1981) *A Matter of Fear: Portrait of an Argentine Exile* (Westport CT: Lawrence Hill and Co.).

Gray, John (1997) 'Britain's Tories Flirting with Self-destruction', *Guardian Weekly*, 28 September 1997.

GUMG (Glasgow University Media Group) (1976) *Bad News* (London: Routledge and Kegan Paul).

GUMG (Glasgow University Media Group) (1980) *More Bad News* (London: Routledge and Kegan Paul).

GUMG (Glasgow University Media Group) (1985) *War and Peace News* (Milton Keynes: Open University Press).

Gustafson, Lowell S. (1988) *The Sovereignty Dispute Over the Falklands (Malvinas) Islands* (New York: Oxford University Press).

Hall, Stuart, Chas Critcher, Tony Jefferson, John Clarke and Brian Roberts (1978) *Policing the Crisis: Mugging, the State and Law and Order* (London: Macmillan).

Hall, Stuart and Martin Jacques (eds) (1983) *The Politics of Thatcherism* (London: Lawrence and Wishart).

Hanrahan, Brian and Robert Fox (1982) *'I Counted Them All Out and I Counted Them All Back': The Battle for the Falklands* (London: BBC).

Harris, Robert (1983) *Gotcha! The Media, the Government and the Falklands Crisis* (London: Faber and Faber).

Harrisson, Tom (1990) *Living Through the Blitz* (London: Penguin).

Hartley, John (1982) *Understanding News* (London: Methuen).

Hastings, Max and Simon Jenkins (1983) *The Battle for the Falklands* (London: Pan).

Hastings, Max (1984) *Overlord: D-Day and the Battle for Normandy* (London: Pan).

Hawkes, Terence (1977) *Structuralism and Semiotics* (London: Methuen).

HCDC (House of Commons Defence Committee First Report 1982–3) (1982) *The Handling of Press and Public Information During the Falklands Conflict*, Volumes I and II (London: HMSO).

Heidel, Gerardo (1982) 'Lo Ganado en el Campo de Batalla no Debía Perderse en los Despachos de los Teoricos', *Gente*, 13 May 1982, No. 877.

Hichberger, J.W.M. (1988) *Images of the Army: The Military in British Art 1815–1914* (Manchester: Manchester University Press).

Holmes, Richard (1985) *Firing Line* (Harmondsworth: Penguin).

Homer (1957) *Iliad*, translated by E.V. Rieu (Harmondsworth: Penguin).

Honeywell, Martin and Jenny Pearce (1982) *Falklands/Malvinas: Whose Crisis?* (London: Latin America Bureau).

Hunt, Rex (1992) *My Falklands Days* (Newton Abbot: David and Charles).

Idriess, Ion (1935) *The Desert Column* (Sydney: Angus and Robertson).

Isherwood, Christopher (1947) *Lions and Shadows: An Education in the Twenties* (Norfolk: New Directions).

Janowitz, Morris (1960) *The Professional Soldier: A Social and Political Portrait* (New York: The Free Press).

Jenkins, Peter (1982) 'Is There Really No Alternative?', *Guardian*, 17 May 1982.

Jenkins, Peter (1987) *Mrs Thatcher's Revolution: The Ending of the Socialist Era* (London: Jonathan Cape).

Jennings, Christian and Adrian Weale (1996) *Green-Eyed Boys: 3 Para and the Battle for Mount Longdon* (London: HarperCollins).

Kasanzew, Nicolas (1982) *Malvinas: A Sangre y Fuego* (Buenos Aires: Siete Días).

Keeble, Major Christopher P.B. (1985) 'The Battle for Darwin and Goose Green, 28/29 May: Attack on Wireless Ridge, 13/14 June', *Above All, Courage. The Falklands Front Line: First-hand Accounts* by Max Arthur (London: Sidgwick and Jackson).

Keegan, John (1976) *The Face of Battle* (Harmondsworth: Penguin).

Kettle, Martin (1998) 'Clinton Fits the Bill in Blair's New World Order', *Guardian Weekly*, 15 February 1998.

Kiszely, Major John P. (1985) 'Assault on Tumbledown Mountain, 13/14 June', *Above All, Courage. The Falklands Front Line: First-hand Accounts* by Max Arthur (London: Sidgwick and Jackson).

Knightley, Phillip (1989) *The First Casualty: From Crimea to Vietnam: The War Correspondent as Hero, Propagandist and Myth Maker*, second edition (London: Pan).

Kon, Daniel (1983) *Los Chicos de la Guerra* (London: New English Library).

Lawrence, John and Robert Lawrence MC with Carol Price (1988) *When the Fighting Is Over. A Personal Story of the Battle for Tumbledown Mountain and its Aftermath* (London: Bloomsbury).

Lawrence, Lieutenant Robert (1985) 'Assault on Tumbledown Mountain, 13/14 June', *Above All, Courage. The Falklands Front Line: First-hand Accounts* by Max Arthur (London: Sidgwick and Jackson).

Leader, Zachary (1988) 'Bergen Man Betrayed', review of *Tumbledown* by Charles Wood, *Times Literary Supplement*, 3–9 June 1988.

Leed, Eric (1979) *No Man's Land: Combat and Identity in World War I* (Cambridge: Cambridge University Press).

Levi-Strauss, Claude (1966) *The Savage Mind* (London: Weidenfeld and Nicolson).

Lozada, S., E. Barcesat, C. Iamocaeno and J. Viaggio (1982) *La Ideología de la Seguridad Nacional* (Buenos Aires: El Cid Editorial).

Lukowiak, Ken (1993) *A Soldier's Song* (London: Secker and Warburg).

MacArthur, John R. (1992) *Second Front. Censorship and Propaganda in the Gulf War*, Foreword by Ben H. Bagdikian (Berkeley: University of California Press).

MacLachlan, Gale and Ian Reid (1994) *Framing and Interpretation* (Melbourne: Melbourne University Press).

Makin, Guillermo (1983) 'The Military in Argentine Politics, 1880–1982', *Millennium: Journal of International Studies*, Vol. 12, No. 1.

Malcolm, Janet (1994) *The Silent Woman: Sylvia Plath and Ted Hughes* (London: Picador).

Marinelli, Peter V. (1971) *Pastoral* (London: Methuen).

Marwick, Arthur (1990) *British Society Since 1945*, second Edition (London: Penguin).

McCracken, Willie (1985) 'Attack on Mount Longdon, 11/12 June', *Above All, Courage. The Falklands Front Line: First-hand Accounts* by Max Arthur (London: Sidgwick and Jackson).

McCullin, Don (1982) 'War Coverage', *The Times*, 17 June 1982.

McCullin, Don with Lewis Chester (1990) *Unreasonable Behaviour: An Autobiography* (London: Jonathan Cape).

McEwan, Ian (1989) *A Move Abroad: Or Shall We Die and The Ploughman's Lunch* (London: Picador).

McGowan, Robert and Jeremy Hands (1983) *Don't Cry For Me, Sergeant-Major* (London: Futura).

McManners, Captain Hugh (1984) *Falklands Commando* (London: William Kimber).

McManners, Hugh (1993) *The Scars of War* (London: HarperCollins).

Mercer, Derrik, Geoff Mungham and Kevin Williams (1987) *The Fog of War: The Media on the Battlefield* (London: Heinemann).

Middlebrook, Martin (1989) *The Fight for the 'Malvinas': The Argentine Forces in the Falklands War* (London: Viking).

MoD (Ministry of Defence) (1982) *The British Army in the Falklands 1982* (London: HMSO).

Morales, Cecilio (1982) 'Why We All Hate Britannia So', *Guardian*, 19 April 1982.

Morgan, Keith (ed.) (1982) *The Falklands Campaign: A Digest of Debates in the House of Commons 2 April to 15 June 1982* (London: HMSO).

Morrison, David E. and Howard Tumber (1988) *Journalists at War: The Dynamics of News Reporting During the Falklands Conflict* (London: Sage).

Mosse, George E. (1990) *Fallen Soldiers: Reshaping the Memory of the World Wars* (Oxford: Oxford University Press).

Myhre, Jeffrey D. (1983) 'Title to the Falklands-Malvinas Under International Law', *Millennium: Journal of International Studies*, Vol. 12, No. 1.

Naipaul, V.S. (1980) *The Return of Eva Peron* (London: Penguin).

Newland, Corporal Stephen C. (1985) 'Attack on Mount Harriet, 11/12 June', *Above All, Courage. The Falklands Front Line: First-hand Accounts* by Max Arthur (London: Sidgwick and Jackson).

Nicolson, Harold (1967) *Diaries and Letters 1939–45*, ed., Nigel Nicolson (London: Collins).

Norris, Christopher (1992) *Uncritical Theory. Postmodernism, Intellectuals and the Gulf War* (London: Lawrence and Wishart).

Orwell, George (1938) *Homage to Catalonia*, The Authoritative Text (London: Penguin, 1989).

Orwell, George (1957) 'Politics and the English Language', *Inside the Whale and Other Essays* (Harmondsworth: Penguin).

Orwell, George (1965) 'Why I Write', *The Decline of the English Murder and Other Essays* (Harmondsworth: Penguin).

Orwell, George (1984) 'My Country Right or Left', *The Penguin Essays of George Orwell* (London: Penguin).

O'Sullivan, Tim, John Hartley, Danny Saunders and John Fiske (1983) *Key Concepts in Communication* (London: Routledge).

Owen, Wilfred (1963) *The Collected Poems of Wilfred Owen*, edited with an introduction and notes by C. Day Lewis, and with a memoir by Edmund Blunden (London: Chatto and Windus).

Panter-Downes, Mollie (1972) *London War Notes 1939–45*, ed. William Shawn (London: Longman).

Parker, Tony (1985) *Soldier, Soldier* (London: Heinemann).

Parry, Gareth (1982) 'Mirages a Threat', *Guardian*, 20 May 1982.

Perkins, Roger (1986) *Operation Paraquat: The Battle for South Georgia* (Beckington: Picton Chippenham).

Perrett, Brian (1982) *Weapons of the Falklands Conflict* (Poole: Blandford).

Piaggi, Italo (1986) *Ganso Verde (Goose Green)* (Buenos Aires: Editorial Planeta).

Plaza, Juan (1970) *Nuestra Proxima Recolonizacion de las Islas* (Buenos Aires: Juan Plaza).

Potash, Robert A. (1980) *The Army and Politics in Argentina, 1945–62* (Stanford: Stanford University Press).

Raban, Jonathan (1986) *Coasting* (London: Picador, 1987).

Reginald, R. and Dr J.M. Elliot (1983) *Tempest in a Teapot: The Falkland Islands War* (San Bernardino: The Borgo Press).

Rimmon-Kenan, Shlomith (1983) *Narrative Fiction: Contemporary Poetics* (London: Methuen).

Roberts, Yvonne and Jeremy Seabrook (1982) 'The Patriots of Pompey', *New Society*, 3 June 1982.

Routledge, Paul (1988) 'Army Threats to Tumbledown Hero', *Observer*, 29 May 1988.

Rowse, A.L. (1977) *Homosexuals in History* (New York: Macmillan).

Schank, Roger and Robert P. Abelson (1977) *Scripts, Plans, Goals and Understanding* (New York: Lawrence Erlbaum Associates).

Seabrook, Jeremy (1978) *What Went Wrong? Working People and the Ideals of the Labour Movement* (London: Gollancz).

Seabrook, Jeremy and Trevor Blackwell (1982) 'Suffering Thatcher for the Sake of her Visions', *Guardian*, 3 May 1982.

Secretary of State for Defence (1982) *The Falklands Campaign: The Lessons* (London: HMSO).

Serra, Alfredo (1982) 'Antes, en Malvinas, Se Vivea Así', *Gente*, April 1982, No. 872.

Shackleton, Lord (1976) *Economic Survey of the Falkland Islands* (London: Economist Intelligence Unit).

Simpson, John and Jana Bennett (1985) *The Disappeared: Voices from a Secret War* (London: Robson).

Smith, John (1984) *74 Days: An Islander's Diary of the Falklands Occupation* (London: Century Publishing).

Speranza, Graciela and Fernando Cittadini (1997) *Partes de Guerra: Malvinas 1982* (Buenos Aires: Editorial Norma).

Squier, Susan, Helen Cooper and Adrienne Munich (eds) (1992) *Arms and the Woman: War, Gender and Literary Representation* (Chapel Hill: University of North Carolina Press).

Sunday Times Insight Team (1982) *The Falklands War: The Full Story* (London: Sphere).

Taylor, John (1991) *War Photography: Realism in the British Press* (London: Routledge).

Thatcher, Margaret (1993) *The Downing Street Years* (London: HarperCollins).

Theroux, Paul (1983) *The Kingdom by the Sea. A Journey Around the Coast of Great Britain* (Harmondsworth: Penguin).

Thompson, Julian (1985) *No Picnic. 3 Brigade in the South Atlantic: 1982* (London: Fontana).

Thwaites, Tony, Lloyd Davies and Warwick Mules (1994) *Tools for Cultural Studies: An Introduction* (Melbourne: Macmillan).

Timerman, Jacobo (1982) *Prisoner Without a Name, Cell Without a Number* (Harmondsworth: Penguin).

Tinker, David, Lieut. R.N. (1982) *A Message from the Falklands: The Life and Gallant Death of David Tinker, Lieut. R.N. from his Letters and Poems* (Harmondsworth: Penguin).

Townsend, Sue (1982) *The Secret Diary of Adrian Mole Aged 13¾* (London: Methuen).

Townsend, Sue (1984) *The Growing Pains of Adrian Mole* (London: Methuen).

Turner, Graeme (1990) *British Cultural Studies: An Introduction* (Boston: Unwin Hyman).

Vaux, Nick (1986) *March to the South Atlantic. 42 Commando, Royal Marines, in the Falklands War*, foreword by Max Hastings (London: Buchan and Enright).

Virgil (1961) *The Eclogues*, translated by E.V. Rieu (Harmondsworth: Penguin).

Walsh, Jeffrey (1992) '"There'll Always be an England": The Falklands Conflict on Film', *Framing the Falklands War: Nationhood, Culture and Identity*, ed. James Aulich (Milton Keynes: Open University Press).

Warman, Robin (1992) 'Robin Warman Joins the Crowds as the Task Force Sails From Portsmouth', *The Falklands War, March–June 1982: Original Recordings from the BBC Sound Archive* (London: BBC).

Weston, Simon (1989) *Walking Tall: An Autobiography* (London: Bloomsbury).

Wiener, Martin (1981) *English Culture and the Decline of the Industrial Spirit, 1850–1980* (Cambridge: Cambridge University Press).

Williams, Philip with M.S. Power (1990) *Summer Soldier* (London: Bloomsbury).

Williams, Raymond (1973) *The Country and the City* (London: The Hogarth Press).

Williams, Raymond (1983) *Keywords. A Vocabulary of Culture and Society* (London: Fontana).

Williams, Raymond (1991) *Orwell*, third edition (London: Fontana).

Winchester, Simon (1983) *Prison Diary, Argentina* (London: Chatto and Windus).

Windschuttle, Keith (1988) *The Media: A New Analysis of the Press, Television, Radio and Advertising in Australia*, third edition (Ringwood: Penguin).

Winward, Walter (1985) *Rainbow Soldiers* (London: Sphere).

Wood, Charles (1987) *Tumbledown: A Screenplay* (Harmondsworth: Penguin).

Wright, Patrick (1985) *On Living in an Old Country: The National Past in Contemporary Britain* (London: Verso).

Young, Hugo (1989) *One of Us: A Political Biography of Mrs Thatcher* (London: Macmillan).

Young, Peter (ed.) (1992) *Defence and the Media in Time of Limited War* (London: Frank Cass).

Zimmerman, J.E (1964) *Dictionary of Classical Mythology* (New York: Bantam).

Index